WOOD FINISHING AND REFINISHING

REVISED EDITION

Wood Finishing and Refinishing

S. W. GIBBIA

 VAN NOSTRAND REINHOLD COMPANY
New York Cincinnati Toronto London Melbourne

Van Nostrand Reinhold Company Regional Offices:
New York Cincinnati Chicago Millbrae Dallas
Van Nostrand Reinhold Company International Offices:
London Toronto Melbourne

Library of Congress Catalog Card Number 70-149255

ISBN 0-442-22667-5 cloth
ISBN 0-442-22668-3 paper

Designed by Jean Callan King

Published by Van Nostrand Reinhold Company
450 West 33rd Street, New York, N.Y. 10001

16 15 14 13 12 11 10 9 8 7 6 5

Contents

PART ONE: PREPARING FOR FINISHING

CHAPTER 1

Woods and Why We Finish Them

A visit to the department store or furniture store will show a large variety of furniture in different styles, woods, and finishes. The appeal of the furniture rests on the style and its finishes.

The manufacturer spends considerable time and effort in producing a finish which blends with the style and creates sufficient eye-appeal to attract the customer. How often have you admired the color and tone of a coffee table? How often have you passed your hands over the top or drawer fronts of a commode and felt the sensation of warmth and smoothness? The finish has accomplished its purpose.

Although the finish was produced by professionals, it is possible for you to obtain similar results in your finishing attempts. No extensive experience is required, only a willingness to apply yourself to the methods and principles discussed in this book. Each type of finish or operation discussed is broken down into short sequential steps, many illustrated, and easy to follow and perform. An attempt has been made to limit the types of materials and equipment to the barest essentials, and in most cases these have been chosen because they are easily accessible and readily available. Their selection will in no way affect the results of the finishing attempt. Finally, in any operation where manual activity is involved, success depends upon good judgment, a willingness to experiment, and persistence.

Finishing to bring out beauty

The finishing or painting of a surface is done for specific reasons. It would be rather foolhardy to leave a mahogany cabinet in the "raw" wood state. All your efforts would go to naught if you did not bring out the beauty of the mahogany grain. Wood in the "raw" state has a flat, dull appearance. It is only after it has been stained and finished that the beautiful grain, the high lights, and the rich tones become apparent. Try this little experiment. Take two pieces of identical wood—let us say oak. Apply a thin coat of oil to one piece and wipe it off thoroughly; then compare it with the piece that has not been oil-stained. Notice the difference in appearance. Notice how the grain of the oiled surface stands out. Notice the light and dark shades which have become very pronounced. Try the same experiment with a piece of crotch mahogany and then feast your eyes on one of the beauties of nature.

Finishing to facilitate cleaning

Have you ever wondered how difficult it would be to clean your furniture if it did not have a finish? Every speck of dust, food, and liquid would stain the surface and it would be next to impossible to remove all of these stains and keep the surface clean. Finishing a surface prevents all this. The finish could be the application of a thin coat of linseed oil or a coat of shellac, but either one of these would seal the surface of the "raw" wood and prevent the stains, dirt, and liquids from marring it. How simple cleaning your furniture and other wood products can be, when the surface is protected by a finish!

Finishing to prevent moisture absorption

Let us take another example. No doubt you have found that the drawers of your chest or cabinet do not open easily during certain times of the year. Do not always place the blame on the construction of the furniture. The reason may be that the surfaces of the woods used in making these drawers were not properly sealed. As you know, wood absorbs moisture when the moisture in the room is greater than that of the wood, and it loses moisture when the moisture in the room is less than in the wood. Consequently, when the drawer absorbs moisture, it expands and, as it does, you have difficulty in pulling it out of the case. When these conditions are in reverse, the drawer opens freely and easily.

Sealing the surface will prevent this constant contraction and expansion of the wood. When a finish like shellac, varnish, oil, or wax is applied to the surface, it seals the pores of the wood and prevents moisture from affecting it. Sealing the surface by finishing it prevents unnecessary splitting and warping of wood, too. Here again, the prevention of moisture entering the pores of the wood keeps the wood in a normal condition.

Finishing to obtain uniform color

Occasionally, it is almost impossible to make an article of furniture with all the parts of the same kind of wood. Some parts may be of walnut, others of gum or poplar. Without the aid of wood finishing this practice would be almost impossible, for each wood would have its own characteristic color. These variations in color in the same piece of furniture would not enhance its appearance.

Through the medium of furniture finishing it is possible to stain or bleach practically any wood to match the color of another. Thus, it is possible to use maple with mahogany and stain the maple to match the shade of mahogany. It is possible to use gumwood and stain it to match the walnut on the same job. Ashwood stained to match oak can be detected only by the very critical eye. The next time you visit your furniture dealer, investigate and see if the mahogany table you are interested in is really made of mahogany wood, or if it has been made of gumwood or poplar. See if your critical eye can distinguish between mahogany wood and a mahogany finish.

SELECTION OF WOOD

You should constantly bear in mind the ultimate finish which is to be applied on the piece of furniture being made. Only then can you intelligently select the kind of wood that will assure the best results. Of course, many other factors enter into the picture—for example, you might want to make a table to match the dinette set you own, or a chest for your bedroom set. In that case, it is best that the wood selected be the same as the wood of the particular piece you are matching. On other occasions, however, where this prerequisite is not necessary, the choice of the wood for your project should be determined by the use to which it is to be put, the cost, and the type of finish to be applied.

If the piece of furniture is to be used in a child's room, the wood chosen should be hard enough to withstand the abuses to which it will be subjected by the child. Hard-textured wood like maple, birch, and ash would be appropriate here. If a bookcase is to be constructed and placed in a corner of the room, woods like gum, poplar, and pine could be used with fine results. These are rather soft-textured woods that will stand up well when not subjected to much wear.

Of course, cost also enters into the picture. Woods like walnut, mahogany, cherry, and birch are rather expensive and can be finished to a beautiful appearance even in a natural shade. However, to the person not in a position to afford this luxury, other more inexpensive woods having similar characteristics can be used. Woods like poplar, gumwood, and pine, if correctly stained and finished, will easily serve the purpose. The ingenuity of the craftsman plays an important part in the proper selection of the wood to be used for his project.

Finally, the type of finish is taken into consideration. If you are going to make a desk and it is to be finished in pickled pine, you are limited in the choice of wood for the job. Pine is the wood that you must use for this type of finish for no other wood can duplicate the characteristics of pickled pine. To cite another example, you are making a kitchen cabinet that is to be painted in white enamel. An inexpensive wood like poplar, gum, or pine would be more appropriate and more economical than the more expensive woods like maple or birch. In this situation the wood is going to be covered with an opaque paint, and any wood used will be hidden by the enamel.

We have seen that the choice of wood depends upon many factors, and these factors should always be taken into consideration if the craftsman is to accomplish a fine job as inexpensively as possible.

CHARACTERISTICS OF DIFFERENT WOODS

The wood finisher should possess some knowledge of the more common cabinet woods so that he can more adequately apply the best finish for the best results. Woods, like any other organic material, have certain visible characteristics which can be readily identified. These are different with different kinds of woods. The most common characteristics of woods are color, grain, hardness, and strength. Color refers to the actual shade of the wood in the "raw." Examine several different woods and you will notice that some of the woods are brownish, others are greenish-white, and others reddish. For identification purposes, color is very important; however, it is of secondary importance to the modern finisher, because he can, by staining and bleaching, remove or add color to match any shade desired. Grain characteristics are indeed very important in aiding one to identify a wood. They are important, too, because the appearance of the grain through the finish enhances its beauty. We refer to the grain of the wood when we note the pores and figure of the particular wood in question. Where the pores of the wood are open and easily visible to the naked eye, the wood is said to be open-grain. Where the pores of the wood are small and close together, but not visible to the naked eye, the wood is said to be a close-grain wood. "Figure" refers to the characteristic design made by the grain of the wood. This figure can be controlled by the method used in cutting the wood. Wood like mahogany can be cut in different ways into boards, and each way will produce a different and distinct figure. Plain-cut mahogany has straight grain. Crotch mahogany, which is the lumber cut at the juncture of the trunk and a limb of a tree, has a wavy, characteristic V-shaped grain.

To the finisher, grain is very important, because the grain of the wood makes the finished furniture either pleasing to the eye or dull. There is no substitute for fine grain; thus, where the appearance is important, the choice of a wood with the proper grain is very essential. Woods like walnut, mahogany, cherry, bird's-eye maple, and oak, in addition to being hardwoods, are known for their beautiful grain.

The hardness of a cabinet wood refers to ability of the wood to withstand abuse without any effect on it. Granted that a wood having a hard texture will last longer and can be more abused than a soft wood, yet the craftsman should also consider the working qualities of the wood. A very hard wood is difficult to work with. It makes tools dull and it requires more labor than is necessary. Cabinet woods are classified according to their hardness, and each one in the classification has a definite use. If you were making baseball bats, you would use a very hard wood like ash. If you were making a kitchen chair, you would use a medium-hard wood like sugar maple. In furniture making, the medium-hard woods are preferred to the very hard woods.

The strength of a wood is also important to the craftsman—especially when making furniture which will be subject to stress and strain. Chairs, for example, require woods which have much strength and resilience. Walnut, maple, and mahogany are fine examples of strong and resilient woods. Thomas Chippendale, one of the world's foremost cabinetmakers and designers, found mahogany to have all the characteristics that make it the exceptional furniture wood. Practically all of his furniture was made of mahogany. Duncan Phyfe, the famous early American cabinetmaker, sent emissaries to Cuba to select the best species of mahogany trees for the furniture he made.

Let us now apply the background which we have just acquired to the actual woods and we shall see how each wood differs from the other. We shall also see that once we know the characteristics of a wood we can identify it without too much difficulty.

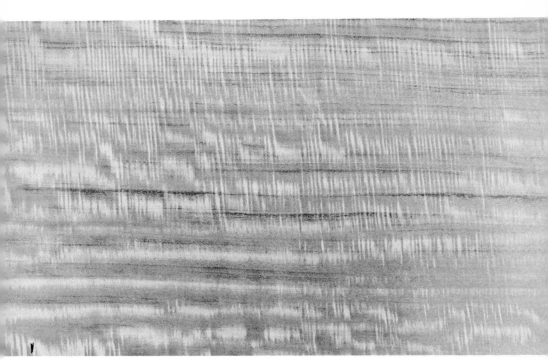

Mahogany (Hardwood Plywood Manufacturers Assn.)

Mahogany (African, Cuban, West Indian)

It is salmon pink in color when freshly cut, but changes to a golden brown when exposed to the air for a time. The pores are noticeably open, and the grain has a beautiful figure ranging from straight stripe to a wavy, mottled effect. It is rather soft in texture and easily worked into any shape or design; yet it is hard enough to withstand many of the shocks to which furniture is subjected. It is excellent finishing wood for it takes stains well—thereby bringing out the beautiful figures of the wood. Mahogany, when properly filled, will receive any type of finishing material like lacquer, shellac, and varnish with equally good results.

Mahogany is the aristocrat of furniture woods; it can be used for any type of project from simple cabinets to very ornate, expensive highboys. This is possible because of the characteristics of this wood.

13

American walnut

Walnut is one of the most versatile of American woods. It can be identified by its soft, gray-brown color, which is sometimes shaded with dark brown. The pores are rather large and noticeable. The grain is of exceptional beauty, ranging from a straight stripe to a very decorative swirl. Here the figure of the grain can be altered by changing the method of cutting the log into lumber or veneer. Very interesting and beautiful effects can be obtained by cutting the log near the trunk of the tree. The so-called burled walnut is lumber or veneer which has been cut from a log near the root. The figure of this walnut consists of many fine curved shapes of contrasting color. Walnut is medium-hard in texture, just a trifle harder than mahogany; but it can be worked rather easily. It takes stains and bleaches well and can be finished in open-grain or close-grain effect. Walnut will rub to a high, lasting gloss when finished with any of the common finishing materials. Because of its texture, beautiful grain, and general appearance, walnut is a very popular furniture wood both in the solid form and in veneered panels. It is used to make the better types of furniture, ranging from chairs to expensive dining-room furniture.

Sound wormy chestnut

Although once common in many parts of the United States, the chestnut has become almost extinct because of an insect blight. Nevertheless, in recent years it has become rather popular as a furniture wood. It is used in the Mediterranean styles and usually finished in dark colors. The natural color is grayish white to almost white. The grain structure resembles plain sawed oak. It is not as hard as oak, however. Some furniture styles lend themselves to the open-grain wormy appearance of the wood. It is used both as a solid wood and as the face veneer of plywood panels.

Sugar maple

Maple is one of the most popular of native-grown woods. It has uses in every type of furniture from the least expensive to the most expensive. Its color ranges from whitish to pinkish brown. The pores are small and close together and consequently are not visible to the naked eye. The plain sugar maple has no distinctive figure and therefore lacks the appeal of mahogany or walnut. However, the bird's-eye maple has a very definite and pronounced figure —small, dark-brown specks distributed throughout the surface of the wood, each speck resembling, as the name implies, the eye of a bird. This type of maple is rather rare and expensive and is found mostly in veneer panels;

American walnut

Chestnut (Hardwood Plywood Manufacturers Assn.)

Bird's-eye maple (Hardwood Plywood Manufacturers Assn.)

15

however, it enriches the appearance of the furniture when used. It is comparatively hard in texture and rather difficult to work with. This need not be a drawback, however, because maple will withstand abuse without too much damage to the surface itself. It is suitable for all types of furniture, ranging from juvenile furniture to the expensive French Provincial pieces. Because of its close grain and hardness, stains do not penetrate too well; nevertheless, it does take any type of finish and can be rubbed to a fine, satin gloss.

White and red oak

Oak as a furniture wood has regained its popularity after a lapse of many years. The modern styles and finishes have made it one of the most desired of woods. It ranges in color from almost white to light brown in the white oak family and to reddish brown in the red oak family, the white color being preferred for the modern finishes. Oak has a very prominent open pore forming a figured grain from straight to quite coarse. It is rather hard wood, and much effort is required in working it. Because of its color, grain, and hardness, oak can be used for the making of all types of furniture from chairs to television cabinets. Although the large pores of the wood require much filling, it finishes very well in any type of style. The wide pores make it exceptionally suitable for the contrasting pickle finish—the grain filled with a light filler and the surface stained a darker shade.

Cherry

Cherry, too, has returned to popularity during recent years. Its color ranges from light to dark reddish-brown; it is often mistaken for mahogany. The pores of the wood are rather close, and the grain has a very slight figure except in the burl cuts. Its texture is medium-hard, similar to that of mahogany; consequently it is a rather pleasing wood to work with. It takes stains well, especially those of a reddish cast. It can be finished to match mahogany, and often it is used with mahogany on various types of furniture. Because of its close grain, it will take varnishes easily and will rub to a high gloss. Practically all types of furniture can be made with cherry wood. Desks and bedroom suites are very common in this type of cabinet wood especially in the Scandinavian and Provincial styles.

Red gum

Gum is abundant in the southern part of the United States. Its cheapness and availability make it a very important furniture wood. The heartwood is brownish, tinged with pink. The sapwood (the newer wood of the tree) is grayish.

16

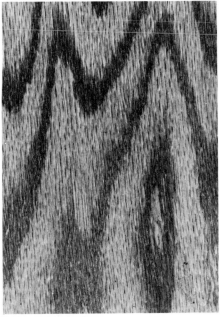

Rotary-cut red oak

Flat-sliced red oak

Plain or flat cut red oak

Cherry

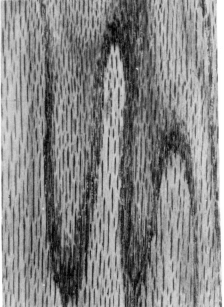

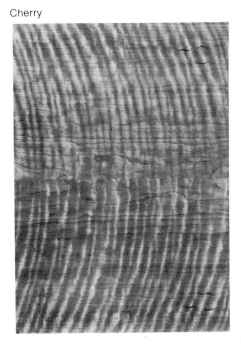

(All photographs: Hardwood Plywood Manufacturers Assn.)

17

It is one of the softest-textured woods used for furniture making and therefore does not stand up well to hard wear. It dents easily and has a tendency to warp. The pores of this wood are very close together, but the grain has distinctive features. The plain-cut gum is plain in figure; however, when quarter-cut, the wood has a very pleasing figured surface. Gum is one of the most simple woods to finish. Because it takes all types of stain exceptionally well, it replaces the more expensive woods in furniture construction. It can be finished to match walnut and mahogany so well that only the experienced eye of the craftsman can recognize the wood when finished. It is combined with the woods mentioned above and finished like them, and the results are so fine that it is used extensively in the manufacture of medium-priced furniture. Gum takes all types of finishes well and, when rubbed, will produce exceptionally good results. Practically every type of furniture can be made with this wood and with plywood having gumwood veneer. The next time you visit your furniture dealer, determine for yourself the amount of furniture that has been made with gumwood, especially the number of occasional tables.

Sugar-knotty pine

Modern design and finishes have made pine indispensable as a furniture wood. It finishes well and is adapted to many types of novelty contrasts. Pine is a whitish, cream-colored wood with very little figured grain. Its popularity is derived mostly from its knotty appearance, which, when finished in the natural finishes, stands out well. The pores are close together and scarcely visible. This characteristic makes possible a fine, smooth finish without the aid of fillers. It is very soft in texture—too soft for many uses as solid wood. However, this is overcome by using the wood as a veneer over hard-core, furniture plywood panels. In this form (plywood), pine is used for tables, desks, credenzas, and other expensive pieces. Pine also takes paints well, and you will find that most painted furniture and kitchen cabinets are made of pine for this reason. Later chapters will give detailed instruction on the finishing of pine.

Poplar (whitewood)

Poplar is another substitute for the more expensive woods. It is quite common in the construction of juvenile furniture, bookcases, and other inexpensive furniture. Poplar is white to yellow with an occasional black streak running along the grain. The pores are close and not noticeable. The grain has almost no figure, and therefore the wood should not be used where grain is an important part of the finished job. Poplar has a very soft texture, so soft that it

Red gum   Pine

Poplar

(All photographs: Hardwood Plywood Manufacturers Assn.)

should not be used for furniture that must withstand much use. A better job will result if poplar plywood is used instead of the solid wood. Poplar is an excellent wood for cabinet interiors, such as drawers, partitions, and shelves. Poplar, like gum, takes any type of finish well, be it transparent or paint. It can be stained to match any of the more popular woods. Mahogany and walnut can be imitated very well by staining poplar to those shades. Like gum, it is used in combination with the more expensive woods on the same pieces of furniture. Because of its close grain it will take paint well without the necessity of filling the surface.

Pecan (hickory)
Pecan is another wood which is becoming a favorite furniture wood. Its strength, color, grain, and hardness suit it to the modern furniture styles, especially the Mediterranean and Provincial. Because of this it can be finished in the natural shades with just a tint of antique stain added. The so-called pecan finish is very popular today. Pecan wood is reddish-brown, often with dark streaks. It has very little figure and can be stained to resemble walnut.The pores, although visible, are not large enough to require the heavy filling used in other open-grain woods.

Beech
Beech is grown in the central part of the United States. Its color is white or slightly reddish. It has no figure. The pores are barely visible, making this wood most suitable for painting. The wood is used in the manufacture of chairs and the exterior parts of furniture. It has the working qualities of maple in strength and hardness and is used in its place in the contemporary furniture styles requiring the "fruitwood finishes."

WHAT WOOD TO USE

From the foregoing discussion it is clear that the choice of wood depends upon many factors. It would be uneconomical, for example, to use mahogany on a surface to be painted, for the beautiful grain of this wood would be hidden by the opaque paint. Then too, assuming that the wood must be painted, the large open pores of mahogany are difficult to seal sufficiently for the perfectly flat surface that is so essential. To cite another example, if you desired a natural finish where the grain would stand out as part of the job, you would not use fir for the panel parts. Despite the fact that fir has a prominent grain, this grain is so vivid that it becomes obnoxious.

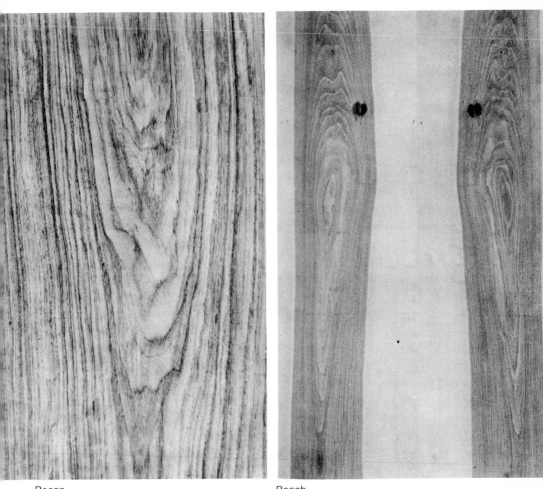

Pecan

Beech

(Both photographs: Fine Hardwoods Assn.)

Another factor to consider is the use to which the wood is to be put. Use hardwoods, hard in texture, for articles that will be subjected to much wear and tear. Use softwoods for articles not subjected to this type of wear.

Finally, the type of finish to be put on the article should help in determining the type of wood to use. Surely, if your specifications call for a wheat-oak finish, oak should be used, in order to obtain this desired effect. If you desire to match a new piece of furniture to the furniture you now possess, you should, if possible, obtain the same kind of wood, with the same grain characteristics, color, etc. You should also remember that there are certain woods, such as gum and poplar, which can be stained to match other woods easily and well.

PLYWOOD AND SOLID WOOD

Occasional mention has been made in this chapter of the use of plywood. The craftsman often must decide whether or not to use it. Shall it be mahogany plywood or solid mahogany? Will either finish as well? Will each take water stain as well as the other? Will each bleach as well? Will water affect either? But before discussing finishing characteristics of plywood, it might be wise to describe the material.

Plywood is the term used to designate a type of manufactured wood which consists of three or more layers each glued at right angles to the other. The face is usually the best surface of the panel, and in hardwood plywood this is usually the finest of wood veneers, like oak, walnut, mahogany, and maple. Plywood panels are always designated by the kind of veneer on the face of the panel. The face veneer is glued over another layer of veneer at right angles, and this is called the crossband. The next layer, the core, gives thickness to the panel and is made of an inexpensive wood like chestnut or white wood. This core is glued at right angles to the crossband. The next layer consists of another layer of veneer also at right angles and is followed by still another layer glued at right angles to the crossband called the back. You can readily see that, by its structure, plywood is exceptionally strong both across the grain and along the grain. Warpage and shrinkage are reduced to a minimum, thanks to this gluing arrangement.

During the past few years great developments have been made in the manufacture of glues and gluing processes which are very important to the manufacture of plywood. Present glues, unlike the older type glues, adhere to wood remarkably well and will withstand heat and moisture without bad effects to the surfaces glued. Thus, the plywood of today is far superior to

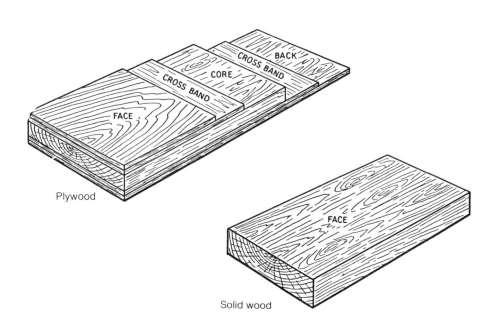

Plywood

Solid wood

the plywood made twenty-five years ago, and it is because of this that plywood is recommended in many cases in place of solid wood of the same thickness and kind. There are, indeed, many other advantages for the use of plywood. Rare woods, such as rosewood, satin wood, ebony, and tulip, would not be practical for use in furniture construction if it were not for the fact that these woods are available as face veneers in plywood panels. Also, it is possible to obtain the more common woods in plywood panels in widths which would not otherwise be possible. Oak, mahogany, walnut, and poplar plywoods can be obtained in widths up to forty-eight inches and more. This eliminates the need for gluing several boards of solid wood, edge to edge, to get the desired width. In addition, plywood is purchased already clean and sandpapered, ready for use. Plywood used for wall paneling now can be obtained prefinished in a multitude of species and colors. No finishing is required and the panels are applied directly to the wall surface. Nails and moldings are available to match.

Of course from the foregoing discussion it should not be assumed that solid wood has no further use in your project. There are many sections in it that require solid wood—parts like rails, legs, aprons, and frames. Wherever possible, however, plywood is recommended.

23

Finishing plywood

Finishing plywood presents hardly a problem. The top veneers have the same characteristics as the solid wood in question, and consequently the finishing procedures are the same in both cases. Water stains, chemical stains, and bleaches will cause no ill effects on the plywood panel. They will not blister or loosen the veneer, and, when applied evenly, they will give the same effects as on solid wood. Any finish film applied, whether shellac or varnish, will adhere to the surface if the usual precautions are taken. There is no fear of checking, pealing, or bleeding of the surface film. The finished plywood surface will rub well with either water or oil as a lubricant and will take a high polish when waxed. Finally, plywood, because it is presanded, will always guarantee a fine, smooth surface which often is not possible where the craftsman must plane and sandpaper the surface by hand. The finishing procedures explained in Chapters 10 and 11, apply to both the solid woods and the plywoods. No distinction is made.

Do not hesitate to use plywood where possible, provided it meets the requirements of your job. Consider the facts already mentioned. Modern furniture manufacturers are for plywood all the way—practically all television cabinets, table tops, and bureaus are made of plywood.

AN INTRODUCTION TO FINISHING PROCESSES

The secret in achieving a fine finish, whether transparent or opaque, depends upon (1) how the surface is prepared and (2) the procedure followed in the finishing operation.

When we talk about a finish we have in mind the finished product. Is the surfaced to be stained, bleached, shellacked, varnished, or lacquered? Is it to be hand-rubbed, with a gloss or dull effect? Are the pores to remain open or closed? These are questions which must be answered, of course. But regardless of the finish desired, the basic steps in all finishing processes are practically identical: The raw surface should be stained or bleached; the pores should be filled and a sealer should be applied; and several coats of transparent film should be applied for protection and appearance.

Staining

As has already been noted, wood is porous and has an affinity for liquids. It will absorb to some degree any liquid applied. It is this absorption which adds color to the wood. Sometimes the stain used penetrates deeply, giving a long-lasting color. With other stains the color is superficial and will eventually wear away with use. Some stains act chemically on the wood to change its color. In practically all cases, stains are applied with a brush or a cloth pad. They are applied in the direction of the grain in long even strokes. Some require wiping after application, others require no wiping, and still others dry so rapidly that extreme care is necessary to apply them evenly. Some raise the grain of the wood, while others do not. (When grain-raising stains are used, the wood must be prepared before the stain is applied. Despite the additional step, many wood finishers prefer to use this stain because of its other qualities.) Whichever type of stain is selected, it is to be applied directly over the raw wood after the surface has been prepared.

Chapter 4 is a complete discussion of the different types of stains.

Filling

Any wood has pores, and some woods have very prominent pores. The old masters solved this problem by a simple but tedious procedure. Coats upon coats of shellac were applied. As each coat dried, it was sanded smooth. As more coats were applied and sanded smooth, the pores gradually began to fill. Eventually, enough shellac had been applied and all the pores were completely filled. With the exception of a few craftsmen who finish furniture to imitate museum pieces, no one uses this method today. Instead, paste fillers are used, and the results are comparable to those achieved with the old method. Chapter 5 discusses the composition and application of fillers. At this point it is sufficient to note that all woods regardless of the size of the pore require some type of filling, and this filling usually follows after the surface has been stained. There is one exception to this rule. Some styles, the Scandinavian, for example require an open-grain finish. Here no filler is used to fill the pores. The finish is applied directly after the stain. The open grains are essential to the style.

Applying the transparent finish

To this point the raw wood has been treated with a stain and filler. To leave the surface in this condition would neither enhance its appearance nor protect the surface. Some type of protective top film must be applied. This could be shellac, varnish, or lacquer. Sometimes the protective film is merely linseed oil, and with some modern staining agents it can be wax. The choice depends upon the use of the furniture. Thus if the piece is a cocktail or coffee table it should be finished in varnish or lacquer; shellac can be used on pieces which do not come in contact with liquid or heat. Then too, the choice may depend upon the facilities available. For example, lacquer is difficult to apply with a brush and should be sprayed on, so one would need spraying equipment. Varnish requires adequate dust-free space for drying and storage, since it dries very slowly.

Shellac may be used as a finish. Two to three coats will produce a fine satin finish. Shellac may also be used only as a first coat, in which case it acts as a sealer, and then two or three coats of either varnish or lacquer are applied. Varnish finish requires at least two coats. These are applied either directly over a shellac sealer or varnish. Each coat must be allowed to dry thoroughly and then sanded before the next coat is applied. Lacquer finish requires at least two heavy coats, sprayed over lacquer sealer or shellac. Here again, each coat must be permitted to dry before the next is applied.

Chapters 6, 7, and 8 discuss in detail the composition and application of each material.

Smoothing and rubbing

Ultimately the transparent material applied should be rubbed with some type of rubbing abrasive to remove brush marks, dust particles, and other irregularities in the surface. This operation is most essential, since it gives the surface the glossy appearance and feel of the fine professional finish. Rubbing is tedious and time-consuming, but the effort seems worth it after the piece has been completed.

There are various types of rubbing agents, and they are discussed in detail in Chapter 9 and elsewhere. Simple rubbing may be done by using steel wool over the surface. This type of rubbing has its advantages and disadvantages. A professional finisher rubs with pumice stone and oil or water. Pumice produces a very smooth satin-gloss surface. Another type of abrasive is rubbing compound. It is recommended for surfaces which have been finished in lacquer. Its advantages and disadvantages will be discussed later.

SUMMARY

We have explained the reasons wood is finished and described various woods and their characteristics. The various operations in the finishing process have been discussed briefly. To summarize, although the finishing steps may vary somewhat, they should proceed in this order:
1. Prepare the surface.
2. Apply stain or bleach.
3. Apply a paste filler to fill the pores.
4. Apply several coats of clear transparent finishing material.
5. Rub with an abrasive to obtain a smooth surface.

CHAPTER 2

Preparing New Wood for Finishing

One of the most important steps in the wood-finishing process is the preparation of the surface. The craftsman—or would-be craftsman—who gives this part of the work scant consideration is due for many disappointments in the finished piece. The minor defects which he neglected to correct, the small scratches which did not seem important, now become very conspicuous and ugly. They definitely cheapen the effort, labor, and material that went into the making of the piece. This must always be borne in mind: it is easier to correct any defect, no matter how trivial, while the wood surface is in the raw state than to attempt repair of these same defects when the surface is in the process of being finished.

All wood products are subject to scratches, dents, bruises, and stains, regardless of the care exercised. It is, consequently, very important that these defects be discovered before proceeding with the job. You should always examine carefully every part of a piece of furniture before you start finishing it. Look at every section from every angle and with ample light. A dark corner of the room is the last place to attempt this inspection unless plenty of good artificial light is available. Dust the surface to be inspected and rub your hands over the area, but, of course, be careful of splinters.

Removing scratches

Scratches along the grain are more difficult to find than scratches across the grain. However, by following and sighting along the grain, it is possible to see these scratches because they are deeper than the grain itself. Scratches across the grain are more noticeable, for this type of scratch has cut across the fibers of the wood, leaving a scar on the surface. In any event, always remove these blemishes before proceeding to the next step.

In the case of any surface scratch, determine whether it can be removed easily or will require much effort. Usually light sandpapering with a fine sandpaper will remove a fine scratch, provided the sanding is done along the grain, and never across the grain. Sandpapering across the grain will just produce more scratches which will be more difficult to remove. When sandpapering a small area, you should always bear in mind that too much sanding will remove too much of the wood, and this will be more noticeable when the finish is applied. A good practice to observe at all times, when sandpapering a scratch, is to sandpaper with the aid of a sandpaper block and to sandpaper not only the scratched area, but the surrounding surface as well.

At times you will find that some scratches are quite deep and will not disappear despite much sandpapering. In cases of this sort removal of a great deal of wood becomes necessary. By using a hand scraper, the excess material around the scratch can be removed until the bottom of the deep scratch has been reached. However, when you are scraping a veneered surface, great care should be exercised to make certain that the thin layer of veneer is not entirely removed for the sake of eliminating the defect. Where you have used the scraper to remove the scratches, always go over this surface with fine sandpaper to remove any marks made with the scraper. As always, sand only with the grain.

A plane should never be used to remove scratches on a surface that is ready for finishing. Greater damage could be done by the improper use of the plane than any benefit which could be derived by its use. Plane marks are difficult to remove by sanding, and, if they are not removed properly, they will look unsightly after the finish is applied.

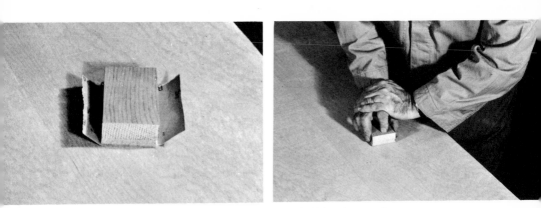

A sandpaper block is very easy to make. It helps to use both hands to apply pressure.

The hand scraper is used for scratches that are too deep to remove easily with sandpaper.

Removing dents

A dent on the raw wood surface can usually be removed without having to scrape or sandpaper the area affected. You will recall that wood is composed of microscopic cells. In a dent, these cells have been crushed out of shape. The fibers of the wood have not been cut or damaged, and consequently the problem is merely to restore the shape of these crushed cells. You can do this by wetting the affected area with a few drops of water and then permitting this water to soak into the wood. As the wood absorbs the water the cells expand and take their original shape. You now allow this area to dry thoroughly and then sandpaper with fine finishing paper to remove any unusual swelling left by the water.

Infrequently, this procedure will not produce the desired results, either because of the hard texture of the wood or the depth of the dent. In such a case, place a few drops of water on the dented area, then touch the water with the hot point of the knife. This action will produce a small pocket of steam around the affected area. The moist, hot steam will penetrate the pores of the wood more readily and cause the affected cells to absorb this hot moisture and then expand. Repeat this operation several times until the area has expanded sufficiently to permit you to sandpaper it flush to the adjacent area.

Sometimes even this does not work and it becomes necessary to fill a damaged area with one of several types of fillers prepared for that purpose. In selecting the correct materials for filling holes, bruises, and dents, it is essential to choose those that will adhere to the wood, not shrink when dry, and will take stains well. Let us examine a few of these closely.

Removing dents with steam. First the knife is heated. Then water is sprinkled on the dent and touched with the hot knife. When the dented area has swelled sufficiently, it is sanded flush to the surface.

Plastic water putty

This type of filler is one of the most inexpensive, yet it is very effective. It is purchased in powder form—usually in one-pound containers. You add about three parts of the powder to one part of water in a clean dish. Then you mix the mixture with a putty knife or flat chisel until it has changed into a soft putty. Do not prepare more than you need for immediate use. Any excess remaining will set quickly, and it cannot be remixed with water to form a new supply of the putty. With a putty knife, put the putty into the hole or crevice. Work it well into the area affected until it fills every part. Do not, however, place more putty on the surface than is necessary, as this excess material will become very difficult to remove. Allow the putty to dry thoroughly (until it is very hard), and then sandpaper the area until smooth. Make certain that every trace of excess putty is sanded off the surface, for traces of putty not absolutely essential will mar the surface not affected by the dents.

Incidentally, this water putty, which has a light cream color when mixed with water, can be changed in shade by adding dry powdered colors to the mixture. These colors are available in many shades and can be obtained from your local paint dealer.

Wood compound paste

This is another material which can be used for the filling in of dents, holes, and bruises. It comes in hard paste form in glass jars and in many of the popular wood shades, like walnut, mahogany, and natural. No mixing with water is necessary; merely scrape out the desired amount with a putty knife or chisel and work it into the defective spot. You then allow about one hour of drying time and sandpaper smooth with fine finishing paper. Here again, care should be taken that not too much of the compound is applied where not necessary. This compound has a tendency to clog the pores of the wood, thus preventing the absorption of the materials which are to be applied later. Therefore, make certain that all traces of unnecessary compound are sanded off well.

Plastic wood

Plastic wood is a very well-advertised common type of filler, popular because of the ease in application and quick setting time. It is made of wood fibers and a plastic binder, and it is available in several of the popular wood shades. It can be obtained in small tubes and in larger quantities from an ounce can to a pound can. Enough of the material is removed from the container with a knife or chisel to fill the affected area. The plastic wood is forced into the

Above: When applying plastic water putty, avoid leaving too much excess on the surface. It dries very hard and is difficult to remove.

Wood compound is worked with a putty knife and forced into the hole.

hole and worked until it has filled the hole. If the area affected is deep, it is best to fill it partway, allow that to set, and then complete the job.

After about fifteen minutes, sandpaper the filled area with fine finishing paper until it is flush. Care should be exercised to make certain that every trace of the plastic wood has been completely sanded from the surface. Any remaining filler will clog the pores, thereby preventing the absorption of the stain or other coats of finish. If this is not done, the spot which remains will be very difficult to hide as you proceed in your finishing operations. Another point to bear in mind is the rapidity with which this material dries. You should, therefore, keep the container tightly closed when not in use, and while you are using it you should avoid letting the can stand open for any longer than necessary. In the event that the plastic wood has dried out, you may purchase a plastic wood thinner. Buy both the plastic wood and the thinner at the same time, and avoid the nuisance of interrupting your job to go to the hardware store.

Oil putty
Although ordinary oil (glazer's) putty is very popular for some uses, it is not recommended for fine furniture finishing. Because of the linseed-oil binder, the putty dries very slowly and leaves an oil mark when applied to a hole. This also prevents any stain or other material from being absorbed into the spot filled with it. However, it has its uses in many types of finishing situations. Where there is ample time to permit good drying, it may be used to fill nail holes and other similar defects on jobs which are to be painted rather than stained. It is a good idea to paint the surface first and then work in the putty. This assures better adhesion of the putty and less chance of it drying or falling out. When this putty has dried hard, it should be sanded smooth and even.

Glue and sawdust putty
This is a simple, yet fine, type of putty to make. Merely mix hot animal glue or vinyl resin with very fine sawdust, usually of the wood used on the cabinet, into a heavy paste and then apply with a chisel or putty knife to the damaged area. Work the mixture well to assure good filling. Allow sufficient drying time—usually one or two hours—and then sandpaper smooth. Here, again, care should be exercised to make sure that every trace of this paste has been sanded off the adjacent surface. Stain penetration will be prevented if any of this glue remains imbedded in the pores of the wood. But if the paste is carefully applied and sanded, the damaged area will become quite inconspicuous.

Glue and sawdust make an excellent putty.

SANDPAPERS AND THEIR USE

No doubt you have by this time realized the importance of preparing the surface for finishing by proper inspection and by proper sanding. You may now wonder what type and kind of sandpaper to use.

Sandpapers for the wood finisher are divided into two classes: cabinet papers and finishing papers. These papers can be obtained in four different types of abrasive coatings—flint, garnet, aluminum oxide, and silicon carbide. Each has its purpose and appropriate use. It will be well to study the features of each type indicated so that you may be in a better position to determine which type to purchase for your special needs.

Cabinet papers

Broadly speaking, cabinet papers are sandpapers used for the sanding of raw wood. They range in coarseness from very coarse for the first sanding operation to very smooth, the final sanding operation. These cabinet papers may be obtained in any of the abrasive coatings already indicated.

Finishing papers

As the name implies, the finishing papers are used most frequently to obtain a fine, smooth surface either on raw wood or on the finished surface. They are used on raw wood only after a coarse paper has been used to smooth the rough and uneven surface. The smooth finishing paper is then used to remove the deeper scratches made by the coarse sandpaper and thus pro- duce a finer surface. On a finished surface the finishing papers serve a dual purpose. When used properly, they reduce the rough shellacked or varnish surface to a smooth, even texture, and they give the finished surface a fine scratch which will permit better adhesion for the coats to follow. These papers are also obtained in any of the abrasives already mentioned. The grade coarseness depends upon the type of coating the paper has.

Flint paper

Either cabinet paper or finishing paper may be obtained with a flint coating. The abrasive in flint paper is quartz or silica, and it can be recognized by the peculiar yellowish cast of the coating This is the type of sandpaper most familiar to the home craftsman and hobbyist, and unless you specify other- wise, your local dealer will invariably give you flint paper when you ask him for sandpaper. It is the cheapest form of abrasive that you can buy, but this economy is not always recommended. It has some drawbacks which make it impractical for fast production work. It wears out after a little use, the flint losing its cutting qualities very quickly. However, for certain types of work like sandpapering to remove an old finish, the use of flint paper is recommended. Here, the old finish clogs the coating quickly anyway; consequently, the cheapest paper is the most economical.

Flint papers are available as both cabinet papers and finishing papers. The cabinet papers range in grit from very coarse to fine. The finishing papers range from fine to extra fine. The most popular grits are medium for the cabinet paper and fine for the finishing papers. However, other grits may be used depending upon the type of sanding being done.

Garnet papers

Due to their many decided advantages both in lasting and in cutting qualities, garnet-coated papers have gained much in popularity during recent years. Garnet paper gets its name from the mineral which is used as the abrasive coating. You can easily recognize it by its color—a tawny red cast. This mineral is noted for its hard, sharp texture. It is one of the best available abrasives for fast cutting on either a raw-wood surface or a finished surface. Both cabinet papers and finishing papers are available with this mineral coating. The craftsman will find that the large choice in grit makes them suitable for any type of sanding work. The grits range from No. 2 (very coarse) to No. 7/0 (very fine). The paper is durable, strong, and economical to use. If you have been accustomed to using flint sandpaper for all your sanding, try garnet paper instead—you will discover its advantages for yourself.

Aluminum oxide paper

Aluminum oxide paper is gradually replacing garnet paper as an abrasive in wood finishing. This paper is coated electrically with a metallic oxide. It has a grayish color. As a finishing paper it is superior to the others because of its fast cutting action and long-lasting qualities. It can be used when sanding shellac, varnish, or lacquer surfaces. The grit or coarseness ranges from very fine (320A) to medium coarse (100). Number 200 is recommended for finish sanding.

Wet-or-dry silicon carbide paper

This is a synthetic abrasive whose grains are very sharp and irregular, thus assuring a very fast cutting action. The grains or crystals are coated on the paper electrically, thereby making the abrasive waterproof. This is rather important from the finisher's point of view, since he now has a paper which can be soaked in water before being used. Soaking the paper in water or in a solvent such as benzine makes it cut quicker and easier. Silicon carbide paper is used essentially for fine sanding. It is used where an extra-fine smooth surface is required on raw wood or in sanding or rubbing the finished coats of shellac, varnish, or lacquer. The grades range from very fine (No. 400) to fine (No. 200).

	Flint	Garnet	Aluminum Oxide	Silicon Carbide
Super-fine work				400
Extra-fine work		280 (8/0)	320-9/0 280-8/0	360 320-280
Very fine work	Extra fine	240-7/0 220-6/0	240-7/0 220-6/0	240 220
Fine work	Fine	180-5/0 150-4/0	180-5/0 150-4/0	
Medium work	Medium	120-3/0 100-2/0	120-3/0 100-2/0	
Coarse work —raw wood	Coarse	80-0	80-0	
Very coarse work	Extra coarse	60-½ 50-1	60-½ 50-1	
Extra-coarse work		40-1½ 36-2	40-1½ 36-2	

How to use sandpaper

There is an art in sandpapering. Although it is considered a very tedious job, it can be done well and easily if a few simple rules are followed. You must remember, at the outset, that the success of your finishing job will depend to a great extent upon the care you exercised in sanding.

Cut the 9" x 11" sheet of sandpaper into quarters 4½" x 5½". This size makes the sandpaper easier to handle both when sanding with a block and when sanding with the palm of your hand. Limber up the sandpaper by rolling the paper side of the paper over the edge of your bench. This step softens the paper, makes it more pliable, and prevents it from tearing when being used. When sanding a flat surface, provide yourself with a block large enough to fit the palm of your hand. A 3" x 5" block made of cork, rubber, hard felt, or wood, with a thin sheet of cork or felt glued to the bottom of it, will prove ideal. Now wrap the sandpaper around the bottom and sides of the block and hold the block in your hand, holding the loose edges of the paper snugly with your thumb and fingers. Do not nail the edges of the paper to the sides of the block.

Flat surfaces. Assuming that you have selected the correct paper for the sanding operation, proceed to sandpaper the surface in straight even strokes along the grain. Never under any condition should you sandpaper across the grain. Continue the operation until every trace of the imperfection has been removed. Occasionally check your sandpaper and block to make sure that no chips have imbedded themselves in the paper or between the block and paper. If any of these are permitted to remain, they will produce deep scratches on the surface as you are sanding. From time to time free the sandpaper of dust by hitting the block against the edge of your bench; you will find that this increases the cutting action of the paper. Turn the paper around the block from time to time to assure even wearing of the paper, and thus economy. Apply enough pressure to your block to obtain good cutting, but never so much that excessive friction and heat results. Avoid tearing the paper while sanding; this often happens when your sandpaper touches the sharp edges of your job. A slow even stroke will prevent this unnecessary waste of paper.

Curved surfaces. When moldings, irregular shapes, or uneven surfaces are to be sanded, the sanding procedure differs somewhat. Where moldings are involved, shape the sandpaper selected so that it matches the contour of the molding. Then hold this shape with your fingers and sandpaper the molding in question. Make sure that you do not alter the shape of molding while you are sanding. When you are about to sandpaper a corner of your job, or the

Sanding a flat surface. Note that both hands are used to apply pressure.

In sanding a curved surface, the fingers act as a sanding block. But be careful—friction means heat.

crevice in a molding, fold your sandpaper so that the paper side is on the inside, hold the paper between your fingers (watch out for splinters), and sandpaper the corner with the sharp edge of the folded sandpaper. Avoid friction, as serious finger burns may result from overzealous sanding of this type.

As a final reminder, unnecessary sanding should be avoided—yet appropriate sanding should always be the rule. You should continue to sandpaper until all traces of marks, scratches, etc., have been removed. Start with a medium-coarse paper to remove most of the marks, and then finish off with a fine paper to eliminate the scratches made by the coarse paper.

How to use portable electric sanders

The labor involved in hand sanding may be reduced considerably by using a portable electric orbital or oscillating sander. These are found in many sizes and styles. Either may be used effectively for finish sanding of raw or finished surfaces. The oscillating type is recommended because the stroke is a back-and-forth movement, thus avoiding the fine oval marks made by the orbital sander.

The portable electric sander saves a lot of time, but because it is so efficient it must be used very carefully.

A sheet of finishing paper of the proper grade is cut to fit around the moving pad of the sander. It is then locked into position at either end of the pad. Make sure that the abrasive is secured tightly around the pad.

Start the power, lower the pad to the surface, and begin to move in a back-and-forth motion with a moderate pressure. Move the pad over the entire surface until it has been sanded to your satisfaction. Replace the abrasive with a finer grade and repeat the operation. Dust off the surface thoroughly.

Some precautions with electric sanders
1. The machine must be in constant motion. Leaving it in one place for any length of time will wear away too much of the material.
2. Move the sander in the direction of the grain, never across it or in a circular motion.
3. Do not apply too much pressure as you near the edges, or you may round them off.
4. Clear the abrasive from time to time for better cutting.
5. Unless the sander is of the double-insulated type, it should be grounded, like any electrical tool.

Sanding finished surfaces

As we shall note in the succeeding chapters, it is very important that a surface having one or more coats of shellac, varnish, or lacquer be sanded with a finishing paper before other coats are applied. This type of sanding differs somewhat from the sanding already described. Here you should not concern yourself with removing scratches, but with preparing the surface for the next coat. This means that your sanding should be done so that burrs, brush marks, and dirt imbedded in the finish are removed. Cabinet papers should never be used in this type of work, because although they cut very rapidly, the scratches they leave on the finished surface are so deep that they are beyond repair. Use a finishing paper with any of the four coatings mentioned—No. 5/0 garnet paper is preferred. Cut sheets into quarters as before, but instead of using a block for sanding, use the flat palm of your hand. The paper is now held flat on the surface. Proceed to sandpaper the surface by moving your palm to follow the grain of the surface you are sanding. Apply just enough pressure to assure sufficient cutting. Do not press too hard or sandpaper too rapidly, as either of these may cause overheating and thus soften the finishing material which you are sanding. If you sand in a circular motion or across the grain, you will create scratches on the surface that cannot be removed.

42

Final examination before staining

Let us assume that you have made the necessary repairs according to the instructions in this chapter. You have sanded the surface with the appropriate papers. You feel confident that your initial preparation has made the job as perfect as can be expected. Now prepare your work bench by dusting it off thoroughly. Dust off your working area. Wet the floor to prevent dust from flying around while you are working. Dust off your project, preferably with a brush and a clean rag. Remove any loose parts of your job, such as drawers, doors, and hardware. You are now ready for the next step—staining, bleaching, or applying a natural finish.

CHAPTER 3

Preparing a Finished Surface for Refinishing

The word "refinishing" implies the removal of the original finish to the bare wood by some mechanical or chemical means, and then the preparation of the surface for a new finish. It also implies the making of simple repairs, like the regluing of loose members, replacement of broken pieces, and removal of deep scratches and dents.

Refinishing a piece of furniture requires much time, labor, and expense. It should not be attempted unless the existing finish is so poor that it cannot be made satisfactory with additional coats of transparent finishes or polishing and cleaning. Refinishing is required, of course, when the shade of the furniture is to be changed—for example, when changing a dark mahogany finish to a natural, or a walnut finish to a fruitwood finish.

METHODS OF REMOVING AN OLD FINISH

There are two methods which may be used to remove an old finish: the mechanical method, with such tools as the steel hand scraper, sandpaper, and the portable electric sander; and the chemical method, with liquid solvents. Mechanical methods are more appropriate when removing paint or varnish on small articles, such as picture frames, chairs, and small case goods.

The hand scraper

The steel hand scraper may be used to remove an old finish. (A piece of window glass may be substituted for the steel scraper. The edge of the glass must be perfectly straight to assure good results, and one must be careful not to break the glass.) The edges of the steel scraper are turned to an angle of approximately 90° to the flat sides. These sharp edges do the cutting when the scraper is moved on the surface. For best scraping results, the following procedure is recommended:

1. Hold the scraper with both hands so that the thumbs are behind the direction of the scraping movement. The thumbs push the scraper forward.
2. Push the scraper at an angle of 45° along the surface. Apply pressure downward and forward in the direction of the grain.
3. Change the cutting angle from time to time to obtain a better scraping action.
4. Continue scraping until the finish has been removed to the bare wood.
5. Finish off by sanding with fine flint paper.

Sandpaper

An old finish may be removed by sandpapering by hand, although it is rather slow work.

1. Select No. 1 flint or No. ½ garnet paper and fold a quarter of a sheet around a sandpaper block.
2. Proceed to sandpaper by following the direction of the grain. Use pressure on the block to assure a good cutting action.
3. Remove as much of the finish as possible by continuing to sandpaper with this coarse paper. Replace the sandpaper when its cutting action decreases.
4. When the wood has been sanded to the bare surface, repeat the sanding with No. 0 paper to remove any deep scratches made during the original sanding.
5. Fold a quarter sheet in half and place between fingers to sandpaper places where the sandpaper block cannot reach, as in the crevice of a molding.

The portable electric sander

As indicated in the previous chapter, the portable electric sander may be substituted for hand sanding. When attempting to remove an old finish with the portable sander, start with a coarse paper—No. 80, for example—and remove as much of the finish as possible. Continue with a No. 120 or 3/0 until you have sanded down to the bare wood.

It should be noted that portable sanders can be used only on flat surfaces. They cannot be used on curved, turned, or molded surfaces.

Chemical removers

These are the most economical and efficient materials to use in the removal of a finish, and they are popular with most wood finishers and craftsmen. Very little equipment is necessary, and the chemicals involved are not too expensive when we consider the type of work they can do. Then, too, very little previous knowledge or experience is necessary to use these chemicals.

These types of removers are grouped into two classes: caustic and solvent.

Caustic (alkaline) types of paint removers

In this group are found a number of chemicals which are common household detergents, like lye, washing soda, and beetsol (trisodium phosphate). When these are dissolved in hot water and then applied to the surface, a chemical action takes place which softens whatever finish may be on the surface. The mixing formulas for each of the above are given below with the instructions for application. *Note:* Use rubber gloves when working with caustic materials.

Lye

Three or four tablespoons of lye are dissolved in a quart of hot water to which has been added a little powdered corn starch. Stir the solution until all ingredients have dissolved.

1. Apply the solution to the surface while hot and allow to stand until the finish becomes soft.
2. Apply additional coats to hasten the action.
3. Remove softened finish with the wide putty knife or coarse steel wool.
4. Wash the entire area with clean water to remove all traces of the caustic material.
5. Use a stiff brush to get into corners.
6. Allow the surface to dry for 24 hours before the next steps are performed.

Trisodium phosphate (beetsol; "Oakite"; "Spic-and-Span")

Two or three pounds of the powder are dissolved in one gallon of hot water. Stir the solution to make certain that all the powder has dissolved.

1. Apply the hot solution to the surface with an old brush and allow it to remain on the surface for a few minutes, or until the finish shows signs of softening.
2. Apply a second coat if the softening action seems slow.
3. Remove the loose grime with coarse steel wool or a coarse rag.
4. Use a stiff brush to remove the softened material from corners and moldings.

5. Apply additional coats of the hot liquid if all of the finish has not been removed.

6. Wash the entire surface with clean water after all of the grime has been cleaned off.

7. Allow at least 24 hours to elapse before sanding the surface for the finishing process.

Advantages of caustic materials

1. Excellent results are obtained when used as directed.

2. The painted surfaces are softened within a matter of minutes. The residue can easily be removed.

3. They are inexpensive. A gallon of the solution costs but a few cents.

4. They are common household chemicals and thus there is no need for scouring the community for them.

Disadvantages of caustic materials

1. Inasmuch as they are water solutions, there always is the danger that the water on the surface may affect the wood. This danger is particularly serious when the furniture is made of plywood. The water may seep through the thin top layer and loosen the glue bond holding the various sheets together.

2. The solvents are quite caustic and consequently must be used with care. Clothing should be protected and so should parts of the body. Rubber gloves should be worn at all times to prevent skin burns.

Solvent types of paint removers

Although the removers just mentioned are used quite extensively, the solvent types to be discussed now seem to be favored more by the professional wood finisher. In most cases these may be purchased ready-mixed and in any quantity desired. If you have the inclination to make your own, however, you may do so by using the following formula:

4 oz.   Benzote
3 oz.   Fusil oil
1 oz.   Denatured alcohol
½ oz.   Paraffin wax shavings

These are mixed together in the order listed and then applied to the old finish.

Another formula which you may use to make an effective paint remover is:

3 parts paraffin wax shavings
50 parts benzol
25 parts denatured alcohol
25 parts acetone

Here again the components are mixed together in the order listed and applied to the surface.

Prepared paint and varnish removers

For the home craftsman it is best to purchase the paint removers already prepared. Usually you do not use a large enough quantity to make it worthwhile to make your own. One quart of remover will remove about 100 square feet of surface. You may buy either the paste or the liquid form. The paste form usually contains either sawdust or starch so that when it is applied to a vertical surface, it will remain there without running off. The liquid form can be used on either a horizontal surface or a vertical surface. The liquid form is more popular.

How to use liquid paint and varnish removers

At the outset it should be emphasized that these materials are very flammable and should be used carefully. The working area should be free of all debris and other material that may be subjected to this hazard. The rags used for wiping off should be removed from the premises at once and destroyed. Prepare the working area by placing newspapers on the floor and near the object whose finish is to be removed. Wear an apron to protect your clothes, and, if possible, wear rubber gloves. Although the removers are not injurious to your hands, they do cause an unpleasant stinging sensation.

1. Pour some of the remover into an open container.
2. Secure an old but soft brush and fill with the remover.
3. Begin brushing the remover on the surface. Apply liberal coats to a small section at a time. *Note:* Do not attempt to cover the entire job at one time since the liquid evaporates rapidly and becomes a part of the old finish.
4. Apply a second coat over the area just covered and work the brush on the wet surface while doing this. This softens the finish and hastens its penetration.
5. Allow about five minutes of waiting time to give the remover an opportunity to soak down to the raw wood.

Paint remover is brushed on liberally. Most of the finish can be peeled off with a putty knife, and the remainder will yield to steel wool. A rag soaked in alcohol or benzene will get the last traces. However, there still may be stain embedded in the pores, and it must be removed by sanding.

49

6. Secure a wide-edged putty knife and begin peeling off the softened material. Place the residue on a sheet of paper. Do not drop on floor.

7. Clean the putty knife as often as necessary. Make sure that the edge of the knife is not damaged in the process. A damaged edge will produce deep scratches on the surface.

8. Rub the surface with No. 1/0 steel wool when all of the residue has been removed with the putty knife.

9. Inspect the cleaned surface carefully, and repeat steps 3 and 4 if traces of the old finish still remain.

10. When the cleaned section is satisfactory, use a piece of cloth to wipe off any traces of the finish from the surface.

11. Use a stiff brush soaked in remover to remove the finish from moldings, turned parts, and carving. Clean off with a dry brush.

12. All rags, residue, and paper used in this operation must be soaked in water and discarded immediately. Paint remover is very flammable and extreme care must be taken when it is used.

Before you can consider the removing operation a success, the surface must be absolutely free of every trace of the old finish. The bare wood should be completely exposed. The fact that the wood may still have the color of the original stain does not mean the surface has not been thoroughly cleaned of the old finish. The remover does not usually eliminate the stain imbedded in the pores. Sandpapering will do that. Once the old finish has been eliminated, however, the surface is ready for the next operation.

All good-quality removers contain wax as part of the mixture. The wax is included in order to permit the remover to remain moist and thus penetrate the finish. This wax has a tendency to imbed itself in the pores of the wood as the remover does its work. It is not entirely eliminated when the surface is cleaned of all the residue. Thus, provision must be made to remove all traces of it; if allowed to remain, the subsequent finishes will not dry thoroughly. So serious would be this situation that the entire new finish would have to be removed.

Avoid this by cleaning the surface of all the old finish. Wash it with a cloth soaked in either alcohol or benzine. Go over the surface thoroughly with this cloth and apply as much pressure as possible. The alcohol or the benzine will dissolve whatever wax remains in the pores of the wood. It is important also to remove the wax from corners and moldings. Soak a stiff brush in either of the two solvents mentioned and work the brush into those places. Remember that all rags, paper, and residue must be destroyed at once. Soak them in water and place them outside the house. Do not store them indoors.

You now allow the piece just cleaned about four hours to dry. After this drying period the surface is sanded with No. 1 flint paper to remove traces of the stain remaining. Check the surface for scratches, dents, and other imperfections and make the necessary repairs as described in Chapter 2. Complete the final sanding with 3/0 garnet paper.

How to use paste paint and varnish removers
Unlike the liquid removers, most of the paste removers are nonflammable. However, hands and clothing should be protected.
1. Pour enough paste remover in a container for the job in question.
2. Secure an old but soft brush and use it to apply the paste to a small section at a time.
3. Apply the paste in one direction only and work it as it is applied.
4. Allow the paste to set for approximately ten minutes or until the old finish shows signs of softening.
5. Begin to remove the softened material with a wide-bladed putty knife or coarse steel wool and place the residue on old newspaper. Do not permit it to fall to the floor or on your clothing.
6. Repeat the application on the remaining parts of the job until all of the old finish has been removed.
7. Additional coats may be applied to areas showing resistance to the remover.
8. Wash surface with cloth soaked in water to remove all traces of grime.

OBSERVING AND CORRECTING SURFACE DEFECTS

Many surface defects appear after the finish has been removed. A careful examination of the piece may show deep scratches, dents, bruises, and blistered and peeled veneers, and there may also be loose joints. All these should be repaired before the refinishing is attempted.

Gluing loose members
All loose parts and members should be detected, removed if practical, and reglued before the new finish is attempted.
1. Remove members, noting the relative position of each.
2. Scrape off the old glue with a knife. Do not damage the joint members.
3. If members fit snugly apply glue (a polyvinyl resin such as Elmer's Glue) and replace in original position. If joint members fit loosely, fit slivers of wood into the joint to make a tight fit before applying glue.

4. Apply pressure with a bar clamp or a rope-tourniquet clamp and remove the excess glue.

Removing dents
Follow the procedure outlined in Chapter 2. Wherever possible the dent should be raised by steaming. If this proves unsuccessful a water putty or plastic wood should be used. Here again the filled area should be carefully sanded and later touched up.

Removing deep scratches
Chapter 2 describes methods for removing scratches in new wood, and the same methods are used when refinishing. The best method to use depends upon the type of surface wood used in the manufacture of the furniture. If the wood is all solid, sanding and scraping is not apt to damage the wood, but if all or some of the wood is plywood, special care is necessary. Plywood can easily be recognized by studying the edges of drawers, doors, and tops. The various layers making up the plywood are easily visible. The face veneer or top layer is quite thin—usually 1/28″ thick—and it is all too easy to scrape right through it. So sanding and scraping should be done only if the scratch or blemish is not too deep. Deeper defects should be filled with a water putter or plastic wood. These fillers should be carefully sanded after they have hardened and later touched up.

Replacing splintered or peeled veneer
Small pieces of veneer splintered or peeled off the edges of a plywood top may be repaired by replacing the damaged section.
1. Select the appropriate species of wood veneer—mahogany, walnut, teak. Many varieties of veneers in small quantities are available in wood hobby shops and lumber yards.
2. Make a V cut around the damaged section with a razor blade or sharp knife.
3. Carefully remove the cut-out veneer section by placing the knife under the veneer.
4. Cut a piece of new veneer to match the cut-out. Make certain that the direction of the grain is the same.

5. Apply glue to both parts and apply pressure with the ball of a hammer or a small handscrew.
6. Allow sufficient time for glue setting, remove pressure, and sand the area.

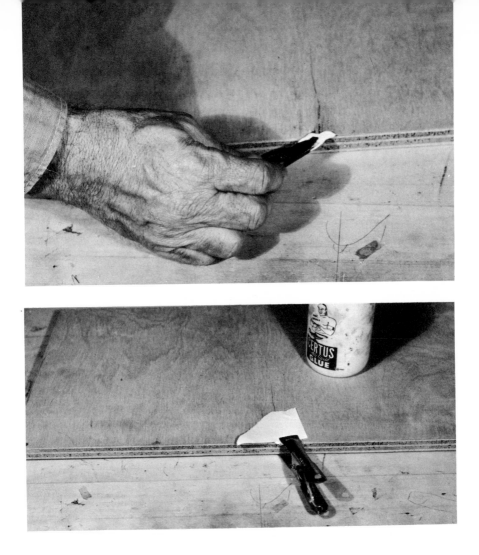

Loose veneer is glued, clamped, and finally sanded.

Repairing blistered veneer

The surface veneer of a top may have blistered. This may have been caused by water or excessive heat. Actually the glue holding the veneer in place has dissolved. Thus, in order to remove the blister, the thin layer of veneer should be reglued.

1. Make a fine cut with a razor blade in the direction of the grain and at the center of the blister. The cut should be deep enough to sever the upper layers of the blister. But do not make the cut any longer than necessary; there will be a slight scar no matter how careful you are.

2. Place a small amount of glue at the end of a pointed knife and force it into the slit, poking it right and left into the air pocket. Be careful not to break the delicate veneer.

3. Use finger tips to force more glue into the slit in the blister.

4. Remove any excess glue from the surface, using a water-damp cloth.

5. Apply pressure to the area with the face of a new hammer or some other clean-faced heavy article. Move the hammer back and forth over the area with moderate pressure until the upper layer of the pocket has adhered to the lower part of the surface.

6. If this method does not prove successful, place a piece of paper over the blister and a small flat block of wood over the paper and apply pressure with a handscrew or clamp.

7. Allow overnight drying time, then sandpaper the area with 3/0 garnet paper.

BLEACHING WOOD

At times, the purpose of the refinishing operation is to change the original color from a darker to a lighter shade. This would indeed present a problem if it were not for the different kinds of chemicals available. The removal of color from an object is called bleaching. In wood, as in other organic material, it is possible to remove all of the color with the aid of bleaching agents. Woods like walnut, oak, mahogany, and cherry, all dark woods, must be bleached of all their color before the so-called modern, blond finishes can be applied to them.

Bleaches are also used to remove stains in bare wood that might affect the appearance of the wood when the finish is applied. Rust stains, glue stains, weather stains, and water stains can be removed very easily with the aid of wood bleaches.

The craftsman and wood finisher have access to many types of wood

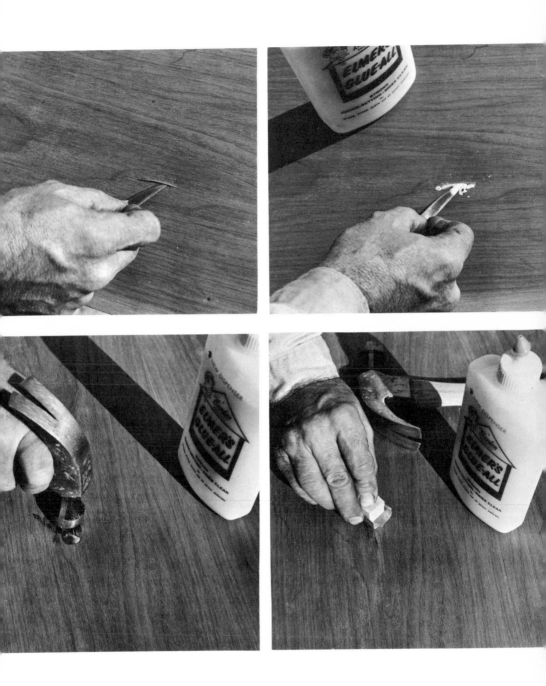

A blister in veneer is delicately sliced with a knife (in the direction of the grain) and filled with glue. Pressure is applied while the glue dries, and then the area is sandpapered.

bleaches. Each has its own characteristics and its own peculiar bleaching qualities. They may be classified as prepared bleaches and as home-prepared bleaches. The following discussion will clarify the differences.

Home-prepared bleaches

1. *Hydrogen peroxide.* Here is one of the most common bleaches available to the craftsman. It is quite an effective bleach and has proved satisfactory because of its power in bleaching wood. Incidentally, the hydrogen peroxide used in this bleach should not be confused with the hydrogen peroxide used in the home. This is a concentrated, 30% solution, which may be obtained from your local wood-finishing supply house or your chemist. The cost is not too high.

Dissolve 4 ounces of lye in one quart of water. Apply a coat of this solution while hot to the entire surface to be bleached. Use rubber gloves while handling the lye. The liquid may be applied with a piece of cotton waste or a clean piece of cloth. Allow this solution to dry on the surface for about thirty minutes and then apply the 30% hydrogen peroxide uniformly over the area. A piece of cotton waste or cloth can be used for this, but make certain that you are wearing rubber gloves. This concentrated peroxide is very caustic, and it will injure your hands.

The peroxide should be permitted to dry on the surface, for it is during this drying process that the bleaching of the wood fibers takes place. The surface is then rinsed with clean water to remove all traces of the chemicals still remaining on the surface before the next step is taken in the finishing process.

2. *Oxalic acid.* Oxalic acid is frequently used as a bleach, but it is not as effective as some of the others. Nevertheless, it is quite inexpensive, easily obtained, and simple to apply. Practically all paint stores and wood-finishing supply houses keep it in stock.

Dissolve 1 to 4 ounces of the salt in one quart of hot water, and store in a glass container. Apply the hot solution to the surface with an old brush or a piece of cloth. Make sure that the surface is covered adequately and evenly. Allow this to dry for about five minutes and apply another coat. More coats may be applied in this fashion until the desired bleached effect is obtained.

When the surface has dried thoroughly, rinse with clean water so that all traces of the salt are removed from the pores of the wood. Allow sufficient time for drying before other steps in the finishing process are added.

It is said that some manufacturers combine oxalic acid with denatured alcohol to produce a stronger-acting bleach. It is worth experimenting with.

However, the alcohol should not be heated to make the salt dissolve quicker.

3. *Oxalic acid and hypo.* The ingredients of this bleach are quite common. Actually the bleaching operation is the result of the application of each of the chemicals at separate intervals. The bleaching results are excellent when used on light woods like maple or pine. These are bleached to almost white. On the darker woods, like walnut and mahogany, the results are good. The bleach produces a much lighter shade in these woods.

Make a solution of oxalic acid by dissolving 1 to 4 ounces of the oxalic acid salt in one quart of hot water. Call this solution A. Make another solution by dissolving 2 to 4 ounces of hypo (this may be obtained from your local photography shop) in one quart of water. Call this solution B.

Apply solution A to the entire surface with a piece of cloth. Allow this to dry for a few minutes and then apply solution B in the same manner. Do not use the cloth used for solution A to apply solution B. This second application is allowed to dry for about ten minutes. Then wash off the surface with a solution made by dissolving about 1 ounce of household borax in one quart of water. This final solution cleans the surface of all traces of the salts left by solutions A and B.

The bleached area should be permitted to dry overnight. The next steps in the finishing process are started after this, drying period.

4. *Household laundry bleach.* Where a mild bleach is desired, as for example in bleaching white pine a shade or two lighter, an ordinary household laundry bleach may be used quite effectively.

Dissolve ½ pint of the bleach in one gallon of water. Apply this solution liberally to the surface with either an old brush or a piece of cloth. Several applications should be made if the desired effect is not obtained immediately. Rinse the surface with clean water to remove all traces of the chemical remaining in the pores of the wood. The surface should be permitted to dry overnight before the next step is taken.

Factory-prepared bleaches

Various manufacturers, following the trend of the times, have placed on the market many types of wood bleaches. Some have developed bleaches which will remove all color from wood with one application of the solution. Others have developed solutions which require the application of two different solutions to obtain the shade desired. Each manufacturer, however, has his own formulas for making these bleaches. Some call them Bleach No. 1 and Bleach No. 2. Others call them Bleach X and Bleach Y. Still others designate them as Color Dissolvent, Decolorant, and Aspen Concentrate. In all cases

Use rubber gloves when applying bleaching chemicals.

Bleached and unbleached wood.

the final result seems to be the same—namely, color is removed from the wood by the chemical action which takes place when these liquids are applied to the wood.

Some of them are very potent. For example, it is possible to remove all the color from mahogany to a shade of almost light buff, and all the color from walnut to a shade of almost gray. The directions given by the manufacturer aid in producing the effects desired.

In the main these bleaches are applied in about the same manner. A word of warning: These bleaches are very caustic and should not be handled unless rubber gloves are worn.

1. Make sure that the surface to be bleached is clean and free from dust.

2. Apply Bleach No. 1 evenly and liberally in the direction of the grain with an old brush or piece of clean rag (white).

3. Apply Bleach No. 2 in the same manner, but with a different rag or brush.

4. If the desired amount of color has not been removed, repeat Step 3.

5. Allow the surface to dry and then wash with clear water or a 2% solution of white vinegar, to remove all traces of the bleaching residue on the surface.

6. After overnight drying, sandpaper carefully with 5/0 finishing paper.

Some hints to assure proper bleaching

1. After the bleaching action has taken place and the surface has been properly rinsed, enough time should be allowed for moisture and oxygen to escape from the work. From six to twenty-four hours should be ample time.

2. The bleached surface should be neutralized with either water or borax or acetic acid to remove the residue of the chemical on the surface. Hundreds of little air bubbles and blisters will appear on the surface after the finish is applied if this step is skipped.

3. The wood to be bleached must be thoroughly clean—free of all dust, glue spots, dirt.

4. Experiment with the bleach on scrap wood before the main job is attempted.

5. Use rubber gloves at all times. These materials are quite caustic.

6. If an acid brush is not available, use a piece of cloth formed in the shape of a ball.

7. Apply the bleach evenly but do not flood on the surface. Uneven bleaching will result unless the chemicals are applied evenly and carefully.

8. Exposing the bleached surface to the sunlight while it is drying will intensify the bleaching process and hasten the drying.

9. All bleach solutions should be kept in cool places and away from sunlight or they will lose their strength.

Preparing bleached woods for finishing

Before the finishing materials are applied, the surface should be thoroughly sanded with 5/0 garnet finishing paper or # 180 aluminum oxide paper. This is a most important step, since the surface grain will have been raised by the application of the bleaches and must be made smooth before the actual finishing begins. Provide ample ventilation while sanding and avoid inhaling the sand dust. The dust is rather caustic and can irritate the nasal passages.

It must be remembered that wood is bleached in order to remove its color, therefore care must be exercised to make certain that the color is not affected when the top coats are applied. These special finishes require the bleached wood to remain in that shade. Before antiquing or glazing is attempted the surface should be sealed with a thin coat of white shellac or water-white lacquer. This will seal the bleached shade of the wood and prevent any of the succeeding materials from penetrating and discoloring the wood. Oil or water stains should not be used directly over the bleached wood. There is, however, one exception to this rule. When a pickled finish is desired, a light, diluted water stain is applied over the bleached wood. This process will be explained in Chapter 10.

PART TWO: SELECTING THE FINISHING MATERIALS

CHAPTER 4

Wood Stains

Undoubtedly, there have been times when you could not decide which stain would be most appropriate for your job. No doubt you have purchased stains, applied them to a surface, and found that they did not color the wood as you expected. You have become quite concerned about your failure and have made up your mind that, before attempting another staining job, you would obtain more detailed information. Many types of wood stains are on the market which can solve any staining problem you may have. All that is necessary is to know what types of wood stains are available, how to use them, and where to purchase them. The following discussion will provide this information. At the outset, this should be made clear—your selection should be conditioned by the following essentials of a stain: the stain should penetrate well; it should apply easily; it should leave a clear transparent surface; it should dry within a reasonable length of time.

PENETRATING OIL STAIN

This is one of the most common types of stains available. As the name implies, it is an oil stain with good penetrating qualities. It is prepared by the manufacturer by dissolving coal-tar dyes in naphtha, benzine, or turpentine and sold in a large variety of shades and in all quantities, from pints to gallons.

Penetrating oil stain is indeed very useful to the craftsman who has neither the time nor the experience to mix his own stains. These stains, ready for use, can be used on all types of wood, but they will not produce the same color on different woods. Thus, if a walnut stain is used, it will stain walnut a deep brownish color; but if applied to maple or pine, the same peculiar brownish color will not be produced. Hence, these stains will give the desired color only on the woods for which they are intended. Another fact to remember is that these stains will penetrate deeper when applied to open-grain woods than they will when applied to closed-grain woods. In selecting the stain, it is an excellent idea to test the stain for shade on a piece of scrap stock of the same wood as you are about to stain.

The variety of shades of the stain offered varies with the manufacturer. Usually the larger the manufacturer, the greater the variety of shades available by that trade name. Whenever possible, purchase these stains from a reliable paint dealer, for then you will be assured of a greater choice of colors. The following penetrating oil stains are quite common and may be procured from the better paint dealers:

Shade	Approximate color on wood of same name
Fumed Oak	dark brown
Golden Oak	light golden brown
Light Oak	yellowish
English Brown	dark chocolate brown
Brown Mahogany	reddish brown
Red Mahogany	deep reddish brown
Golden Maple	yellowish
Reddish Maple	pumpkin red
Light Maple	creamish white
American Walnut	brown (dark)
French Walnut	brown (light)
Ebony	black onyx (any wood)

This list is not all-inclusive. It is possible to obtain other shades by shopping from one dealer to another. You may combine several of these stains to obtain variants of them. A little experimenting with some of these will prove quite interesting.

When you are ready to select your oil stain, obtain a color card from your dealer and study the shades. If possible, test the stain you intend to purchase on a sample of the wood. This will assure you of the correctness of the shade. Then, too, experimenting with a piece of scrap wood will save you much time and annoyance. Surely, it will not be necessary to restain the entire job if the stain you applied did not turn out as you expected.

Advantages of penetrating oil stain
This type of stain can be purchased ready for use in a fairly large variety of shades from your local dealer. This is indeed an important fact to consider, especially when the craftsman is in a hurry. The shades are clearly indicated on the color card, thus giving the finisher an idea of what color to expect if applied to a surface. These stains can be purchased from time to time without fear that the shade in one container will differ from the same shade in another container. As long as the same manufacturer makes the stain, the shades will remain constant. It is a comparatively simple stain to apply—no special skill is required. It is a deep penetrating stain, which will soak into the wood surface very quickly, giving the stained wood a clear and transparent look. The grain will show through clearly. It is a non-grain-raising stain; therefore it is not necessary to sponge the wood before staining.

Disadvantages of penetrating oil stain
One of the weaknesses of this type of stain from the standpoint of the finisher is the fact that the shades available are limited. No more than about fifteen shades are available, and these from only the more reliable manufacturers. Because of their oil base, these stains require at least twenty-four hours of drying time before any other coat can be applied. Paste fillers and varnishes cannot be applied directly over these stains, for the oils in these materials will tend to soften the oil stain on the surface, leaving a muddy appearance. A wash coat of shellac (refer to Chapter 6) is always advisable over an oil-stained surface before the other materials are applied. Finally, penetrating oil stain has a tendency to seep (bleed) through a varnished or lacquered finish, causing a change in the color of the finish. Have you ever applied a light paint over a stained door? Have you wondered why the color of the stain came through the paint and changed the color of your paint? Oil stain of the

finished door combined with the paint and thus changed the color of the paint after it had been applied. Where a stained door must be painted a light shade, this reaction can be prevented only if the door is first painted with a metallic paint, such as aluminum paint. This paint seals the surface and prevents the stain from bleeding through. Any pastel paint applied directly to the aluminum paint will not be affected by the stain.

Applying penetrating oil stain

You should always bear in mind the importance of preparing the surface before attempting to stain. The surface should be inspected for scratches and other imperfections, which should be removed. Final sandpapering with No. 3/0 garnet finishing paper is recommended. Clean your surface thoroughly before staining.

Make certain that you have ample work space, free from dust and other encumbrances. Allow yourself plenty of room to move about the object you are about to stain. Good lighting is also important. Select an appropriate brush (a wide, flat, bristle brush is suggested for staining large surfaces). Make sure that the brush is clean, free from dust, oil, grease, or previous stain. Now study the nature of your wood. Soft woods and open-grain woods will absorb more stain than hard-textured and closed-grain woods; therefore, when applying the stain, remember to allow the proper amount of penetration before wiping off the excess. If there is any exposed end grain on any part of your job, apply a thin coat of shellac or linseed oil. This step will seal the very porous end grain and prevent the absorption of too much stain. If this step is not taken, any section having exposed end grain will appear much darker than any other section of the piece of furniture. Of course, the shellac or oil used to seal this surface must be thoroughly dry before the stain is brushed on.

1. Fill the brush with stain, but not dripping full.
2. Place the brush about two inches from the edge and in the center of the surface and begin brushing to the left and right in long even strokes. Always follow the direction of the grain.
3. Refill the brush and again start about two inches from the last brush mark and brush in long even strokes toward the ends of the surface. Move toward the previous brush mark as the brushing continues.
4. Continue refilling the brush and brushing as indicated until the entire area is covered.
5. If possible stain the entire surface with one brushful. This eliminates the chances of overlap marks.

It is good practice to stain one section of your piece at a time. Do not jump from one area to another, but continue in a normal sequence. Start staining the sides, then the front, then the back, and finally the top. Again you should be reminded that all brushing should follow the direction of grain. Brushing across the grain will cause uneven absorption of the stain, leaving unsightly light and dark streaks on the surface. Another good practice to remember is that you should never permit the brush to rub against the end of your work, for this will cause an unusually large amount of stain to collect at that point, which will dry much darker than the remainder of the job. Avoid brushing additional stain to an area which has just been stained. This care will assure a uniform stained surface free from dark and light streaks.

After the stain has been applied to a section, wipe off the excess with a clean cloth, but be careful that you wipe with the grain and not across the grain. To assure uniform color throughout the piece of furniture, allow an equal amount of drying time for each section stained before wiping. More time for one section and less time for another will result in one area drying darker or lighter than the other. All rags used in this operation must be soaked in water immediately or destroyed. Oily rags should not be permitted to accumulate in your workshop as these will, by spontaneous combustion, begin to burn within a short time.

Oil stain is brushed on in the direction of the grain.

WATER STAIN

To the professional wood finisher there is no better stain than water stain. This popularity is the result of its many fine qualities, as a stain, which are unknown to the average amateur finisher. You will do well to consider the many advantages of this stain before deciding what kind of stain to use for your job.

Its most important feature is its ready absorption by wood. This results in the deep penetration of the stain, which is actually colored water. You can see the advantage of this deep penetration to the finisher who is anxious to obtain a clear and permanently stained surface.

As the name implies, the solvent in this stain is pure water. In this water a coal-tar or vegetable dye (powder) is dissolved. Water stain cannot be purchased in a prepared form as is the penetrating oil stain. The dyes (anilines) for this stain are obtained from a reliable paint dealer. The solution can be prepared easily and quickly. Boil a quart of water and pour into a metal container. Then add slowly to this hot water one ounce of the aniline powder, stirring the solution as you add the powder. Allow the solution to cool and the stain is ready for use. Be sure that the powder you purchase is water-soluble. Other powders are available for making of stain that are not soluble in water, and if these are used for that purpose, they will not produce the desired solution. The label on the package designates the type of liquid that will dissolve the powder. Read it carefully before making the stain.

No other type of stain can produce such a large variety of colors. The powders can be obtained to make stains in almost any color on the color wheel, thus assuring the user a range of shades to meet his every need. These colors are brilliant and more transparent than those of any other type of stain.

Available colors

The modern wood finisher likes to blend his own powders to obtain the particular shade for his job, and his knowledge of formulas and colors is such that he can combine powders to produce such stains. Lately, however, manufacturers, noting the increased demand for special colored stains, have begun to blend their own powders to get these effects, and they have placed them on the market for distribution to all. Now, the home craftsman need know only the particular shade of stain he requires and he can purchase the powder to make that stain. Very little blending is required. If a darker shade is needed, merely add more powder to the water. If a lighter shade is needed, add more water to the solution. Note the large variety of colors which are available for your staining problems.

Black—Jet
Blue
Brown Bismark—Reddish
Brown Bismark—Yellowish
Brown—Seal
Brown—Adam
Brown—Sheraton
Green—Olive
Green—Light
Mahogany—Light
Mahogany—Brown
Mahogany—Pinkish
Mahogany—Red
Mahogany—Yellowish
Maple—Antique Light
Maple—Yellowish
Maple—Reddish
Oak—Weathered
Oak—Early English
Oak—Fumed
Oak—Reddish
Oak—Golden Dark
Oak—Flemish
Orange
Red—Scarlet
Red—Medium
Red—Blood
Red—Rose
Red—Eosine Yellowish
Rosewood
Silver Gray
Violet—Purple
Walnut—Circassian
Walnut—Medium
Walnut—Dark
Yellow—Lemon
Yellow—Canary

More shades can be produced by combining two or more of these powders in a solution. For example, Red Mahogany powder (aniline) dissolved in water will give you a reddish stain, too red if what you want is a reddish-brown shade. Merely add to this stain enough Brown Mahogany powder to produce the desired reddish-brown color. Of course, test the solution from time to time to assure the proper blend.

Advantages of water stain
As indicated previously in this chapter, water stain is very popular with the skilled finisher. The large variety of powders available make any shade possible. These stains are deep-penetrating and, consequently, will give stained surfaces that will not fade when subjected to strong light for any length of time. When applied to any wood surface they will produce a clear, transparent film and will help bring out the beauty of the wood grain. They will not leave a muddy surface even if the excess stain is not wiped off. The solutions made with these anilines are crystal-clear and, consequently, will leave a brilliancy on the wood that is possible with no other stain. Water stain is quite inexpensive. An ounce of aniline, enough to make one quart of water stain, costs about twenty cents, and it will cover about 150 square feet of surface—suf-

ficient for the average piece of furniture. Water stain, unlike oil stain, will dry within a few hours, and the surface will then be ready for the next step of the finishing process.

Disadvantages of water stain

Possibly the most important drawback in the use of water stain is the time required to prepare the surface for the staining operation. As you know, when water is applied to a wood, it raises the grain slightly, causing a rough, fuzzy surface. This is also true when water stain is applied directly to the bare wood. The rough surface which results is not suitable for proper finishing results; and, if this condition is eliminated by sanding, the sanding will wear off part of the stain on the wood, leaving an uneven stained surface. To prevent this, the wood to be water-stained should be first wet with clear water, allowed to dry, and then sanded smooth with No. 3/0 garnet paper. It is this additional labor and time that, at times, influences the finisher to use another type of stain—a non-grain-raising stain.

Greater care must be exercised in applying these stains than in applying oil stains. Streaks and lap marks are quite common when the stain is not applied properly. A little practice is suggested before beginning the actual staining.

Lastly, water stain cannot be used on a surface from which the finish has been removed. The stain will not penetrate a wood which has been finished before, even if every trace of the old finish has been removed.

Applying water stain

Before you begin to stain, make certain that your work area is clear of all obstructions. Now make sure that your job has been checked for defects and these defects removed. Dust off your job, and proceed to sponge every section with clear water. A piece of cloth may be used instead of a sponge, but no matter which you use, do not soak it too much with water—just enough water to wet the surface of your job evenly, and without dripping. It is a good practice, when wetting the surface, to follow the grain. Make sure that every part of the job is properly wet. Spots which are not wet will dry rough when the water stain is applied. Allow the job to dry thoroughly—at least one hour—and then proceed to sandpaper with No. 3/0 garnet paper until the fuzz has been removed. Use a block for the flat surfaces and the palm of your hand for the curved areas and moldings. When you are satisfied with the smoothness of your work, you are ready for the staining operation itself.

At the outset of the actual staining, remember that it is better to apply two

70

Coat end grain with shellac before applying water stain, or it will be much darker than the rest of the surface. When applying the stain be careful not to splatter parts of the surface you have not reached yet.

coats of light stain than one coat of dark stain. In this way it is easier to control the shade of your stain.

1. Secure a wide stiff-haired brush. A soft flaccid brush is not recommended because it will not work the stain into the pores of the wood. A nylon brush is suggested.

2. Fill the brush, but not dripping wet.

3. Place the brush about two inches from the edge and in the center of the surface and begin brushing to the left and the right following the direction of the grain.

4. If necessary refill the brush and again start about two inches from the last brush mark and brush in long even strokes toward the end of the surface. Move toward the previous brush mark as the brushing continues.

5. Do not attempt to stretch the remaining stain on the brush. Refill the brush to assure an even coat.

6. Apply stain to corners, crevices, and carvings in the same manner. Remove excess stain accumulated in these areas by tipping a dry brush into the crevices.

Occasionally, you will discover that the stain you are applying seems rather light for your purpose. You can easily make the shade darker by going over the surface with another coat of the same stain. However, avoid this whenever possible. It is a better practice to check your stain on a scrap piece of wood before applying it to your finished piece. Incidentally, you will note that the stain has a darker appearance when wet than when dry on the surface. This is natural and should be no cause for concern, because the shade of your stained surface will become darker when the other finish coats are applied.

During your staining operation avoid spattering the stain on the other parts of your job. These splatter marks will become very noticeable spots when that part of the project is stained and allowed to dry.

Continue to stain the other parts of the job, but leave the top and drawer fronts, if any, for the last. Where possible, stain all pieces by placing them in a horizontal position to assure better brushing and a more even distribution of stain. When the job has been completely stained, allow at least four hours for drying before the next coat is applied.

SPIRIT (ALCOHOL) STAIN

Spirit stain is another class of stain which deserves a detailed explanation. In addition to its use as a wood stain, it is indispensable as a touching-up stain. As the name indicates, this stain is made by dissolving alcohol-soluble

72

powders in alcohol. The concentration of the stain depends upon the amount of powder dissolved in the alcohol. For an average stain, about ½ ounce of powder is dissolved in one quart of alcohol; but the craftsman can use a different proportion so long as he obtains the correct concentration. These dyes will dissolve almost immediately, producing a very clear and transparent stain. However, care should be taken that the powder purchased is soluble in alcohol, and not in water. Water-soluble dyes will not dissolve well in alcohol, and consequently will not give the shade of stain required. Therefore, again look at the label on the package to make sure that you are getting the correct dye. There are a few dyes that will dissolve in both water and alcohol with the same results. In that case, either liquid can be used. The label should tell.

Unlike water stain, the variety of shades of alcohol stain is limited. There are, however, enough colors to meet practically all the needs of the home craftsmen. The following list indicates the choices available to the finisher.

Black—Nigrosene	Mahogany—Yellowish
Blue—Violet	Mahogany—Adam Brown
Bismarck Brown—Reddish	Maple—Reddish
Bismarck Brown—Yellowish	Oak—Fumed
Brown—Seal	Oak—Reddish
Brown—Adam	Oak—Golden Yellow
Green—Sage	Oak—Dark
Green—Yellowish	Orange
Silver Gray	Walnut—Circassian
Mahogany—Medium	Yellow—Lemon

The powders listed give a clear indication of the shades of alcohol stains that can be made. You will note that the more common wood shades can be easily made merely by dissolving the powder in the alcohol; and it is possible also to combine two or more of these powders to obtain other shades. To illustrate, if you add Black Nigrosene to Reddish Bismarck Brown, the resulting stain will be a very deep, dark red; if Seal Brown is added to Circassian Walnut, the ensuing color stain will be a brown walnut. The craftsman should experiment with these powders and note the possible color combinations. Acquire the habit of mixing small quantities at first; this will prove both economical and time-saving.

Advantages of alcohol stain

The fact that this stain is a fast-drying liquid makes it a very appropriate stain to use when the craftsman is pressed for time. The stain, which dries by evaporation, will dry almost immediately when applied to raw wood. Thus a job may be stained and filled within a matter of minutes, while other types of stains require hours and days to dry. Next in importance is its ability to penetrate a finished surface. In other words, it is possible to apply this type of stain over a shellacked, varnished, or lacquered surface and it will penetrate and stain that surface. Better results will be assured if a little shellac is added to the stain before applying it. It is for this reason that this stain is used for touching up. Chapter 15 discusses this operation in more detail. Consider also the fact that this stain, when applied to wood, will not raise the grain as does water stain. The necessity of wetting and sanding the surface before staining is eliminated. The stain may be applied directly over a smoothly sanded surface. Lastly, it is transparent, leaving a beautiful brilliant surface after the stain is applied.

Disadvantages of alcohol stain

As already indicated, the fact that this stain dries very rapidly when applied is an advantage, but it can also be a disadvantage if the user does not apply it properly. The stain dries so rapidly that it becomes almost impossible to stain a large area without lap or streak marks. Even the experienced wood finisher has difficulty. Thus, the use of this stain on large surfaces is not recommended unless it can be applied with a sprayer. However, on small objects, like picture frames, jewelry boxes, and novelties, it cannot be surpassed, because one section of the article may be stained with one brushful without leaving any unsightly marks on the surface. Then, too, alcohol stain fades with time. Alcohol stain does not penetrate the wood too deeply; consequently, it is not fast to light.

Applying alcohol stain

The surface to be stained should be sanded carefully and cleaned before the staining operation is begun. Secure a stiff-bristle brush large enough for the surface to be stained. A 3″ flat brush is suggested for the large areas; a 1″ flat brush for small picture-frame moldings or other small areas. In selecting the brush, consider that, if possible, the brush should be large enough to cover the complete area to be stained with one brushful. Remember, too, the important fact that the stain dries very rapidly as applied.

1. Fill the brush to capacity, but not dripping wet.

74

Alcohol stain must be applied rapidly and surely, or there will be streaks and lap marks.

2. Place brush in the center of the surface and begin brushing from right to left and following the direction of the grain.

3. Work the brush as rapidly as possible without attempting to stretch the stain.

4. Refill the brush if you note difficulty in spreading the remaining stain. Start about two inches from the previous brush mark and at the center of the surface. Work toward the brush mark in long even strokes from left to right.

Avoid going over a surface that has just been stained, as this additional stain will darken that area considerably with lap marks and unsightly streaks. The secret of a successful stain job, when using alcohol stain, is to use as large a brush as possible and to work as quickly as possible, making sure that you are covering all of the surface. You cannot work the stain as you do oil stain or water stain; the more you work alcohol stain, the darker the surface becomes.

The staining schedule, when using alcohol stain, is the same as when you are using any other type of stain. Stain one section at a time before proceeding to the next. Stain the sides or legs first, then stain the front, then the top, and finally the drawers or other members that have been removed from the piece. Whenever possible, have pieces in a horizontal position when staining, with the light coming from the front of you.

Sometimes an already-finished surface can be darkened with alcohol stain.

Applying alcohol stain on a finished surface

Occasionally it becomes necessary to darken or change the color of a surface already finished. Rather than refinish the article, which requires much effort and time, the color may be altered by redoing with an alcohol stain. Of course, the explanation which follows is not recommended in all cases of this type; nevertheless, when the finished result is not to be a first-class job, the following process may be used.

Blend the alcohol-soluble powders to the desired shade (experiment on a small section of the surface before attempting the complete job) and then add a little white shellac to your solution to make it adhere better to the surface. Sandpaper the surface to be recolored with a fine, garnet-finishing paper, No. 4/0 or No. 5/0, to remove any dirt, grease, or other marks. Dust off with a piece of soft cloth moistened with alcohol, and then apply the stain, already prepared, to the surface. Follow the procedure that was used in staining the raw wood; however, make certain that you brush with the grain and try to cover as much of the surface as possible with one brushful. Do not go over a section just stained with additional stain. Allow this to dry thoroughly, and then apply the other finishes.

PIGMENT OIL STAIN

The craftsman has another choice of wood stain in pigment oil stain. Here, again, we have a stain that cannot be purchased ready-prepared and ready for use, but must be made by the finisher. It is indeed one of the most simple stains to use and also to make. You need only a little experience and a knowledge of the required ingredients:

76

Color—paste ground in oil
Thinner—turpentine or benzene
Oil—boiled linseed oil
Drier—japan drier
Let us discuss each of these ingredients in detail.

Color is the most important of all the ingredients, for it is this material that will eventually color the wood. It is the same oil color that is used for art work or for tinting wall paints. Usually, oil colors are purchased in ounce tubes or in pint containers. They are prepared by mixing the ground color in linseed oil to form a paste. Go to your local dealer and ask for a color chart of oil colors. The chart contains about fifty different colors, ranging from white to black. You should become familiar with these, for a knowledge of the various shades will help you immeasurably in making the different colors of stains you may need. Incidentally, these colors are standard, and the names applied to each will always refer to the same color regardless of the manufacturer. The most common of these oil colors are grouped in the various color classes.

Pigments	Approximate color
Yellows	
Chrome Yellow Light	lemon yellow
Chrome Yellow Medium	reddish-yellow
French Ochre	tan
Wash Ochre	brownish-yellow
Blues	
Cobalt Blue	purplish-blue
Ultramarine Blue	deep blue
Prussian Blue	indigo blue
Permanent Blue	blue
Reds	
Venetian Red	brick red
Turkey Red	brownish-red
Vermilion Red	brilliant red
Rose Pink	purplish-red
Browns	
Raw Sienna	tannish-brown
Burnt Sienna	reddish-brown
Raw Umber	brown-grayish
Burnt Umber	chocolate brown
Vandyke Brown	deep brown

Pigments	Approximate color
Greens	
Chrome Green Light	pea green
Chrome Green Medium	sea green
Chrome Green Dark	bluish green
Blacks	
Lamp Black	grayish-black
Ivory Black	blackish-black
Whites	
White Lead	yellowish-white
Lithopone	snow-white
Zinc White	white

Thinners. The paste color alone could not serve as a stain because of its heavy consistency. It must be reduced to a liquid by dissolving the paste in a thinner, such as turpentine or benzene. These oil colors will dissolve very easily in either of these two liquids because of the oil vehicle used in making the paste. When dissolved, the color becomes dispersed very thinly in the new liquid. There are other thinners which are used for this purpose, thinners like naphtha and benzol, but these are not recommended because of their cost. However, any can be used with equally good results. All will penetrate the wood surface.

Oil. Boiled linseed oil is recommended as the ingredient to keep together the loose color dissolved in the thinner. Boiled oil is recommended, because it has a tendency to dry faster when applied to the wood than the raw linseed oil. The oil is easily recognized by its dark amber color. It cannot be mistaken for the raw oil, which is very light by comparison.

Drier. The fourth ingredient is japan drier. This is a fast-drying varnish which is added in a small quantity to hasten the drying of the stain. Oil dries by oxidation; the oil combines with air to form an oxide—a very slow process indeed. The drier hastens this oxidation. However, do not add too much drier just for the sake of shortening the drying time. Too much drier will cause the stain to become too gummy on the surface and consequently it will not wipe off easily.

Recipes for pigment oil stains

Let us now see how all of these ingredients are combined to form the stain in question. Proportions of the latter three ingredients—namely, the turpentine or benzene, oil, and drier—always remain constant regardless of the color of stain. The amount (by weight) of color used always remains the same;

The basic ingredients of pigment oil stains.

thus, once the craftsman becomes familiar with these proportions he can mix any shade of stain he desires. A series of the more common wood stains with their appropriate oil color combinations are listed. The formulas given are for one quart of the stain. You will note, too, that the amount of each material is the same regardless of the shade. Let us illustrate: for one quart of any shade of stain, mix, to ½ pound of color, one pint of turpentine (or benzene), 6 ounces of boiled linseed oil, and about ½ ounce of drier. Note how the ingredients for each shade of stain comply with the proportions just illustrated.

79

Cherry Stain
8 ounces Burnt Sienna
1 pint turpentine
6 ounces boiled linseed oil
½ ounce drier

Pumpkin Brown Maple
8 ounces of Burnt Sienna
A trace of Ultramarine Blue
1 pint of turpentine
6 ounces boiled linseed oil
½ ounce drier

Yellowish Maple
6 ounces yellow (French) Ochre
1 ounce Burnt Sienna
1 ounce Ultramarine Blue
1 pint turpentine
6 ounces boiled linseed oil
½ ounce drier

Dark Oak
4 ounces Raw Sienna
2 ounces Burnt Umber
2 ounces Burnt Sienna
1 pint turpentine
6 ounces boiled linseed oil
½ ounce drier

Brown Mahogany
6 ounces Vandyke Brown
2 ounces Rose Pink
1 pint turpentine
6 ounces boiled linseed oil
½ ounce drier

Cherry Stain Light
4 ounces Raw Sienna
4 ounces Burnt Sienna
1 pint turpentine
6 ounces boiled linseed oil
½ ounce drier

Honey Brown Maple
6 ounces Burnt Sienna
2 ounces Ultramarine Blue
1 pint of turpentine
6 ounces boiled linseed oil
½ ounce drier

Light Oak
6 ounces Raw Sienna
2 ounces Raw Umber
1 pint turpentine
6 ounces boiled linseed oil
½ ounce drier

Red Mahogany
6 ounces Burnt Sienna
2 ounces Rose Pink
1 pint turpentine
6 ounces boiled linseed oil
½ ounce drier

Walnut
4 ounces Vandyke Brown
4 ounces Burnt Umber
1 pint turpentine
6 ounces boiled linseed oil
½ ounce drier

Dark Walnut
8 ounces Vandyke Brown
1 pint turpentine
6 ounces boiled linseed oil
½ ounce drier

Silver Gray
4 ounces Lamp Black
4 ounces White Lead
1 pint turpentine
6 ounces boiled linseed oil
½ ounce drier

Fruitwood
6 ounces Vandyke Brown
2 ounces Burnt Umber
1 pint turpentine
6 ounces boiled linseed oil
½ ounce drier

How to mix pigment oil stains

Let us take a concrete example. Suppose you desire to stain a table a red mahogany, and you intend to use a pigment oil stain. Refer to the formula for making red mahogany stain, and note that Burnt Sienna and Rose Pink oil colors are required. Secure an empty tin container and pour into it one pint of turpentine or benzene, then slowly add 6 ounces by weight of Burnt Sienna, stirring as you add the color. When all of the Burnt Sienna has dissolved, add 2 ounces of Rose Pink, also stirring as you add the color. Then add the boiled linseed oil, also stirring the mixture as you add the oil. Finally add the drier to the stain. Check the stain on a small piece of scrap wood and see if the color is satisfactory. If the stain is not the color shade, add a little more of either of the oil colors until the correct shade is obtained. It should be noted that the formulas given are not exact; they are approximations. A little experimenting with your colors should always be done before accepting the stain that you have made as the best possible.

Advantages of pigment oil stain

Of all the stains discussed, this is the most simple to apply. You merely put it on the already-prepared surface and wipe off the excess. More will be said of this later in this chapter. It is not a fast-drying stain and, consequently, need not be applied with the haste and care required for other stains. A reasonable length of time may elapse before wiping off the excess. Then, too, the ingredients for making this stain are common household supplies; and, where they are not available at home, they can be purchased from your local paint dealer. The oil color pastes are not wasted if they remain unused. They can be stored for future use without losing any of their strength.

This stain is important also as a blending and antiquing medium. When a dark stain is applied to a light-finished surface and then wiped off lightly, a contrasting soft color will result. See Chapter 13 for further details.

Disadvantages of pigment oil stain

The main weakness of pigment oil stain lies in the fact that it is not a deep penetrating stain; it is a superficial stain just covering the top layer of the wood surface. It fades when subjected to light for a long period of time and, consequently, is not recommended for very fine work. Also, it does not possess the clarity and transparency of the other stains mentioned and must be wiped off after it is applied to assure some showing of the wood grain. On soft woods like pine and gum, the stain has a tendency to darken the wood more than if used on hard woods like maple or birch; therefore, a good practice is to coat these soft woods with a wash coat of shellac or linseed oil before applying the stain. More uniformity of color will also result. As with the penetrating oil stains, fillers cannot be applied directly over the surface stained with pigment oil stain. The filler will combine with the stain, forming a muddy film over the surface. The stained surface should be coated with a wash coat of shellac in order to protect it before the filler is applied. Finally, the length of time required for drying should also be considered. At least twenty-four hours should elapse before any other material is applied.

Applying pigment oil stain

The piece to be stained should be thoroughly prepared with the usual sanding and checking. Then you must prepare the desired shade of stain according to instructions.

1. Use a stiff, flat bristle brush. Fill it to capacity, but not dripping wet.

2. Apply the stain to one section of the job. Direction of brushing and amount of stain applied is not important at this stage.

Pigment oil stain is brushed on, then the excess is wiped off with a rag. Use a dry brush to get the excess stain out of crevices.

3. After an entire section has been stained, take a soft clean piece of rag and wipe off the excess stain by rubbing in the direction of the grain. Use uniform pressure in wiping off the excess and wipe stain off evenly.

4. Other sections of the piece are stained in the same manner. Compare the color of the different sections stained. Restain if color is too light, or wipe off additional stain if area is too dark.

5. If an area remains too dark after additional wiping, soak a piece of cloth in turpentine and use it to wash off some of the dark color remaining.

6. Use a clean dry brush to pick up accumulated stain in crevices and carvings. Tip the dry brush into the crevices.

CHEMICAL STAINS

Chemical stains are not familiar to the average wood finisher, but are nevertheless indispensable in obtaining certain types of wood effects. The chemicals are either acid or alkaline. They combine chemically with the wood, causing a reaction to take place which colors the wood permanently. Only those will be mentioned which are easily available and applied. Among these are many of the ordinary household chemicals used in the home laundry and kitchen.

Some of these chemicals are available in crystal form or powder. A few are in liquid form. Those that are not in liquid form may be dissolved by adding 4 to 8 ounces of the crystal or powder to one gallon of warm water. The depth of shade can be easily controlled, either by adding more water to the solution if the stain is too dark, or more chemical if the stain is too light. A little experimentation is recommended. After the solution has been made, it should be stored in glass containers—*never* in metal containers, because of injurious chemical reactions.

When you are mixing or using these stains, bear in mind that they are very caustic and can injure hands and clothing. Wear old clothing and rubber gloves.

Permanganate of potash

A violet-colored crystal which, when dissolved in water at the ratio of 2 ounces of crystal to one quart of water, will produce a stain which colors wood a medium brown. Of course, if a deeper or lighter shade is desired, the amount of crystal may be proportioned accordingly.

84

Lye
Household lye, when dissolved in water, will produce a liquid which will color wood a light brown. Note above for proportion.

Sal soda
A white powder used in the household for cleaning when dissolved in water (2 ounces to one quart of water) will stain wood a yellowish brown to brown depending upon the type of wood being stained. Oak, for example, will stain to brown.

Acetic acid (vinegar)
The chemical result of combining vinegar with iron filings or nails will produce a stain which will color pine a beautiful, weathered gray. Place the iron filings or pure iron nails in a container and then pour in about one pint of cider (white) vinegar. Allow this to stand overnight. Strain the solution and then apply to the surface with a brush. At first the color on the wood will be light, but it dries to antique gray.

Ammonia (26%)
This chemical is a gas but, when mixed in water, it produces a very strong ammonia water. When applied to oak with a brush it will combine with the chemicals in the wood to stain the wood a deep brown color. This ammonia must not be confused with the household type found on the grocer's shelf. It must be purchased from your paint dealer. However, household ammonia may be tried. Ammonia stain has regained its popularity with the introduction of wormy chestnut as a furniture wood. Many furniture pieces and interiors are now being constructed of this species of wood. Ammonia when applied to chestnut or oak will stain them in a beautiful soft warm brown.

Applying chemical stains
The preparation of the surface is similar to the preparation of the surface when water stain is to be used—namely, the job to be stained is sponged with clear water, allowed to dry, and then sanded with No. 3/0 garnet sandpaper. If this were not done, the grain of the wood would become fuzzy after the application of the chemical stain.

The stain is applied in the same manner as is water stain, but with an inexpensive brush. The chemical stain will harm the hair of any brush; consequently, use one that is clean but of little value. Use rubber gloves while handling the stain. Allow at least four hours for drying before proceeding with the next finishing material.

WAX STAINS

A recent addition to the wood-stain market is the product developed by such companies as Minwax and U.S. Plywood. These stains usually consist of a mixture of penetrating oil stains mixed with wax and a drying agent. When applied to a raw wood surface, they will produce a pleasing hand-rubbed finish. These stains are manufactured in most of the popular colors and finishes, such as Early American, Cherry, Driftwood, Colonial, Maple, Walnut, and Mahogany. A study of a color chart is suggested before a selection is made. It should also be remembered that these stains work best with the woods intended. Colors should be tested on sample woods before used.

Advantages of wax stains
They are comparatively easy to apply. They are applied with a brush or cloth. They bring out the true beauty of the wood, since the stains become a part of the wood itself and give a rich soft wax finish. They are penetrating stains and are not grain-raising.

Disadvantages of wax stains
The stains do not in any way fill the pores of the wood. An open-grain effect is the result, with a smooth satin effect. Although it is possible to add a paste filler to the stain, the results are not comparable to those obtained when a filler is applied over a stained wood. This stain is not recommended where a "piano finish" or a hand-rubbed lacquer finish is required.

Applying wax stains
1. Apply first coat with a brush or cloth, preferably in the direction of the grain.
2. Allow to stand for five to ten minutes, until the stain has sufficiently penetrated the wood.
3. Remove the excess stain with a clean cloth.
4. Allow to dry overnight and apply a second coat in the same manner.
5. Allow twenty-four hours drying time and apply a paste finishing wax and buff.
6. No other coating is necessary, however several coats of white shellac may be applied if a protective satin appearance is desired.

VARNISH STAINS

Many a craftsman has from time to time purchased varnish stain with the dual purpose of staining a surface and applying a varnish coat at the same time,

Wax stain is wiped or brushed on, and then after a few minutes the excess is wiped off.

all in one operation. The results of this attempt do not always turn out as desired. You discover that you have neither stained the wood properly nor applied a good coat of varnish. The reason for this should be quite obvious. The properties of a good stain are penetration and clarity. The varnish stain has neither of these qualities. It does not penetrate the surface, and the varnish diminishes its transparency. The result of using this stain is a muddy, streaky surface on the wood. Yet these stains are used by many, because it is believed that time and money are being saved.

As the name implies, varnish stain is a mixture consisting of varnish and penetrating oil stain. These are combined in a proportion to produce a colored varnish capable of coloring wood when applied. These stains can be purchased at any department, paint, or hardware store, ready to use and in many popular shades ranging from oak to walnut. They are sold in containers ranging in size from a half pint to a gallon. The cost is rather high. If the craftsman desires, he can mix his own varnish stain by adding penetrating oil stain to clear varnish. A large variety of choices thus becomes possible.

Advantages of varnish stains

Very little can be said in favor of these stains from the standpoint of obtaining professional results in staining. However, there is a use for them that is quite practical. They can be applied to surfaces like interiors of cabinets or closets, where appearance is not essential, but all that is required is the coloring of the surface to make it inconspicuous. Staining and giving a protective coat in one operation is indeed economical for this type of work.

Disadvantages of varnish stains

Most of the disadvantages have already been mentioned; however, this should be added. A skilled hand is required when the stain is brushed to the surface. The brushing must be done so that the stain is spread on evenly without overlapping. Despite all the care exercised, it dries streaky, with a rough surface, and a semi-gloss finish. Additional coats will not improve the surface.

Applying varnish stains

The surface to be stained should be prepared as any other surface undergoing a similar operation. It should be thoroughly sanded and cleaned. Prepare your stain by pouring it into a container large enough to accommodate the brush you are using.

1. Fill the brush to capacity, but not dripping wet.
2. Begin brushing from the center of the area and brush to the left and right in long even strokes.
3. Refill the brush if necessary and start brushing about two inches from the last brush mark to the left and to the right.
4. Pick up any excess stain by brushing over the area with a dry brush.

Take these additional precautions when applying this type of stain: Make sure that the brush you are using is free from oil or grease; if your brush is not clean, the stain will become affected and will not dry. Do not go over a section just stained with another coat of the material, because overlapping and streaks will result. Always brush with the grain; brushing across the grain will produce uneven color and lap marks. Inasmuch as this stain contains varnish, care should be exercised to see that the project stained is stored in a dust-free room while it is drying. This will eliminate much of the trouble associated with varnishing a surface—namely, the settling of dust on the wet surface.

CHAPTER 5

Wood Fillers

All wood is composed of millions of little cells, giving the particular characteristics to the wood which we call grain. Regardless of the size of these cells or pores, some ingredient is required to fill them and make them even with the surrounding surface. This filling is a necessary evil, for without it the surface could not possibly have the appearance that we admire so much in fine pieces of furniture. A lack of knowledge of this principle of pore filling can cause the craftsman much inconvenience and expense.

The process of filling the pores of wood, either before or after the wood is stained, is called filling. The material used for filling is called filler. There are two types of wood fillers—paste wood filler, used for filling the pores of open-grain wood; and liquid filler, used for filling the pores of close-grain wood.

PASTE WOOD FILLER

You should bear in mind that a wood filler has a specific function—namely, the filling of the pores of the wood. It must have qualities that will do this job well. The filler must adhere without shrinking, crumbling, or cracking when it dries in the pores of the wood. In addition, the filler must dry hard and not rubbery within a reasonable time—let us say twenty-four hours. The material having all these qualities is Silex, the commercial name for crystal quartz. This quartz is ground into a very fine powder and then mixed with boiled linseed oil to form a grayish-white paste. Pure quartz powder and linseed oil plus japan drier is known as natural wood filler—a filler having a neutral color. This is the type of filler that is used to fill the pores of raw wood surfaces, because this filler does not impart any color to the bare wood. However, this type is not recommended for stained woods. In that case, the shade of the filler should match or be a trifle darker than the color of the stained wood. In order to tint paste filler, oil color is added to the natural filler. The combination of oil colors and the amount of each added will depend upon the shade of the stained surface that the filler is to match. In short, the following ingredients are found in colored paste filler:

Silex powder—the solid base material

Linseed oil—the binder to keep the Silex in a paste form

Oil color—to color the filler to the desired shade

Japan drier—to hasten drying of the filler once on the surface

The craftsman need concern himself with these ingredients only insofar as they give him an idea of the materials used in the filler. Fillers can be purchased ready-made in practically every color of stained wood surfaces.

Colors of paste filler

The wood finisher must consider several factors when he is about to buy the paste filler for his job. First of all, he must make sure that the label clearly indicates the ingredients. Do not purchase a filler whose label does not clearly show this information, for there are many fillers which use corn starch, plaster, and flour as substitutes for the Silex. These are all inferior and should be avoided.

In deciding on the color to select for your particular job, remember that the color of filler selected must be close to the color of the stained wood surface, and not the color of the natural wood. If possible, the color should be a slightly darker shade than the stained wood, for when the filler dries in the pores it will dry a little lighter than the original color of the filler, and thus it will stand out lighter than the surrounding surface. There are a few exceptions to this rule. For example, where a pickled finish is contemplated, the filler used to fill the pores should be lighter than the stained surface—for here the particular finish requires a contrasting color. More will be said about these special cases in Chapter 10.

These paste fillers may be purchased from your local supplier in practically all of the popular stained-wood shades. Below is a partial list of the more common ones.

Black—for ebony
Gray—for silver gray
Red Mahogany
Brown Mahogany
Golden Maple
Golden Oak
Brown Oak
American Walnut
Circassian Walnut
Antique Maple
White

Any of the above-mentioned colors may be purchased in any quantity required, from pint containers to gallon containers. It is more economical to purchase a quantity sufficient for your needs than a larger quantity. Just remember that one gallon will cover about 480 square feet.

Occasionally, no prepared colored filler will be suitable for your needs. This should not cause too much concern, for it is rather simple to change the color of any filler. Merely add to it a sufficient amount of the correct oil color to obtain the desired shade. To illustrate: if a dark-brown-mahogany filler is needed, add enough Vandyke Brown oil color to the Brown Mahogany filler on hand to obtain the dark-brown color. Again, if a gray filler is needed, and only white filler is available, add enough black oil color to the white filler to get the desired shade of gray. Remember, however, too much oil color should not be used in changing the color of the filler, for an excess of color will have a tendency to discolor the stained surface when it is applied to it. Just enough color should be added to make the necessary changes in the filler.

What woods require paste filler
With a few exceptions, all open-grain woods require paste filler to fill their large, open pores. The few exceptions are finishes like mission oak, weathered oak, Scandinavian oil finish, and fumed oak, which require no filler,

92

despite the large pores of the wood. Under normal requirements, the following open-grain woods require paste filler.

Ash	Mahogany, Honduras, African
Oak	Mahogany, Philippine
Chestnut	Walnut, American
Elm	Rosewood

How to apply paste filler

As I have said, paste filler is purchased factory-mixed and in a variety of colors. If the color is not right, it may be corrected by the addition of the appropriate oil color. The ready-mixed filler as found in the can is much too heavy for good brushing to the stained surface. It is necessary, therefore, to reduce or thin this heavy paste with benzene to the consistency of cream— just heavy enough to spread easily with a brush. Avoid thinning the filler too much, because such a filler cannot serve the purpose for which it was intended. In other words, the filler should be heavy enough to fill the large pores with one application.

Before applying the filler you have just reduced to the proper consistency, you must make sure that the stain on the surface has dried thoroughly. If the surface was stained with water, alcohol, or chemical stain, the filler is applied directly; but if the surface was stained with oil stain, a wash coat of shellac must be applied and permitted to dry before applying the filler. Then the steps are as follows:

1. Select a wide brush and begin to apply the filler to a section of the piece. (Direction of brushing is not important. However, care should be taken that the filler covers all areas.)

2. Allow several minutes' drying time, or until the filler begins to lose its luster on the surface. Filler is not to be removed until it has all turned to a dull appearance.

3. Obtain a coarse material, like excelsior, sea-grass, horse hair, or burlap, and form it into a wad.

4. Begin removing the surface filler with this coarse material by rubbing across the grain. This procedure hastens the removal of the surface filler and forces more filler into the pores.

5. When all of the surface filler has been removed in this manner, take a wad of clean soft cloth and again wipe the surface, but in the direction of the grain. Continue to do this until the rag shows no further evidence of excess filler remaining on the surface.

6. Check surface with finger tip. The finger will pick up no color if all of the

Paste filler can be purchased in various shades, and oil colors can be added to it. It is brushed on liberally and allowed to dry for a few minutes. Then it is wiped off, first with a rough burlap rag and then with a soft cloth. Cloth wrapped around a pointed dowel is used to remove the filler from crevices and moldings.

surface filler has been removed. A semi-gloss sheen should appear on the surface if the filler has been removed properly.

All flat surfaces on your job are filled and cleaned in the same fashion. A little problem presents itself when curved, turned pieces, and moldings require filling. In such cases, the burlap alone will not do a thorough job of removing the surface filler, because it cannot fit into the crevices and corners of these parts. The filler remaining in the corners may be removed by scrubbing with a short-haired, stiff brush. You will find that most of the filler will be picked up by the brush. Clean the brush from time to time as you continue.

Some finishers prefer another method for removing this excess filler. This method is more foolproof than the method just discussed. Here the craftsman secures a piece of ⅜" dowel or stick and sharpens the end to a point, like a pencil point. A piece of cloth is wrapped around this point and it is then run along the corners and crevices. The sharp covered point fits snugly into these places and pushes out the excess filler. The cloth covering the point of this pick stick should be changed from time to time, as constant use fills it with filler and it will no longer be useful. Bear in mind that if this stick is handled carelessly it may scratch the surface and cause considerable damage to the molding or corners.

It should be emphasized that every trace of filler not lodged in the pores must be removed, regardless of where it may be. Care should be exercised when removing the excess filler from the surface, but the corners and moldings should not be neglected. As already indicated, any trace of filler remaining will alter the color of the stain and will leave a grayish, muddy film on the surface which cannot be removed easily after the filler has dried hard.

Some tips when using paste filler

1. Make sure that you stir the filler periodically while you are using it. The heavy material in the filler tends to settle at the bottom, and all you will be brushing on the surface will be the oil which has risen to the top.
2. Make certain that the filler is brushed into the pores of the wood. Work the full brush across and with the grain. It is important that the filler settle into the pores. The correct working of the brush will remove the air pockets within the pores and permit the filler to enter.
3. Apply the filler to a small area at a time. Allow a few minutes' drying time and then remove. If the entire job is covered with filler at one time, too much time will have elapsed between the start and finish of the operation. It is very difficult to remove filler that has dried too hard. Paste filler sets rather quickly, and, once it sets, has a tendency to stick to the surface. If a condition such

as this arises, soak a wiping rag in benzene and go over the surface with it. The damp rag will soften the hardened filler and make it easier to remove.

4. If you discover that the filler dries too rapidly even when doing a small area, add a little linseed oil to the mixture. This will cause the filler to dry more slowly. But if you add too much linseed oil the filler will take much longer to dry than is practical.

5. When using burlap or excelsior to start the removal across the grain, take care not to scratch the surface. Scratches across the grain, no matter how small, will become very conspicuous when the other finishing materials are applied.

6. Make sure that the filler has not been thinned too much by benzene. A thin filler will not fill the pores in one operation. Several applications will then be required.

7. Destroy all wiping materials used when cleaning the surface. Avoid spontaneous combustion.

8. A wash coat of shellac must be applied to surfaces which have been stained with any type of oil stain. This wash coat must dry thoroughly before the filler is applied.

9. Filler has a tendency to darken the stained wood somewhat when it is applied directly over the stained surface. Some finishers prefer to apply a wash coat of shellac on any stained surface before applying the filler. This practice will tend to leave the stained surface in its original color despite the application of the filler. A wash coat of shellac is made by adding 7 parts of alcohol to 1 part of 5 lb. cut shellac. Chapter 6 will discuss this more fully.

10. Inasmuch as a paste filler contains oil and consequently dries slowly, at least twenty-four hours must elapse before any other material is applied to the filled surface. Shellac or lacquer applied over a freshly filled surface will seal the surface and prevent the filler from drying adequately. Damage to the finished surface will result from this premature finishing.

LIQUID FILLERS

Liquid fillers serve the same purpose on close-grain woods as the paste fillers do on the open-grain woods. The smallness of the pore does not require the same amount of preparation and work in filling. Nevertheless, this type of wood requires some form of treatment which will seal the surface and prevent the absorption of the finishing materials like shellac or varnish. These materials are liquids that fill the close grain and leave a film over the surface.

Unlike the paste fillers, these liquids require no wiping off or cleaning.

96

They are applied directly to the stained surface and permitted to dry. The succeeding coats are applied over this film after it has dried sufficiently. The list of close-grain woods below require liquid fillers for the purpose of sealing their surfaces:

Bass	Beech	Cherry	Gum	Poplar
Birch	Cedar	Fir	Pines	Spruce

Types of liquid fillers

There are several liquid fillers which can be selected by the craftsman for sealing the surface of a close-grain wood: shellac, varnish, lacquer sealer, and dilute paste filler. You can use whichever one is convenient.

As these are transparent liquids, with the exception of the dilute paste filler, no choice of color is needed. Any of them can be used on any shade of stained surface without a noticeable effect on the color. Only when the dilute paste filler is used should consideration be given to the shade of the filler and the shade of the stained job. Both should match for good results.

How to apply liquid fillers

Shellac may be applied as a liquid filler on all types of finishes. However, where a job is to be finished entirely in varnish, varnish should be used for that purpose. When shellac is to be used it should be thinned half and half— one part of shellac to one part of alcohol. It is then brushed onto the stained surface with straight even strokes. You allow two hours for drying and then the other coats may be applied. Of course, light sanding with No. 4/0 garnet paper should precede the second coat of material. Remember to apply white shellac as a liquid filler to surfaces stained in light or natural shades, and orange shellac to surfaces stained in dark shades. Chapter 6 will discuss this matter further.

When varnish is to be used for this purpose, a little more care should be exercised in its application and drying. You must remember that varnish is a slow-drying liquid and you should, therefore, find a place where the varnished surface can dry without too much dust accumulating on it. The varnish is applied directly over the stained surface and permitted to dry about twenty-four hours. It is then sanded and dusted, and the succeeding coats of varnish are applied. Do not under any circumstances use varnish as a liquid filler when either shellac or lacquer is going to be used as the final coat. The varnish sealer will cause the succeeding shellac coats to crack badly. If lacquer is applied over a varnish sealer, the lacquer will act as a solvent and it will soften and remove the varnish sealer.

Lacquer sealer

This type of liquid filler is highly recommended if you have a spraying outfit. Lacquer sealer is a mixture of heavy solids and acetates. When applied to a wood surface, the heavy solids will fill the small pores of the woods and seal the surface as well. The sealer is sprayed directly over the stained surface. It is allowed to dry for at least an hour and then sanded. Succeeding coats of lacquer are applied over the lacquer sealer. Do not use a lacquer sealer on any finished surface other than one to be entirely finished in lacquer. The dangers noted in the preceding paragraph apply here as well.

Dilute paste filler

Many wood finishers prefer a very dilute paste filler to seal the pores of the close-grain wood. They believe, and rightly so, that the paste filler, even when diluted, will fill the small pores better than the other type of liquid fillers. It colors the wood slightly and leaves a better and smoother surface.

The proper shade of paste filler is diluted to the consistency of varnish by the addition of benzene or turpentine. It is then brushed on the surface in the usual manner. Wipe it off when a section begins to show signs of dullness. The same precautions should be considered when using this type of filler as when using the regular paste filler. The same procedure is followed in all the steps which lead to a perfectly clean, filled area. Refer to the section above on application of paste filler for a full explanation of this step.

The proper choice of the filler and the correct application of it are very important. The success of your finishing job will depend on the care you exercise in this step of the finishing process. Poor results, although not at first noticeable, will become very pronounced as the other finishing materials are applied.

CHAPTER 6

Shellac

Shellac is one of the oldest types of finishing materials. Throughout the centuries it has been one of the mainstays of the wood finisher because it is fast-drying, protects well, and is long-lasting. Look at the antique furniture exhibited at any museum, and you will see many fine examples of furniture finished with shellac. The finish has lasted through all these years and still has beauty and mellowness. With the advent of the more modern fast-drying finishes, shellac has lost some of its popularity, but it still holds a very important place not only in the wood-finishing field but in other industries as well.

Shellac, as we know it, is an organic material made from the residue of a small red bug, called the lac bug, which inhabits parts of Ceylon and India. The lac bug lives and breeds on trees found in those countries. It exudes a hard shell-like material which eventually envelopes the bug and causes its death. Local harvesters gather the encrusted twigs and remove the shell-like material from them. This residue is then crushed and ground into granules, placed in cloth bags, and heated over an open fire until it begins to melt. This melted material is gathered and stretched while still soft into very fine, thin sheets. After these sheets have cooled and hardened, they are crushed again into flakes. These flakes are placed into 100-pound bags and shipped to all parts of the world. Your shellac dealer dissolves this lac flake in denatured alcohol in a specific proportion and then puts it in glass or metal containers of various sizes.

Cut of shellac

To the craftsman, the cut of the shellac will prove quite important, because it gives him an indication of the amount of lac flake that has been dissolved in one gallon of alcohol. Naturally, the less lac flake dissolved in the alcohol the cheaper the cost and the thinner the shellac. The standard cut of shellac is 5-pound cut, which means that 5 pounds of lac flake are dissolved in one gallon of alcohol. It is natural that a 5-pound cut should be more expensive than a 3-pound cut. The price of a quart of 3-pound cut should, by this reasoning, be less than the price of a quart of 5-pound cut. Thus, when you purchase shellac, note the label and observe the cut of the shellac. The label on the container purchased from a reliable dealer will always indicate the cut.

When you purchase shellac, it is recommended that you purchase the 5-pound cut and then thin it down with alcohol to the consistency desired. It is more economical to purchase it this way. For normal use, the consistency of the shellac should be about 3-pound cut. You can very easily reduce 5-pound cut shellac to 3-pound cut by adding one pint of alcohol to one quart of shellac. The following table will help you, in reducing shellac to any consistency required. Use it for good results.

To convert	Add denatured alcohol
1 quart 5-pound cut to 3-pound cut	1 pint to quart
1 quart 5-pound cut to 2-pound cut	1 quart to quart
1 quart 4-pound cut to 3-pound cut	½ pint to quart
1 quart 4-pound cut to 2-pound cut	¾ pint to quart

There should be no problem when quantities other than quarts are to be reduced. Just bear in mind the ratio in one quart, and then add the alcohol in the correct proportion. The proper consistency of shellac is very important to good brushing results. As will be noted later, the thinner the shellac, the easier it is to apply and the better the brushing results.

Orange and white shellac

In addition to knowing the proper cut of shellac, you should be able to choose the appropriate color for your specific needs. The natural color of shellac is a transparent orange, and, when it is applied to a surface, it will tend to discolor the surface slightly. It is not good practice to apply orange shellac to a bleached or natural finish, first because it will definitely alter the color of these light woods and second because any uneven brushing or lapping will show up badly. Use orange shellac on dark stained surfaces like walnut, mahogany, or mission oak. There the color of the shellac will not appreciably affect the shade of the stained surface.

White shellac is made by adding a bleaching agent to orange shellac to remove the orange color. White shellac is eggshell in color—not white as the name indicates. It is also transparent and, when it is applied to a surface, will alter the color of the surface very little. It can be used on dark surfaces, but it is recommended on all types of light surfaces, bleached or stained, where the shade of the wood must remain as is. White shellac, however, has certain disadvantages which make it impractical for use under certain conditions. It has a tendency to turn a milky white when subjected to moisture, giving the surface a cloudy and muddy appearance. Then, too, because of the bleaching chemicals added to it, the life of the shellac is shortened somewhat. It loses its drying qualities when stored for six to twelve months and should be discarded.

Whenever possible, orange shellac is recommended for general finishing. If white shellac must be used, make certain that you buy just enough for your job and that the amount you purchase is fresh. Many reliable manufacturers date the labels on their shellac containers, thereby assuring the purchaser of its freshness.

THE USES OF SHELLAC

Let us now discuss the many uses of shellac. You will then appreciate the versatility of this finishing material.

Shellac as a sealer

As has already been indicated, shellac serves as an excellent sealer when used either on raw wood or over a stained surface. It leaves a hard, transparent undercoat for any other finish which will be applied over it, whether it be varnish or lacquer. Shellac seals the surface so well that paint and enamels applied over it will not soak into the wood. How often have you patched a plaster wall and then painted over the new hardened plaster, only to find that the paint seeped through the new patch, leaving a dull, matted surface? If you had sealed this fresh plaster patch with a coat of shellac after it had dried, the paint that you applied would have been as glossy as the remainder of the wall. The shellac seals the minute pores of the plaster and prevents the paint from seeping through.

When using shellac as a sealer it should be thinned down to a 2½ pound cut by adding denatured alcohol to the mixture if necessary. A heavier coat will leave a very thick film on the surface, and this heavy film may cause the succeeding coats of material to crack. Get into the habit of using your shellac as thin as possible.

Shellac as a final finish

Shellac as a final finishing material is most popular with the amateur finisher, and rightly so. Three to six coats of white or orange, applied very thin at intervals of at least two hours, will produce an excellent film on the surface. When this surface is rubbed with either steel wool or pumice stone and oil after it has dried sufficiently, a durable and beautiful finish will be produced. Whenever possible this type of finish is recommended over the other types, because of its relative ease in application, its fast drying time, and its excellent results.

Shellac as a french polish

The finish produced by this method of shellac application is beyond expression. This was the type of finish which the masters of old used for finishing all of their furniture. The results obtained by French polishing have been imitated but never surpassed. In French polishing, the shellac is applied to the surface with a wad of lint-free linen. The shellac-dampened pad is rubbed briskly on the surface until the desired effect is obtained.

Chapter 14 will describe in detail the procedure involved in French polishing.

Shellac as a pigmented paint

If you refer back to the section on alcohol stains, you will note that there are dyes and anilines that will dissolve in alcohol to produce alcohol stains. If these anilines are dissolved in shellac, the same results will be obtained, but instead of having a colored stain you will have made a colored shellac that can be used as a paint. This type of paint is very useful in coloring the interior of cabinets and other inconspicuous places, where the need for staining and filling is not essential. However, it should not be used on surfaces that require stains and finer finishes.

This pigmented shellac has another very important use for the wood finisher. It is used as a fast-drying paint to cover small surfaces, spots, edges etc., which have been rubbed bare during the rubbing operation. This process is called touching up. Assuming that such a spot is found on your furniture after you have rubbed it, it would indeed be time-consuming to stain, fill, and finish this small area to get it to match the surrounding surface. With the aid of the colored shellac made to match the color of the furniture, you can very quickly and easily paint the defect to match the surrounding surface. Only the critical eye of the master would be able to see the difference in the patch just colored.

102

Shellac should be applied in long even strokes.

Occasionally, in refinishing a piece, where the removal of the finish is not essential, it is possible to alter the color of the finish by going over it carefully with a colored shellac. Refer to Chapter 15 for additional information regarding this process.

APPLYING SHELLAC WITH A BRUSH

At the outset, you must bear in mind that shellac dries very rapidly, once it is applied to any surface, and consequently should be applied with as much speed as possible.

Brushing shellac on flat surfaces
1. Dust off surface with brush or lint-free cloth.
2. Mix shellac to 2½ pound cut and pour in wide-mouthed container.
3. Secure a double chisel fitch brush wide enough for the surface to be shellacked. A 3″ brush should be used when shellacking such areas as wide tops and cabinet sides.
4. Place piece to be shellacked so that the light is in front of you.
5. Fill brush with shellac, but not dripping full.
6. Center yourself in front of the piece and start brushing from left to right and about 2″ from the top edge. The strokes should be long and even from one end to the next. Avoid short choppy strokes.
7. Refill the brush as before and start about 2″ from where you just left off. Using the same stroke as before, brush toward the shellac applied and away from it.
8. Continue this procedure until the entire top has been covered.

After applying shellac to a curved piece, use the dry brush to pick up the excess.

Brushing shellac on turnings, etc.

1. Fill brush as described above, but use judgment as to the amount of shellac required for the area to be covered.

2. Brush around the turning until a section has been covered. Work down in this fashion until the entire turning has been shellacked.

3. Pick up excess shellac by drying the brush and then using the dry brush. This should be done while the shellac is still wet. Always work around the turning and not up and down.

4. The procedure is similar when shellacking irregularly shaped pieces, such as cabriole legs and split turnings and carvings.

Additional suggestions when brushing shellac

1. Use as wide a brush as possible for the job.
2. Always brush in the direction of the grain and in full long strokes from one end to the next.
3. Fill the brush to capacity and cover as much as you can without forcing the brush to stretch any remaining shellac.
4. Always begin the next brushful about 2'' from the last. Work toward it and away from it.
5. Never start a new brushful where the other ended. This will build up the shellac at that point and leave unsightly lap marks, which will be difficult to remove. Remember, shellac is fast-drying and it does not spread as paint or varnish does.
6. Do not attempt to cover skips by brushing shellac over the spot. Wait until the next coat is applied and make sure that ample shellac is brushed to that spot.
7. Return all unused shellac to a covered container for eventual reuse.
8. Clean the brush by washing in alcohol solution and allow it to dry.

Shellac dries dust-free within minutes, but this does not mean that it has dried sufficiently to permit the application of another coat. At least three hours should elapse before the second coat is applied. A good way to test the dryness of the shellacked surface is to sand a small area with fine finishing paper; if a powdery film is deposited on the paper and on the surface while you are sanding, you may assume that the surface has dried sufficiently and is ready for the next coat.

When you have made this test and you are certain that the surface has dried sufficiently, proceed to sandpaper the entire job with 5/0 garnet finishing paper, using the palm of your hand to apply the pressure. A good suggestion in using finishing paper for this purpose is to wet the back of the sandpaper (not the abrasive side) with clear water. Do this by soaking a sponge in water and then rubbing the wet sponge on the paper side. You will notice that the paper will limber up and become pliable and soft. Paper prepared this way will prevent the scratching of the fine, finished surface. Place this sandpaper in the palm of your hand and, in full strokes and following the direction of the grain, proceed to sandpaper every section of the shellacked surface. Be extremely careful while sanding. Do not overdo it. Remember that sandpaper cuts a finished surface very rapidly and, if care is not exercised, you may sand off all of the shellac from the surface. If this should happen, you will have removed not only all of the shellac but the filler and stain as well, thereby leaving a bare, irreparable spot. The sandpapering should be done solely to remove any fuzz or brush marks on the shellacked surface and never to remove all of the shellac.

When all the sanding has been completed, clean the surface of every trace of dust and prepare for the next coat. If your job is to be finished in shellac, proceed to apply the second coat as you did the first, remembering of course to follow the steps enumerated above. Allow this second coat to dry at least three hours before resanding, and then apply the third coat. Continue in this fashion until the desired number of coats have been applied. As a final word, it is better to apply two thin coats than one heavy coat. The results will make the extra labor worth while.

APPLYING SHELLAC WITH A SPRAY GUN

Equally good results may be obtained when shellac is applied with a spray gun. However, there are several factors that should be kept in mind. The appropriate spraying equipment should be available and the operator should know how to use this equipment. As in the brushing of shellac, the surface must be clean, free from dust, oil, and grease. The spray gun must be absolutely clean and free of any paints or other finishing materials. The shellac should be thinned to about 2-pound cut.

The article to be sprayed should be placed on a turntable, so that it may be turned with ease to any side desired. When spraying the shellac, care should be taken not to have the spray gun closer than seven inches from the surface. A distance greater than this will not permit an even flowing stream of shellac to settle on the surface. A distance less than seven inches will cause too much of the shellac to flow on the surface, thereby causing ugly sags and runs, which will be difficult to remove. The spraying should be done along a straight line and not in an arc. As you are spraying, maintain an even distance from the surface at all times. Altering this distance along the line may cause unevenness in the amount of shellac being applied to the surface. Continue this procedure until every section has been covered with shellac. You may, if you wish, go over the surface already sprayed with another coat provided the surface previously applied has set somewhat; but exercise care, for too much material on a given surface will result in runs, and these are very difficult to remove. The top should be sprayed after all other sections have been covered. Chapter 8 will discuss this phase of the finishing operation in greater detail.

The best way to shellac a turned piece is to pad on the shellac while the piece is turning in the lathe.

APPLYING SHELLAC WITH A PAD

Still another method of applying shellac should be noted. This method is called padding. The shellac is first soaked into a piece of cloth and then the cloth is rubbed on the surface to be shellacked. Here, again, a degree of skill should be developed before this method is attempted, but good results can be achieved if the craftsman exercises a little care. This method can be used on a flat surface as well as on wood turnings.

Let us suppose that you have just turned a lamp base on your wood-turning lathe and that you are now ready to finish it. Finishing it while the lamp base is turning between the centers of your lathe is the most appropriate way. The stain and filler may be applied in the usual way—by brushing—but the shellac finish is best applied with a pad while the piece is turning in the lathe.
1. Provide yourself with two shallow saucers. Fill one with alcohol and the other with 4-pound cut shellac. White or orange may be used.
2. Secure a piece of lint-free cloth and arrange it into an oval shape.
3. Dip the oval pad into the alcohol and work the liquid into the pad by rubbing the surface with the other hand.

4. Dip the pad into the shellac and work the liquid as with the alcohol.

5. Press the saturated pad on the turning lamp base, moving your hand back and forth as the pressure is applied. Make sure that the contour of the turning is followed.

6. Continue this movement until the pad runs dry, then refill the pad as before and continue the operation.

7. The surface is to be padded until a smooth glossy appearance is evident on the object.

It is important to note that the more shellac applied, the more body and the better the appearance. Judgment must be exercised regarding the amount of shellac to be padded. Twenty-four hours should elapse before the turning may be rubbed to a smooth soft sheen. Saturate the pad in boiled linseed oil and press it on the object while it is turning on the lathe.

When padding shellac on a turning, consider these simple rules and good results will be assured:

1. Do not soak the pad too much, as this will leave too much material on the surface being padded, causing a smeared and muddy appearance.

2. Keep the pad moving at all times while on the turning. This will assure an even coat on all parts of the turning. It will also prevent the overloading of one section at the expense of another. And, too, leaving the pad at one section too long will soften that section and remove any material which has been padded on.

3. Do not use too fast a speed on the lathe, as this will heat the shellac and leave an uneven surface.

4. Make sure that the pad you are using is made of a piece of lint-free cloth. A piece of washed linen is preferred, for then the pad may be used with the shellac and there will be no fear of lint settling on the softened shellac.

The procedure for padding a flat surface, usually referred to as French polishing, will be explained in detail in Chapter 14.

RUBBING A SHELLACKED SURFACE

With the exception of the surface which has been padded with shellac or French-polished, all other shellacked surfaces should be rubbed smooth after the final coat.

By rubbing is meant wearing down the surface so as to produce a fine, even, and satin-gloss finish. There are several methods which will produce these desired results. Among these are steel-wool rubbing and pumice-stone-and-oil rubbing.

Rubbing a shellacked surface with steel wool will produce a fine satin-gloss finish.

Rubbing with steel wool

1. Select a piece of 2/0 steel wool and roll it into a wad large enough to fit the palm of your hand.

2. With a moderate amount of pressure begin to rub the surface in long even strokes.

3. Progress laterally from left to right as the rubbing is continued.

4. Continue rubbing while changing the steel wool from time to time until all the brush marks, dust particles, and other imperfections have been removed.

5. Check the surface periodically by cleaning off the white residue with a soft rag. Cease rubbing when the finish has acquired the smoothness required.

6. Remove all the accumulated residue with a clean cloth.

7. Wax polish or oil may be applied as the final preparation. Wax will produce a high-gloss finish. Oil will result in a satin-gloss appearance.

The method which has just been explained will produce a relatively smooth surface. However, for those who are more demanding and who require a much smoother, finer, and more satiny appearance, pumice-stone-and-oil rubbing is recommended. Chapter 14 discusses this phase of rubbing in more detail. However, the basic steps are as follows.

109

Pumice stone and oil will produce a very fine finish. The pumice-stone residue should be wiped off with a soft cloth in the direction of the grain.

Rubbing with pumice stone and oil

1. Place a small portion of powdered FF pumice stone in a shallow dish.
2. Cut a piece of flat rubbing felt to approximately 2" x 3". A folded part of an old felt hat may be substituted.
3. Place several ounces of crude or light machine oil in a shallow pan.
4. Soak the felt in the oil and then place this saturated felt in the pumice stone.
5. Place the impregnated felt in the palm of the hand and with moderate pressure begin to rub, following the direction of the grain.
6. Rub in long even pressured strokes from one end to the other. Move laterally as the rubbing progresses.
7. Wipe off the grime carefully from a corner of the surface and check the condition of the rubbed section.
8. If imperfections still appear, continue rubbing. Replenish the felt pad from time to time.
9. Make another visual inspection of the surface at different points. Continue rubbing if necessary.
10. Carefully wipe off the grime with a clean soft rag when the desired appearance has been accomplished. Make sure that the cleaning is done very carefully and in the direction of the grain.
11. Polish with a wax polish, or for a higher gloss an oil polish.

Precautions while rubbing

1. Check frequently by removing the grime from various sections of the surface.
2. Remember that pumice is a fast-cutting abrasive and that it is cutting away part of the finish as you rub.
3. Rub all parts evenly. It is a good practice to count the number of strokes as you move laterally.
4. Always rub in the direction of the grain. Circular rubbing will leave circle marks which will be difficult to remove.
5. Use a clean soft rag when wiping off the residue. Clean in the direction of the grain. Change the rag from time to time.
6. Use more oil on the felt if you feel that the pad is not moving freely.
7. Refill the pad with pumice stone if no cutting is taking place while rubbing.

ADVANTAGES OF SHELLAC

Much space has been devoted to the uses of shellac and how it is applied, but very little mention has been made of the advantages of using this material.

Let us, therefore, note some of the qualities which make this finishing material so important to the wood finisher.

One of the outstanding qualities of shellac is its durability and strength. If properly applied and maintained, it will last indefinitely on the surface. It is for this reason that shellac is used as a floor finish, as a finish for bowling alleys, and for other places where abuse and wear are common. There is no fear of it cracking after many coats have been applied because it is so elastic and flexible. Thus accidental shock from spoons, keys, and other objects being dropped on the shellacked surface will not crack or mar the finish.

As already indicated, rubbing with either steel wool or pumice stone leaves a fine velvety smooth feel to the surface, with a mellowness that cannot be duplicated with other materials.

Shellac is fast-drying, and this fast-drying quality makes it the appropriate material to use where time is important. No special drying facilities are necessary, because it dries dustproof in a matter of minutes. Several coats may be applied within hours of each other.

Used as a sealer, it cannot be surpassed. It spreads evenly over the porous surface, leaving a film which prevents the absorption of other materials. Any material applied to the shellac sealer will adhere well, without any fear of checking or blistering.

Then, too, it is unsurpassed as a furniture polish when used as a French polish. You will obtain a beautiful, lasting, lustrous finish that requires no additional polishing or rubbing. It is no wonder that French polishing has been popular since the seventeenth century.

Finally, its use as a touching-up ingredient makes it almost indispensable. No other material will combine with alcohol anilines and then adhere to a surface with such rapidity as shellac. It becomes a part of the finish and, when properly applied, cannot be distinguished from the surrounding surface.

DISADVANTAGES OF SHELLAC

It should not be assumed that shellac is the all-perfect finishing material, which can be used under all conditions and for all types of jobs. There are some drawbacks which should be considered before the final selection of the finishing material is made. A few of these should be considered.

Shellac is not waterproof. It will not withstand moisture without turning white. Therefore, it should never be considered where outside finishing is to be done. Garden furniture, for example, should not be finished in shellac. Shellac is not recommended for the finishing of coffee tables, kitchen tables, and the like, which may be subjected to water at some time or another.

Shellac is not heatproof. When it is subjected to heat, as when a hot dish is placed on a table, it will soften up and mark the surface, which is then beyond repair. When the heat applied is extreme, the shellac will blister and crack. Thus, a piece that will be subjected to heat should be finished in materials other than shellac.

Naturally, because shellac is made with alcohol, it will absorb any trace of alcohol placed on it. It is not alcohol-proof and should not be applied to furniture like cocktail tables or bars, where liquor is apt to be present. The liquor accidentally spilled on a shellacked surface will act as a solvent and remove the finish to the bare wood. There are other finishing materials, like varnish and lacquer, which are alcohol-proof and can be substituted for shellac.

Liquid shellac is not a very stable material. When stored in metal containers for any length of time, it will deteriorate, discolor, and lose its drying qualities. This is especially true of white shellac. The chemicals used in bleaching orange shellac to white affect the drying qualities after the shellac has aged for six to twelve months. Shellac that old should be discarded and not considered for any finishing purpose. Shellac stored in a metal container for a considerable length of time will become discolored due to the chemical actions which take place between the chemicals in the shellac and the metal. Shellac should be purchased in glass containers when it is not to be used immediately, for it will not discolor so readily. Metal containers should be used only when the shellac is to be used immediately.

CHAPTER 7

Varnishes

For thousands of years varnish has been used in one form or another as a wood finish and preservative. The Egyptians used it to decorate their tombs. The Greeks used it as a wood preservative to protect their ships from the elements of the sea. Not until the last few centuries, however, has varnish been used as a furniture-finishing material. Through the years wood finishers have found in oil varnish many characteristics not shared by shellac—for example, its hard-drying qualities, its ability to be rubbed to a high gloss, and its ability to withstand moisture. Until the introduction of fast-drying lacquers, varnish was used quite extensively for many finishing purposes, and it was found to be satisfactory wherever it was applied. It is still used today not only in the shop but in the home as well. There are many different types of varnish—it is not as simple a substance as shellac.

Oil varnish—slow-drying

The composition of oil varnish is rather complicated. The ingredients are natural resins or fossilized gums, which serve as the body; an oil such as tung oil or linseed oil, which serves as the vehicle; a thinner such as turpentine, which reduces the mixture to a workable liquid; and finally a drier to quicken the drying once the varnish is applied.

Oil varnishes have a long history of use. However, they require at least 24 hours of drying time, and this creates serious problems. Special drying facilities are necessary if good results are to be obtained. The temperature and humidity must be controlled, or the varnish will not dry sufficiently hard. The synthetic resin varnishes do not have many of these shortcomings.

Four-hour varnish—fast-drying

In recent years new types of varnishes have appeared. With the discovery of synthetic resins it has become possible to produce varnishes which have the same working qualities as the older type varnishes, but will dry in a few hours. These are the varnishes you will find at the local paint store, department store, and wood-finishing supply house. They are sold as rapid-drying or four-hour varnishes.

The ingredients in these varnishes include synthetic resins such as bakelite, alkyds, formaldehydes and polyurethane which serve as the body; China wood oil as the vehicle (this oil, incidentally, also hastens the drying of the mixture); and volatile thinners, such as varnalene and xylol, which help to reduce the mixture to a workable liquid. Oil varnish dries by oxidation—a rather slow process—but four-hour varnishes dry rather rapidly because of their chemical composition. The volatile thinners dry by evaporation, the china wood oil dries by means of a modified oxidation, and the combination of all produces a chemical reaction called polymerization, or the chemical combination of the china wood oil and synthetic-resin molecules. These physical and chemical reactions allow a speed in surface setting and final drying and a hardness previously unknown. Consequently this kind of varnish has gained in popularity and has replaced the older type of varnish.

These varnishes are manufactured to meet the needs of any finishing problem. Varnishes are made for interior and cabinet finishing. They are also made for exterior and marine finishing. A brief description of each follows.

Cabinet varnish

This varnish contains more resins than oil by proportion. It is a general all-around varnish which can be used on all types of interior work. It spreads easily on the surface and dries rather hard. It may be rubbed with either pumice stone and water or pumice stone and oil with equally good effects. It can be polished to a high gloss. Cabinet varnish is recommended for the craftsman because of its versatility.

Rubbing varnish

This varnish, like the cabinet varnish, contains more resins than oil by proportion. Its main characteristic is that it dries hard to permit extensive rubbing. It, too, may be rubbed with pumice stone and oil or water with good results assured. Rubbing varnish is excellent where a surface is to receive an exceptionally fine, smooth, high luster.

Flat varnish

Flat varnish is another short-oil synthetic varnish which dries dull or with a semi-gloss. No rubbing is required on this type of varnish to produce the desired dull effect. It is applied as the final coat over a full gloss varnish. In other words, several coats of cabinet varnish are applied first, and the flat varnish is applied as the final coat. This will dry dull or with a semi-gloss.

Interior spar varnish

This type of varnish is recommended for the finishing of cabinets, tops, and bars that are subjected to such abuses as the accidental spilling of water, scratching, and nicking. It dries very hard and is not affected by the conditions just mentioned. It can be rubbed reasonably well to a satin gloss.

Exterior spar varnish

Although some manufacturers combine the interior and exterior varnishes into one, actually they have different characteristics. It is suggested that the craftsman request the appropriate one for his job. Exterior spar varnish is a long-oil varnish, which dries slower than the interior varnishes. It is excellent for all types of exterior finishing. It is waterproof and, consequently, protects the surface from the outside elements. It has a light body, flows easily, and sets with a high luster within several hours. It will not turn white or powdery with age. Although spar varnish is recommended for all types of exterior woodwork, it should not be used for interior cabinet work because of its slow drying and elastic qualities. It cannot be rubbed to any degree of luster.

When using spar varnish for exterior work, no other type of finishing material should be applied as the first coat. The exterior surface should be finished with spar varnish throughout from the first coat to the last. Another material will cause the varnish to blister and crack. Under no condition should shellac be used as an undercoat or sealer.

Polyurethane UVA varnish

UVA means "ultra-violet absorbing." Polyurethane UVA varnish produces a very tough and flexible surface on both interior and exterior wood surfaces. It is highly resistant to hot and cold water, acids, alkalis, grease, and alcohol. It dries dust-free in an hour, and can be rubbed after three hours.

HOW TO APPLY VARNISH

There are certain preparations you must make before varnish can be applied properly. The room where the varnishing is to be done must be prepared. The temperature must be controlled. The drying conditions must be considered. Let us discuss these in some detail.

Room conditions

Because varnish dries slower than shellac, it is important that the craftsman prepare the room in which the varnishing is to take place. Synthetic, four-hour varnish becomes dustproof in about two hours. This length of time between application and drying is indeed quite long for the wet surface to be subjected to dirt and particles of dust. The removal of these imperfections, once they have settled on the surface, is difficult. Consequently, every effort should be made to prevent dust from accumulating on the surface while it is drying. All windows and doors should be kept shut while varnishing and during the drying period. The floors should be swept clean and, if possible, should be oiled to prevent dust from rising while you are moving about. There should be some ventilation in the room, but the ventilation should not be caused by drafts or air blowing through the area.

The temperature of the room should also be controlled. Any temperature below 65°F. will hamper the flow of varnish as it is applied. Any temperature above 85°F. will cause the varnish to flow too freely, and this may cause it to run or sag. The room temperature should be controlled not only during the brushing-on process, but also while the surface is drying. Too low a temperature will prevent the varnish from spreading smoothly on the surface. This may later cause blistering and checking of the varnish. A temperature between 70° and 80°F. should be maintained.

Preparing the surface

Extreme care should be exercised when preparing the surface for varnishing. Most varnish troubles can be attributed to carelessness in preparing the surface. Some of the basic principles to bear in mind before beginning the operation follow.

The wood surface should be thoroughly cleaned with benzene to remove all traces of dirt, grease, and oil. If traces of any of these remain on the surface and the varnish is applied, you may discover later that the surface will not dry as you expected, even after waiting the specified drying period. In some cases the varnish film will have to be removed because it will not dry. Any dust on the surface must also be removed. Use a clean dust brush and then wipe off the surface with a damp, lint-free cloth.

If a coat of varnish has already been applied and is later sanded in preparation for another coat, make certain that every trace of the sandpaper dust

117

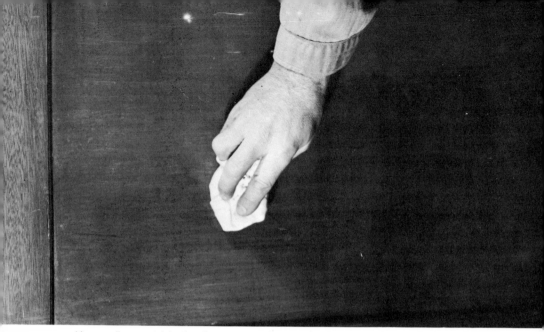

After sanding a varnished surface, use a tack rag to dust the piece before applying another coat.

has been removed. A good procedure to follow, to assure a clean surface, is to provide yourself with a piece of washed linen and sprinkle on it a few drops of the varnish you are using. Work the varnish into the cloth until it becomes tacky with the varnish. This is called a "tack rag." Now hold the tack rag in your hand and rub it over the surface to be cleaned. The sticky tack rag will pick up all traces of grime and dust as you rub it along the surface. When you are through, store the rag in a closed container so that it remains moist and ready for use when needed again.

When an old varnish surface is to be revarnished, more than the usual amount of care should be exercised while cleaning, in order to assure proper adhesion and drying of the new coat of varnish. The old surface should first be cleaned by using a soft rag saturated with mild soapy water. Go over the entire surface with this rag and then remove any trace of soap by washing the surface again with a cloth dampened with clean water. Wipe off any trace of water remaining on the surface. Under no condition should water be permitted to remain for any length of time, because if it soaks into the finish the wood itself may be affected. When the washed surface has dried thoroughly, sandpaper it with a fine grade of finishing paper. Clean the surface as already indicated and apply the new coat of varnish.

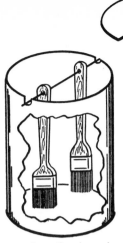

Varnish brushes can be stored in brush-keeper varnish so that they do not have to be cleaned after each use. They should be suspended in a closed container as shown.

Preparing the brush

When varnishing, considerable care is necessary even with the brush. A brush that is dirty, full of dust, grease, or oil should not be considered for any varnishing purpose. A dirty brush will seriously affect the surface being varnished, for the brush will spread the dirt and other impurities on the surface and also contaminate the varnish.

When a new brush is being used in varnish for the first time, it should be cleaned before it is immersed in the varnish. Hold the brush in one hand by the handle and then hit the bristles against your other hand. This will shake off any dust or loose hair. Another good method is to soak the new brush in turpentine or benzene, then work the wet brush in your hand. Dry it thoroughly and then dip it into the varnish container.

Not only should the brush be clean before and while it is being used, but it should also receive care after use. A varnish brush that is to be used again for the same purpose should not be cleaned and stored away. It should be stored in a special container with a hinged cover. The brush should be suspended in the container so that the bristles do not touch the bottom, to avoid clogging the bristles with any residue at the bottom and also to prevent the bristles from curling. The container should contain enough brush-keeper varnish to cover the bristles of the brush. A brush stored in this fashion will remain clean and soft and will be ready for use whenever needed.

When a brush is not going to be used again in varnish it should be cleaned immediately. Work the brush in benzene until you are sure that all of the varnish has dissolved. The brush should then be wiped clean and dry. If paint and varnish remover is used for cleaning the brush, make certain that every trace of wax, which is part of the paint remover, has been washed out of the brush after it has been cleaned. Wash the brush in benzene or alcohol before storing.

Applying the varnish

1. Place the piece to be varnished so that the light is directly in front of you.
2. Select a double chisel camel's hair or fitch brush wide enough for the area to be covered. A 3-inch brush is recommended for large tops and sides.
3. Fill the brush with varnish to capacity. Do not overfill the brush.
4. Begin flowing varnish by moving across the grain in long full strokes.
5. Refill brush and continue flowing on the varnish, starting about two inches from the point just completed. Work toward that point and away from it.
6. When the entire area has been covered, dry the brush over the edge of the varnish can and begin brushing the surface in the direction of the grain.
7. Continue drying the brush and brushing until the area has been covered.
8. Dry the brush again and again go over the surface in the direction of the grain. During the final brushing, the brush is held in an almost vertical position and just the tip of the brush is used. The "tipping" is a brush stroke for the purpose of smoothing the varnish. The stroke starts at the top and continues to the opposite end. The brush is then carried to the top and another stroke is made. This continues until all of the surface has been "tipped."

All other parts of the job in question are varnished in the same manner. It is suggested that you varnish the most important surfaces, such as the top, drawer fronts, and aprons, last. Do the inconspicuous places first. This makes handling the furniture easier. It is also suggested that, whenever possible, the brushing be done with the article in a horizontal position. This makes brushing easier, and it prevents the varnish from running or sagging. Sags and runs should always be considered as you are applying the varnish. Prevent them, if possible; but if they do appear on the surface, remove them by going over them with a very dry brush. The dry brush will pick up this excess varnish. Get into the habit of examining your freshly varnished work as soon as you complete a section. It is much easier then to remove any of these faults than when the varnish has begun to set or when it is dry. The examination may also reveal spots which have not been covered with varnish. Go over these with a full brush before the varnish sets.

The second coat of varnish is applied in a similar manner but first the surface must be prepared. Above all, the first coat should dry at least six hours before the second coat is applied. A good way to check the dryness of the varnish is to press your fingernail at different places along the varnished surface. If no impression is made with the sharp fingernail, you may assume that the surface is hard enough to receive the next coat. If an impression is made, allow more time before applying the next coat.

Varnish is flowed on the surface *across* the grain. When the surface is covered, the brush is dried over the edge of the varnish can, and the dry brush is used *with* the grain. Then the brush is dried again and just the tip of it is used to make long even strokes with the grain.

Sanding the undercoat

A varnish coat, even if dry, must be sandpapered before another coat is applied. This will assure a smooth, even body before the next coat is applied. It will also assure better adhesion of the next coat. There are several methods of sanding a varnished surface. Any method may be used as long as the desired results are obtained. Sandpapering may be done with No. 3/0 garnet finishing paper or with No. 500A "wet or dry" paper. To hasten the cutting action, the garnet paper, if used, may be soaked in gasoline or benzene. Not only does this hasten the cutting action, but it acts as a lubricant and prevents clogging the paper and scratching the varnished surface.

When the "wet or dry" aluminum oxide paper is used, soaking it will also hasten the cutting action. In this case, either benzene or water may be used for the soaking purpose. You will note that water was not mentioned when the garnet paper was referred to. There is an obvious reason: water would dissolve the glue holding the garnet to the paper.

Of course, either paper may be used dry. If it is used dry, the back of the paper should be dampened with water so that it becomes more pliable. This assures even cutting and prevents surface scratches.

1. Select the desired finishing paper and cut sheet into squares.
2. Soak in the appropriate lubricant and place in the palm of your hand, holding the edges with thumb and small finger.
3. Begin sanding by using a moderate pressure and moving in the direction of the grain.
4. Continue sanding until the brush marks and other imperfections have been removed. Check periodically. Do not sand more than necessary.
5. Change the finishing paper from time to time to assure adequate cutting.
6. Clean surface carefully after surface has been sanded to your satisfaction.
7. Use tack rag after sanding if additional varnish coats are to be applied.

RUBBING THE TOP COAT OF VARNISH

The hardened final coat of varnish will show an unsightly gloss, marks, and specks. These must be removed. With the help of a mild powdered abrasive (pumice) and a lubricant, the gloss and other defects give way to a fine even satin surface.

Rubbing with pumice stone and oil

1. Secure a piece of ¼'' rubbing felt approximately 2'' x 3''.
2. Place a portion of FF pumice stone in a shallow tray.
3. Pour about 2 ounces of crude or light machine oil in a shallow tray.
4. Soak the pad in oil and press into the pumice stone.
5. Place the saturated pad in the palm of your hand and begin rubbing.
6. With a moderate pressure on the pad rub in the direction of the grain. Start from one end and work to the other end in long even strokes.
7. Move the pad laterally as you are rubbing from end to end.
8. Replenish the pad with oil and pumice as the need arises.
9. Wipe off the grime from a small section of the surface and check the condition of the rubbed area.
10. Continue rubbing until the entire area has acquired a smooth, even gloss sheen.
11. Carefully wipe off the grime with a soft clean rag, in the direction of the grain.

Rubbing with pumice stone and water

When pumice stone and water are used for rubbing a varnished top coat, the steps are similar to those used in the previous method. There are, however, several precautions to consider.

1. When water is used in place of oil as a lubricant, additional care must be taken and less pressure must be used. Water makes the pumice cut faster than oil.
2. The water should not remain on the surface too long, since there is always a tendency for the water to soak through the thin layer of varnish.
3. Visual inspection of the surface should be frequent as the rubbing proceeds. Wipe off a corner of the area by using your thumb as a squeegee. This will show how the rubbing is proceeding.
4. Stop rubbing promptly when the surface has acquired the desired smoothness and sheen.
5. Clean off grime by washing off with a sponge soaked in water.
6. Remove excess water by wiping with a soft chamois or Turkish towel.
7. Remember to follow the direction of the grain in every step of the operation.

Rubbing varnish with pumice stone and water. The damp pad impregnated with pumice stone is used until the desired smoothness is attained. Then the grime is wiped off with a wet sponge, and finally a chamois is used to pick up the excess water. All these operations should be performed with the grain—not an easy task on the tabletop shown.

MORE PRECAUTIONS WITH VARNISH

It should be clear by now that great care is necessary to achieve a professional varnishing job. It might be well to run over some of the precautions that have already been mentioned and add a few more.

1. The varnish should be used as it comes from the container: In other words, no thinning is required in most cases.

2. If the varnish feels heavy, the cause may be that the varnish is cold. Varnish thickens at temperatures lower than 65°F. Do not thin this varnish with turpentine or any other thinner. Place the varnish into another container holding hot water. The heat will thin the heavy, cold varnish. It should be applied in this texture. Do not place the varnish container over an open flame under any condition.

3. Where thinning of varnish is necessary, use turpentine if the varnish being thinned is oil varnish, or use the thinner recommended by the manufacturer if the varnish is synthetic.

4. In order to prevent blistering of the varnish (small raised spots or air pockets of varnish on the surface), make sure that the surface is free of oil, grease, and wax. Also make certain that shellac is not used as the undercoat on the surfaces that are to be varnished and then exposed to sunlight and the weather.

5. Avoid cloudy effects (bloom) on a varnished surface by applying varnish only when the atmospheric conditions are favorable—that is, temperate and dry. Warm, humid days are unsuitable.

6. To avoid future cracking of the surface, apply the varnish only when the temperature is above 70°F. Cold makes varnish brittle and inelastic, causing it to crack.

7. Do not apply varnish over an undercoat that has not dried hard. Sweating, a condition where a luster appears in spots on a surface after it has been rubbed, will result if the undercoat is not thoroughly dry.

8. Another reason that a surface should be thoroughly cleaned free of oil, grease, and wax, especially when the furniture to be varnished has been previously finished, is that otherwise the new varnish will undoubtedly not dry well and will have a tacky feeling when touched. If this condition arises, it will be necessary to remove the entire finish and begin again. The surface which is to be revarnished should be washed with soapy water, rinsed, and then sanded.

9. Prevent runs and sags by watching your surface carefully as you brush the varnish. Work your brush to spread all excess varnish which may have

accumulated along the edges and moldings. If these faults cannot be removed without damage, wash off the varnish while still wet with a clean cloth soaked in turpentine and then revarnish the area.

10. At least three coats of varnish should be applied over a surface to assure a good film. Each coat should be thoroughly dry and sanded before the next coat is applied. The final coat should be brushed on slightly heavier than the others. Sufficient time should elapse before the rubbing is attempted.

11. A good clean brush of appropriate size will help in getting a good job. Keep it clean before, while, and after using it. Place the brush in brush-keeper varnish when not in use.

12. Place the freshly varnished job in a dust-free room while it sets.

ADVANTAGES OF VARNISHES

It has already been noted that these finishing materials are unsurpassed on a surface under certain conditions. They are a decided improvement over the shellacs discussed in Chapter 6. They do not require spraying equipment, as do lacquers (discussed in Chapter 8).

Varnishes have excellent flowing and leveling tendencies. They provide the wood surface with an excellent body and depth of finish. They are transparent, but amber in color, and when applied will not discolor the natural or stained surface of the wood. The film, when thoroughly dry, will produce an exceptionally hard surface, which is waterproof, alcoholproof, and heatproof to a great extent. Thus, varnish may be used on all types of wood surfaces which could be affected by the conditions just mentioned.

Oil and synthetic varnishes rub well with either water or oil and pumice stone. It is possible to produce the degree of luster required for the job. The surface rubbed will be long-lasting and will withstand much abuse.

Varnish provides a protective film which not only enhances the beauty and depth of the wood, but also protects it against many of the dangers to which wood is subjected. Spar varnish, for example, is excellent for the protection of all types of exterior woodwork.

The large varieties of varnishes available for many different purposes make them suitable for any finishing problem. There are varnishes for floor finishing, outside finishing, high-gloss rubbing qualities, etc.

Four-hour varnish has advantages which make it very practical to use, the most important being the fact that it dries dustproof in about two hours.

DISADVANTAGES OF VARNISHES

The most evident disadvantage is the length of time required for hardening, especially when we compare this time with shellac and with lacquer. Oil varnishes require at least twenty-four hours between coats, synthetic varnish at least four hours. It has already been indicated that great care must be exercised in preparing the room before the varnishing begins. Many craftsmen do not have the ideal facilities for proper varnishing results and for proper drying. Hence, they must accept whatever result they can obtain.

CHAPTER 8

Lacquers

To the craftsman who possesses a spraying outfit, there is no better finishing material than lacquer. This modern, fast-drying finishing material has revolutionized the furniture, automobile, and metal-finishing industries. It has reduced the finishing operations in these industries to hours instead of days and even weeks. To cite an example: it would take at least a week to finish a piece of furniture in varnish, including the drying time between coats. Today the same article of furniture can be finished in lacquer in two days at the most.

Modern lacquer has made possible mass-production finishing techniques which have not only hastened the finishing of the article but have also decreased the cost. Of course, all this could not have been possible without the development of the spraying machine. This equipment is required. The fast-drying qualities of lacquer make it almost impossible to apply with a brush. But so popular is this type of finishing that many amateur finishers and home craftsmen use it exclusively and take pride in being the possessors of a portable home spraying outfit. There are also some lacquers that can be applied with a brush—although they have certain disadvantages—and some that come in aerosol spray cans.

128

Composition of lacquer

Lacquer is a complicated combination of many chemicals. It was first developed commercially immediately after the First World War. There was a surplus of nitrocellulose, also known as guncotton at the time, which had not been used for the manufacture of gunpowder. Research showed that this surplus material, when combined with resin gums, could be used as a finishing material having fast-drying tendencies and long-lasting qualities. At first the material did not prove as effective as claimed, for it lacked adhesive qualities, and it had a tendency to turn white upon drying. Further research and study revealed that the addition of other chemicals made the finishing material suitable for all types of finishing demands. Today lacquers have so improved that they possess all the qualities of a good oil varnish and the added quality that they are fast-drying.

The brief discussion of the chemical composition of lacquer is presented here merely to show the intricate and complicated type of material that it is. Obviously, it cannot be mixed by the user in the manner that shellac is. It is purchased ready-prepared from the lacquer manufacturer, who specializes in these types of chemicals. No doubt you are familiar with some of the more advertised brands—Duco, Egyptian, Sherwin-Williams, Benjamin Moore, H. Behlen, and so on.

There are five main ingredients required in the manufacture of lacquer: nitrocellulose, resin gums (synthetic and fossilized), solvents, softeners, and thinners. Nitrocellulose or pyroxlyn is refined cotton which has been treated with nitric acid and sulfuric acid. It is combined with alcohol to remove any water in the nitrocellulose solution. After it has been treated in this way, it becomes soluble cotton. This material is then combined with varnish resins, like Damais, Copals, and Sandarac, or with synthetic resins like Esters, Malayic, and Vinylite, to become the solid base material for the lacquer. This combination alone does not give us lacquer as we know it. It must be dissolved in still other chemicals to make it a usable liquid. These additional chemicals are called solvents.

Solvents, too, are a combination of several chemicals. Among the chemicals combined to make the lacquer solvents are ethyl and amyl acetates, acetone, and methyl alcohol. Some of these are combined and blended with the base material already mentioned to form an amber-colored liquid. This liquid, as such, could not be classified as a lacquer, because it lacks the proper adhesive qualities. In other words, if this material were applied to a surface and allowed to dry, it would eventually peel or chip off. To prevent this, other chemicals in the form of softeners and plasticizers are added. One of these chemicals added is a form of castor oil. The addition of this oil makes the resultant solution more flexible and causes it to adhere to the surface without peeling off.

Finally, to all this is added a thinner or reducer. Here, again, we find that this thinner is a compound of several chemicals. Coal-tar derivatives, such as toluene, benzene, and xylene, are blended together to form the basis of a lacquer thinner. The addition of the thinner to the solution makes it workable and usable for spraying. In other words, it thins the lacquer to the proper consistency for application.

Types of wood lacquers

The large variety of lacquers available makes it possible to perform practically any type of lacquer finishing. A description of each follows:

Clear gloss furniture lacquer

This is a transparent amber-colored lacquer that dries hard with a very high gloss. It dries dustproof in a matter of minutes but should not be sanded for at least an hour after application. This lacquer, even if scratched or dented, will not chalk or scratch white. The lacquer will not be seriously damaged. The final coat may be rubbed with any of the common rubbing agents to a high gloss. It may be used successfully for any finishing job regardless of purpose. For example, it may be used to finish all types of furniture, wood products, and surfaces which are subjected to moisture and heat. It is considered a general all-round finishing material.

Clear, glossy, water-white furniture lacquer

This lacquer has the same working qualities as the clear, glossy lacquer just mentioned, with the added characteristic that it is water-white. The advantage of this lacquer is that it may be applied to a bleached or natural surface without affecting the color of the surface; it dries to an almost invisible film. It is, therefore, the appropriate material to use where the shade of the wood must remain without change. Other lacquers have a tendency to discolor the lighter finishes slightly.

Flat furniture lacquer

Flat lacquer has the same qualities as clear lacquer with one exception: it will dry flat or dull when applied to a surface and permitted to dry. It may be mixed with glossy lacquer to obtain any degree of dullness desired. For example, one half pint of flat lacquer mixed with one quart of glossy lacquer will produce a lacquer which will dry semi-gloss on the surface. Flat lacquer is exceptional when used on sides of cabinets, legs, and other inconspicuous places where a rubbed appearance is required and smoothness is secondary. Furniture finishers spray glossy lacquer on the important parts of the furniture, like the top and drawer fronts, and then spray the other parts with flat lacquer. The top and fronts are then hand rubbed, giving them the same appearance as the surfaces sprayed with the flat lacquer.

Furniture lacquer sealer

This is a special-purpose lacquer which, because of its composition, is used exclusively for sealing the surface of the wood. It is not as clear and transparent as the clear lacquers, because of the solids added to it. However, when applied to the surface, it does not affect the color of the finish. It can be sanded smooth very easily, and the lacquer remaining seals the surface in preparation of the next operation. When several coats are sprayed on an open-grain wood, the sealer acts as a filler and fills the open pores of the wood as well.

Lacquer sealer should be applied to the surface after the stain or filler has dried. The succeeding coats of clear, glossy lacquer are applied directly over the sealer coat.

Shading lacquer

This is a transparent colored lacquer which is sprayed directly over a natural or stained wood to produce a high-lighted shaded effect. This lacquer is sprayed on after several coats of clear, glossy lacquer have been applied so that it will adhere to the surface better and produce a better antique or high-light effect. Shading lacquer is available in many common finishing shades. The most popular are Brown and Dark Brown, Black, Honey Maple, Wheat, Blond, and White.

Furniture white undercoat lacquer

This is another special-purpose lacquer, indispensable when finishing a surface in colored lacquers. This lacquer is white in color and opaque. It acts like the lacquer sealer already mentioned. It is applied directly to the bare wood and then sanded. It serves as the sealer and as the undercoat for the next coat of lacquer. If the wood to be lacquer-enameled is an open-grain wood, several coats of the undercoat, slightly tinted to the color of the enamel, are applied. Each coat is sanded thoroughly before the next coat is applied. This undercoat should not be used on a surface that is to be finished in a natural transparent shade, because it will cover and hide the wood surface.

Furniture lacquer enamels

These are specially prepared, colored lacquers that are applied over the lacquer undercoat. The variety of colors in which these enamels can be obtained is so great that no mention of the individual colors need be made here. Your local paint supplier has ample color cards from which you may choose.

These lacquers are sprayed on a surface, leaving a hard, durable, glossy color. This enamel may be washed with water and soap without injuring the surface. Lacquer enamels are recommended for all types of furniture that require a painted finish, provided, of course, a spraying outfit is available.

Lacquer thinners

Thinner is the liquid which dilutes the lacquer and makes it suitable for spraying or brushing. As has already been noted, these thinners are a combination of many chemicals. Each manufacturer of lacquer has his own peculiar formula for his thinners. Consequently, best results are assured when the thinner used is made by the manufacturer of the lacquer. If another brand of thinner is used, it may not dilute the lacquer as required, with the consequent effect that the finish will not act properly on the surface. Good flowing, spreading, and covering qualities may be sacrificed when the correct thinners are not used.

Lacquer thinner is water-white in color, and it should be used to dilute whatever type of lacquer you may be using. Some lacquers, like sealers and undercoats, require more thinner than the transparent glossy or flat lacquers. Under normal conditions, about 30% of thinner should be added to a lacquer to obtain the correct spraying mixture. Of course, experience will dictate the correct proportion to add.

Retarders

Retarders are special-purpose thinners, whose purpose it is to slow the drying of the lacquers sprayed on the surface. Under certain atmospheric conditions, like hot, humid weather, lacquer has a tendency to "blush" (turn white and cloudy). This is caused by the absorption of the moisture in the air by the lacquer as it is drying. In order to prevent this, retarders are used in place of the thinners. The retarder in the lacquer permits the lacquer to dry more slowly and thus prevent this rapid absorption of moisture.

Some lacquers can be applied with a brush. It must be flowed on rapidly and cannot be worked like varnish.

APPLYING LACQUER WITH A BRUSH

Recently lacquer manufacturers have developed a lacquer that can be applied with a brush instead of a sprayer. This lacquer is much slower in drying and thus may be brushed on without too much difficulty. It is not entirely satisfactory, because it is quite difficult to slow the drying time without in some way affecting the efficiency of the lacquer. Nevertheless, such lacquers are available and you can use them with some degree of success if a little care is exercised.

Brushing lacquers are not found in as large a variety of types as the spraying lacquers. You may obtain them as clear glossy lacquers, as flat lacquers, and as lacquered colored enamels. The description of these lacquers is similar to the one given earlier in this section. Brushing lacquers are ideal when lacquering small objects, like picture frames, knickknack shelves, small tables, and such; for then the lacquer may be brushed on a small section at a time with no danger of the lacquer pulling as it is being applied. The steps are as follows.

133

1. Pour enough lacquer for the job into a clean container. Make certain the surface to be lacquered is free of dirt, grease, and oil.

2. Fill the brush to capacity and, holding it at a 45° angle, begin to flow the lacquer on the surface. Begin about 2 inches from the edge and work toward the edge and away from it.

3. If the entire area is not covered with one brushful, refill the brush and proceed as in previous step. Excessive overlapping at points where one brushful meets the other should be avoided. The brush should always be full. The lacquer is flowed on and not worked as varnish.

4. Complete flowing lacquer to one section before going to the next. Continue flowing on the lacquer until the entire surface is covered.

5. Allow at least two hours before the second coat is applied.

APPLYING LACQUER WITH A SPRAY GUN

The best lacquering results are obtained when the lacquer is sprayed to the surface. Primarily, lacquer is a spraying material. Its fast-drying qualities make the sprayer indispensable for obtaining good results. Before the actual spraying technique is described, let us describe briefly the equipment and conditions necessary for adequate spraying.

A spraying outfit is an excellent piece of equipment to own, especially if you have the appropriate space and the appropriate ventilating system. You must remember that the spraying outfit itself requires little space, but much space is required for the article to be sprayed so that you can get around it; and, too, ample space is required so that the spray dust and fumes may be dissipated without any danger to you and without danger of fire. Remember that the fumes carried off into the air may be annoying to your neighbor. Therefore, consider all of these incidentals before the purchase is made.

Simply stated, the spraying outfit consists of two important parts: the spraying gun with a cup to hold the material, and the air unit which supplies the gun with air pressure.

The spray gun

The spray gun should have an attached container for the liquid to be sprayed. This container or cup is fastened by means of a threaded collar to the underpart of the spray gun. There are two types of spray guns which you should consider—the bleeder type and the non-bleeder type. The bleeder type con-

134

An industrial spray gun and its compressor unit.

stantly emits air. This prevents the undue accumulation of air in the storage tank and keeps the air at a constant pressure. The spray of the liquid in the cup is controlled by the pressure exerted on the trigger of the gun. This bleeder type of gun is suitable for a compression unit, small in size, which has no pressure control valve. This type is usually found in the home-craftsman outfits. The non-bleeder type of gun shuts off the air when the trigger of the gun is released. Here the compression tank has a pressure-control valve that automatically cuts the compression when a certain pressure is attained. Either type is suitable provided the correct compression unit is obtained with it.

Another difference in spray guns is the manner in which the liquid is fed to the gun. These are of two types—the suction feed and the pressure feed. In the suction type of gun, a vacuum is created which draws the liquid to the tip and sprays it out by the air pressure. In the pressure type, air pressure is forced into the container which, in turn, forces the material in the container to the tip of the gun and then sprays it out. Of the two, the suction type is ideal for the small spraying units and when finishing liquids like shellac, varnish, or lacquer are used in the spraying. This type, however, does not work well for spraying heavy materials, such as fillers and undercoats. The liquids are too heavy to be drawn to the tip. In that case, the pressure type is more appropriate.

The nozzle of the gun should also receive consideration. It consists of several parts which direct the air into the stream of material, break up this material, and then form it into an appropriate spray pattern. These nozzles or caps are divided into two types: the external mix cap and the internal mix cap. In the external mix cap, the air is ejected through two spreader horns and a center opening. In the internal mix type, the air and liquid are mixed inside and then are ejected through a slot. The external mix type is used on both suction and pressure-feed guns. The internal type is used only with the pressure-feed type of gun. This type is normally found with the smaller spraying outfits because a great deal of pressure is not required.

The selection of the cap or nozzle should also be determined by the volume of air and pressure available in the spraying outfit, the type of feed system selected—whether the pressure or the suction type—the type of material to be sprayed, and the size of tip required. The cap should be selected so that it will not allow more air to be ejected at a given time than is being collected. If this should occur, the spraying will have to halt from time to time to allow the further accumulation of air in the storage tank. The manufacturer's description of the outfit will indicate this in more detail.

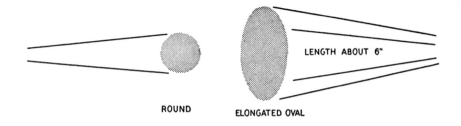

The nozzle of the spray gun should be adjusted so that the spray pattern is an elongated oval.

The air unit

The air unit which supplies air at the desired pressure to the gun consists of the following parts:

a. The compressor, which collects air and compresses it into a storage tank, if one is available.

b. The storage tank, which stores the air and makes it available when needed.

c. A motor or a gas engine to supply the power to work the compressor.

d. An air filter and condenser, which cleans the air of impurities, like dust, oil, and moisture, and smooths the pulsations of the compressor.

e. A pressure gauge, which shows at a glance the air pressure in the unit.

f. An automatic cutoff valve, which shuts off the power as soon as the desired pressure is obtained in the tank.

g. A connecting rubber hose, which directs the air to the gun.

For the home craftsman a small portable spraying outfit is recommended. A unit with a ¼-h.p. motor sufficient to drive a small compressor which will attain a pressure of 100 pounds per square inch is large enough. The average pressure required for lacquer spraying should be between 45 and 60 pounds. These pressures can be obtained with a small, portable outfit.

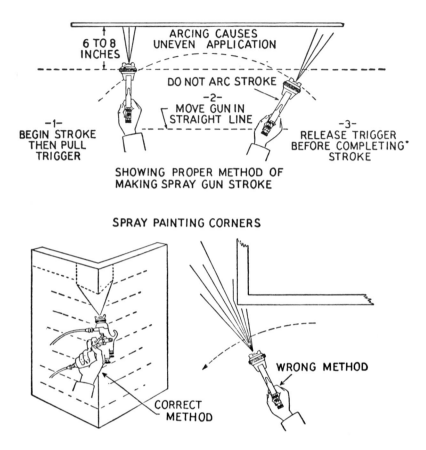

6 TO 8 INCHES

ARCING CAUSES UNEVEN APPLICATION

DO NOT ARC STROKE

−2−
MOVE GUN IN STRAIGHT LINE

−1−
BEGIN STROKE THEN PULL TRIGGER

−3−
RELEASE TRIGGER BEFORE COMPLETING STROKE

SHOWING PROPER METHOD OF MAKING SPRAY GUN STROKE

SPRAY PAINTING CORNERS

CORRECT METHOD

WRONG METHOD

Right and wrong methods of spraying. (Courtesy De Vilbiss Co.)

Spraying the lacquer

The job to be sprayed should be thoroughly clean, free from trace of grease, oil, or wax. It should be placed on a turntable if possible, so that it may be turned to any side desired while spraying. The turntable should be high enough from the floor to prevent dust from being blown on the wet surface. Whenever possible the article should be illuminated with daylight, but if this is not available, artificial illumination properly protected against possible fire should be used. Plenty of ventilation should also be provided. If an exhaust fan is not available with the outfit, some form of ventilation should be devised to remove all spray dust from the work area. It is very flammable and also dangerous to inhale.

138

Prepare the lacquer by thinning it in accordance with the instructions of the manufacturer and fill the spray cup. Lock the cup in position. Before starting the actual spraying, check the pattern of the spray to make sure that it resembles an elongated oval. You may obtain this pattern by adjusting the nozzle of your spray gun. When you have obtained the correct pattern, proceed with the actual spraying as follows: Hold the gun from 6 inches to 8 inches from the surface to be sprayed. This distance is very important. A closer distance will cause too much lacquer to accumulate in a limited area, and it will run and sag as it accumulates. A farther distance prevents the liquid from collecting and leaves a rough and dusty surface.

1. Hold the gun 6 to 8 inches from the surface.
2. Hold it at right angles and begin spraying across the grain. It is important that the gun be kept at the set distance and parallel to the surface while spraying.
3. Overlap each coat about 50 percent as the gun is moved back and forth. Do not stop at the edge of the piece as you move along. Continue the stroke until the gun has passed the edge.
4. When the entire area has been sprayed in this manner, repeat the operation, but now spray in the direction of the grain. This second coat will assure adequate coverage of the lacquer at all points of the piece.

It takes practice to spray properly. Remember to observe all the following precautions:
1. Test the spray pattern before spraying the surface. The pattern should be fan-shaped.
2. Make certain that the gun is never closer than 6 inches from the surface.
3. Do not stop at the edge. Always pass beyond that point and return.
4. Make certain the spray movement is always parallel to the surface. Arching causes more lacquer to deposit as the gun gets closer to the surface.
5. Do not permit the gun to pause on the surface. The movement of the spray gun must be constant as you move from end to end.
6. When spraying corners, aim the gun so that only 50 percent of the lacquer is directed at that point.
7. Additional coats may be overlayed while lacquer is still wet. Do not use excessive lacquer, however, as unsightly runs and sags may result.
8. Allow at least two hours of drying time before the coat is sanded for the next application. The lacquered surface should be sanded carefully with No. 5/0 garnet paper and cleaned thoroughly after the correct drying time has elapsed. The succeeding coats are applied as was the first coat.

On flat surfaces the spray gun is moved parallel to the surface. On corners it is held so as to spray both surfaces at the same time.

A disassembled spray gun. The gun must be cleaned after each use.

Cleaning the gun

It is important to clean the gun after you are through using it. In the suction type of gun the procedure is quite simple. Fill the clean cup with clean thinner and fasten the cup to the gun. Place your finger over the nozzle and pull the trigger to force the liquid back into the cup, then pull the trigger again and allow as much of the thinner as possible to eject, to clean the internal parts of the gun. Remove the cap from the gun and place in the solvent. Do not under any condition place the entire gun in the lacquer thinner, because continued contact of the gun with the thinner will cause the packings in the gun to deteriorate.

COMMON FAULTS IN LACQUERING

1. *Orangepeel.* This is a surface condition of the lacquer which has the appearance of orangepeel. It is caused when the gun is too far from the surface and the air pressure is not high enough to permit the proper breaking up (atomizing) of the lacquer. It may also be caused by the gun being too near the surface. The air pressure causes ripples of the wet surface as the gun moves from place to place.

2. *Dry spray.* This is recognized by a sandy appearance on the sprayed surface. It is the result of lacquer from the gun hitting places not intended. The remedy is quite simple: permit the sprayed lacquer to hit only those places which are to be covered with lacquer. Spray from the finished to the unfinished surface.

3. *Pinholes in the finish.* These are easily recognized on the surface after it has been rubbed. Hundreds of pinhole specks appear on the lacquered surface. This condition is caused by the lacquer not being thinned properly before it is applied. It may also be caused by the improper handling of the gun. The gun may be too close to the edges, allowing too heavy a coat to be deposited at these points. Avoid this by cutting off the fluid supply slightly as you reach the ends.

This condition may also be caused by too much air pressure, which prevents the lacquer from atomizing correctly as it touches the surface.

4. *Sags and runs.* These are caused by the accumulation of the material at different points. The lacquer, not being able to remain in position, runs and sags. This condition may be prevented by reducing the air pressure, increasing the speed of the stroke, and always keeping the gun in motion.

5. *Blushing.* A condition caused by the accumulation of moisture in the lacquer as it is being applied. It may be avoided by using a lacquer retarder instead of thinner to thin the lacquer or by not spraying on warm muggy days.

RUBBING A LACQUERED SURFACE

Clear glossy lacquer, when sprayed and allowed to dry on the surface, leaves a very high luster. In order to remove this high luster and also to remove surface imperfections, the surface is rubbed down with a rubbing agent.

Lacquer may be rubbed in the same manner as varnish. Any of the rubbing agents discussed in Chapter 9 may be used effectively on a lacquered surface. However, the use of rubbing compound is suggested, because it has a tendency to cut the lacquer film quicker and with better results.

Rubbing compound is an abrasive of recent development used mostly for the rubbing of lacquered finishes. It is similar to automobile cleaner, with which you are probably familiar. This compound is available in many different colors to match the surface being rubbed. It may be purchased in any quantity desired. If you are not able to obtain some from your local supplier, automobile rubbing compound may be used just as effectively.

1. Dampen a piece of fine rubbing felt or rag with water.

2. Scoop some of the compound on the felt or rag.

3. Begin rubbing the surface with a moderate pressure in the direction of the grain.

4. Replenish the pad with the compound and continue rubbing, moving the pad laterally from left to right in the direction of the grain.

5. Wipe off a section of the surface and make a visual inspection of the rubbing results. A fine smooth appearance is evidence that the surface has been adequately rubbed.

6. Remove grime with a soft rag. Be careful to rub in the direction of the grain to avoid scratching.

7. Wax may be applied if a higher gloss is desired.

ADVANTAGES OF WOOD LACQUERS

There are many decided advantages in the use of wood lacquers. There is no doubt but that the advantages enumerated here far outshadow the disadvantages.

1. The drying time after the lacquer is applied is very short. It is possible to apply several coats within hours, thus eliminating the need of special drying rooms and equipment. It also permits the handling of the material sprayed within a few minutes after the lacquer has been applied.

2. It is somewhat heatproof thus making it practical for use on furniture which is subjected to heat, like kitchen tables, coffee tables, and cocktail tables.

3. It will withstand moisture well. It will not turn white when water is allowed to remain on the surface for an extended period. Thus lacquer is a fine finishing material to apply over surfaces of bar tops, kitchen tables, and occasional tables.

4. Special lacquers may be obtained which are alcoholproof.

5. Unlike some other finishing materials, lacquer does not oxidize or change into a powder with age. A piece of furniture, properly finished and properly lacquered, will last indefinitely and without any appreciable change in composition.

6. Because they are so transparent and clear, lacquers help to bring out the mellowness and beauty of the surface without in any way affecting the surface itself, whether finished in the natural shades or in the stained woods. And when this film is rubbed, a satin-smooth film is obtained that is very pleasing.

DISADVANTAGES OF WOOD LACQUERS

1. Because of its fast-drying tendencies, lacquer cannot be applied well with a brush. Despite the introduction of brushing lacquers, spraying is the best means of applying lacquers. The craftsman is therefore prevented from using most of these lacquers unless he possesses the necessary spraying equipment.

2. Lacquer cannot be applied directly over a varnished or a painted surface. If this is done, the lacquer will act as a remover and soften the undercoat. It is thus suggested that lacquer should never be applied over an unknown finish. It is better to use shellac.

3. Lacquer should not be applied over a surface whose finish has been removed with paint remover unless the surface just cleaned is free of all traces of the remover and the wax contained in the remover.

4. Lacquer should not be applied over a surface stained with penetrating oil stain, unless the surface has first been sealed with shellac. If the oil-stained surface is to be colored with lacquer enamel, it should first be sealed with an aluminum lacquer paint. The enamel is then applied directly over the aluminum surface. In this way, bleeding through of the oil stain will be prevented.

NOVELTY FINISHES WITH LACQUER

Many novel and interesting finishes may be obtained when special-purpose lacquers are used. The finishes obtained from these lacquers are excellent for children's toys, wood novelties, and knickknack shelves and other articles of furniture. Best results, however, are obtained when these lacquers are sprayed on the surface. The lacquers with the finishes they produce follow.

Crackle spray lacquer

Crackle lacquer is one of the many types of novelty lacquers available for wood finishing. Mention of this lacquer is made in order to familiarize you with the many possibilities in lacquer finishing. The surface is first sprayed

144

with a coat of lacquer enamel and permitted to dry. A crackle lacquer of contrasting color is sprayed over the first coat. Within a few minutes the crackling lacquer begins to split and crack into many uneven interesting designs over the entire surface. A coat of clear, glossy lacquer is applied over this to protect the surface.

Wrinkle lacquer finish
This special-purpose lacquer may be used equally well on wood and metal. The surface is first sprayed with an undercoat to seal it. This is allowed to dry and then is sanded smooth. The wrinkle lacquer of any desired color is then sprayed over the surface. The lacquer begins to dry with a rough wrinkled texture. If desired, an antique stain may be applied to give the wrinkle surface a more mellow appearance.

Flocking lacquer
Here the special lacquer acts as an adhesive for a special type of stranded fiber which is applied over the lacquer. The effect of this process is an imitation suede covering over the surface. It is excellent for interiors of drawers, boxes, lamp bases, and novelty pieces of furniture. The suede-like fiber strands are available in many popular colors, among which are brown, pink, blue, yellow, wine, gold, silver, buff, and black. The lacquers used as the adhesive are usually colored to match the fibers to be applied. Some manufacturers recommend that a special flock-spraying gun be used to apply the fine fiber. However, if one is not available, good results may be obtained merely by sprinkling the fiber on the adhesive.

AEROSOL LACQUER SPRAYING

Lacquer and other finishing materials may now be applied with the aid of the aerosol pressure can. The liquid is stored in a sealed pressure container which is activated by shaking the can vigorously and depressing the fingertip control. As pressure is applied to the spray button a smooth spray of the liquid is emitted.

Not only are lacquer and lacquer sealers available in the spray can. There are also colored lacquers, enamels, and liquid bronzes in gold, copper, and aluminum. In addition, matching stains already discussed in Chapter 4 may be obtained from the local woodfinishing dealers. These come in a variety of shades, among which are Brown Mahogany, Red Maple, Reddish Walnut, American Walnut, Provincial Fruitwood, Silver Gray, and Danish Walnut.

Lacquer and many other finishing materials are now available in aerosol cans. They are somewhat expensive but are a great convenience for small jobs.

These containers are ideal for spraying lacquers on small areas and for patching-up purposes. For best results the spray can should be held between 10 and 16 inches from the surface. While the button is depressed, spray back and forth in a slow even stroke. The can should be kept at the same distance while spraying. Slowing the movement or getting too close to the surface will cause a heavy accumulation of lacquer, thus causing unsightly runs and sags. It is best to practice on scrap wood before the spraying is attempted on the finished piece.

CHAPTER 9

Rubbing and Rubbing Materials

In the previous chapters, methods were discussed for rubbing down a particular type of finishing material. No general discussion was made of the basic principles involved in the rubbing process. This chapter will indicate the various rubbing procedures and the values of each.

Many years ago it was stylish to have as high a gloss as possible on furniture. The image of a person was easily reflected on the surface. Within recent years, the trend has been toward a more subdued and conservative type of gloss—the semi-gloss, satin, and dull finishes. These blend better with the modern and contemporary furniture styles of today.

Any gloss material, be it shellac, lacquer, or varnish, can be rubbed down to the desired effect if enough coats of material have been applied to the surface, and if the surface has been allowed to dry hard enough. Consequently, it is recommended that at least three coats of the material preferred be applied, and that at least 24 hours elapse before rubbing.

Whichever material is applied, it will not dry smooth, free of dust, and free of all brush or spray marks. Then, too, with the exception of the flat-drying materials, all materials will dry with a high gloss, which is not entirely suitable as the finished job. Thus, some operation must be performed which will remove all imperfections and provide the type of gloss desired. This operation is rubbing.

Actually, when a surface is rubbed down, part of the finish is being worn away. The process may be compared to the sandpapering of a piece of wood. The sandpaper cuts away fine pieces of wood and smooths the surface as well. The sandpaper dust is evidence of the fact that material is being scratched away. Sandpaper cuts by producing scratches—naturally, the coarser the paper, the wider and deeper scratches and the more material worn away; the finer the paper, the narrower and shallower the scratch. The former leaves a somewhat rough surface; the latter, a smoother and more polished surface. When a finished surface is rubbed down, the same situation prevails. Instead of sandpaper, other abrasives may be used. These, too, can be obtained in different textures to produce a wide or a narrow scratch, a gloss, or a flat surface. Naturally, the coarser the abrasive, the faster the surface will be worn away.

In rubbing a finished surface, a material (abrasive) must be used that will cut away part of the finish as quickly as possible without damaging the delicate film of the job. There are several methods for this purpose. Each has its advantages and shortcomings. Each has its appropriate place in the final finishing operation. The use depends upon the end result desired. Is an exceptionally fine smooth surface required? Is a quick, smooth job desired? Is a very dull finish needed? Are there ample time and materials available to rub as desired? The answer to these questions will determine the type of rubbing to choose. Let us examine the various rubbing methods so that we may be in a better position to make our decision.

RUBBING WITH STEEL WOOL

One of the simplest ways of rubbing down a finish is with steel wool. Steel wool consists of rolls of steel shavings of different grits, ranging from No. 1 or No. 2 (very coarse) to No. 3/0 and No. 4/0 (very fine). The very coarse grades are not used for furniture rubbing, because they scratch the delicate surfaces too deeply. They are used mostly for floor cleaning and polishing. For ordinary finish rubbing, No. 2/0 or No. 3/0 steel wool may be used very effectively, for a very pleasing, satin-smooth surface.

Dry steel wool
1. Roll the cut piece into a ball and press to the surface with the palm of your hand.
2. Move the steel wool back and forth with a moderate pressure in the direction of the grain.

148

Steel wool is one of the basic rubbing materials.

3. Continue to rub in this manner until the entire area has been covered. Turn the steel wool around from time to time to assure better cutting.

4. Replace steel wool if necessary and continue to rub until the surface is free of dust specks, brush marks, and other imperfections.

5. The surface is considered rubbed when in addition to the above, it has a semi-gloss sheen and is smooth. Do not rub more than is necessary, for you must remember that the more you rub the more material is worn away and, consequently, the greater the possibility of damaging the finish. Moldings, corners, edges, and other pieces having sharp edges should be rubbed with extreme care to avoid wearing away the finish.

6. Clean off the dust and residue produced by the steel wool with a soft brush, again following the direction of the grain. For a thorough cleaning, wipe off the surface with a clean soft wiping cloth. Furniture oil or furniture wax may be applied to bring out the desired sheen. Whichever is used must be completely wiped off after it has been applied.

Steel wool and oil

The steel wool pad is soaked with any light oil, like machine or crude oil, and then used to rub the surface in the same manner as in the dry-rubbing method. The surface must be dried clean of oil and grime after the rubbing operation has been completed. No other polishing device is necessary since the oil remaining on the surface serves as the polishing agent.

Advantages of steel wool

1. It is a simple and yet an effective way to obtain comparatively smooth surfaces.
2. The material is easily handled and readily available.
3. This method of rubbing is not too time-consuming.
4. It can be used as the first step in other forms of rubbing. For example, the surface is first steel-wooled and then rubbed with pumice stone and oil.
5. It may be used for the rubbing of small pieces of furniture, like boxes, small tables, chairs, and picture frames.
6. It may be used for rubbing out-of-the-way places where smoothness alone is required.

Disadvantages of steel wool

1. It is not possible to obtain a perfectly uniform, smooth surface, because the steel wool has a soft texture-and will adjust itself to whatever irregularities are found on the surface. To cite an example, the steel wool rubbing will not remove the ridges on the surface caused by the brush, because the steel wool will take the shape of the ridges as it is rubbed along the surface.
2. There is always the danger of steel slivers injuring your hand.

RUBBING WITH SANDPAPER

The width of the scratch produced by the abrasive determines the amount of luster resulting on the surface. Thus, if a series of very wide scratches are made on the surface, a very dull appearance will result; and if a series of very fine scratches are made, a gloss surface will result. No scratch at all should produce a mirrorlike surface.

Where a very dull, flat finish is required, sandpaper-and-oil rubbing is recommended. A No. 5/0 garnet finishing paper is suggested. Any coarser grade will cause scratches that are too deep, and the damage done to the surface by the deep scratches will be beyond repair.

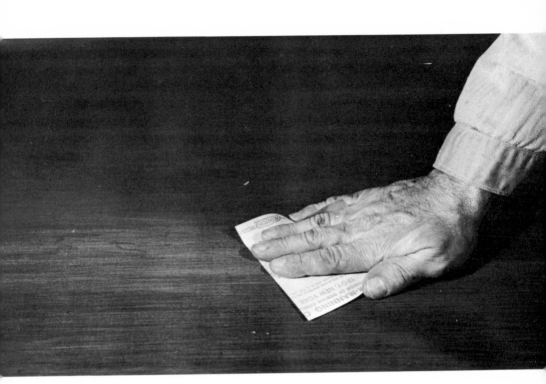
Rubbing with sandpaper and oil.

Sandpaper and oil

1. Cut the finishing paper into quarters and soak a section in crude or light machine oil.

2. Place in the palm of hand and with a moderate pressure begin moving the paper back and forth, following the direction of the grain.

3. Check the effect of the rubbing action from time to time. Remember, the sandpaper cuts very rapidly.

4. Resoak the paper and continue to rub. Remove the grime from a section and check very carefully.

5. Cease to rub when the surface has acquired a smooth, dull appearance, free of brush or spray marks and other surface imperfections.

6. Clean the surface with a soft clean cloth, moving in the direction of the grain.

Sandpaper and water

This method of rubbing is limited to surfaces finished in varnish or lacquer. It should never be used on a surface finished in shellac, because the water will affect the shellac. Flint and garnet paper cannot be used with water, because the glue backing of these papers will wash off. Only aluminum oxide "wet or dry" paper may be used, and of these the fine No. 400 or No. 320 are recommended. The others are too coarse for this purpose and will damage the surface.

The abrasive is soaked in water and then rubbed on the surface in the same manner as in the oil-rubbing method. However, there are several important precautions. The inspection of the surface must be more frequent, since the water has a tendency to cut the surface finish down faster; the water must not remain on the surface too long, since there is a tendency for water to soak through the finish, especially when the finish coats are thin.

After the surface has been rubbed to the desired condition, remove the grime with a sponge soaked in clean water. Wipe off the water with a dry cloth or chamois. Waxing and/or oil polishing may be resorted to as a final step.

Advantages of sandpaper

1. This type of rubbing, if done carefully and expertly, will result in a very smooth and dull surface.
2. This form of rubbing is time-saving when performed on inconspicuous surfaces, like the insides of cabinets, shelves, and other interiors.
3. As already indicated, it is a labor- and time-saving device when performed as the initial rubbing step and then followed by pumice stone or steel-wool rubbing.
4. It is a simple procedure to follow, and good results are assured if the few minor precautions are taken.

Disadvantages of sandpaper

1. Unless care is used while rubbing, serious damage may be done to the film. In some cases this damage may be beyond repair.
2. Although the scratches produced are not visible if they follow the direction of the grain, they will become very conspicuous if the direction is altered. A slight scratch across the grain will mar the appearance of the entire job.

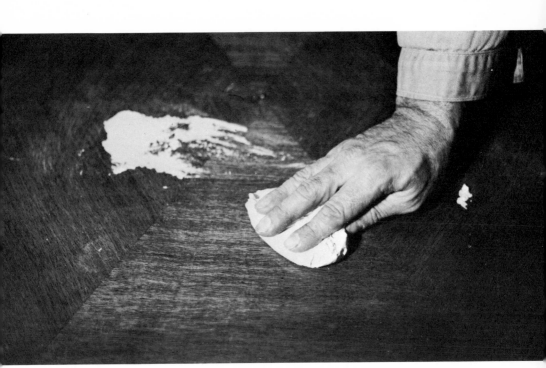

Rubbing compound, the same substance that is used to clean automobiles, is excellent for rubbing a lacquered finish.

RUBBING COMPOUND

In Chapter 8 mention was made of this method of rubbing. It has gained much popularity in recent years because of the excellent results obtained on lacquer finish. Rubbing compound is a paste abrasive consisting of several ingredients, among which may be included pumice stone and wax. The compound is available in different textures. The coarser the compound, the faster it will cut and the more dull the resulting finish. It is suggested that a medium-coarse compound be used for the initial rubbing, followed by a fine compound. In this way the cutting will be quicker at the beginning when it is most needed. Very little cutting takes place during the polishing stages with the fine compound.

The label on the container of the rubbing compound usually indicates the mixture of the material and the solvent used for thinning it. This information will be of assistance to you, especially when the final cleaning is done. In some types, benzene is used as the solvent; in others, water is used for removing the grime. The label will indicate which to use.

Chapter 8 details the steps in rubbing a lacquer finish with rubbing compound. However, there are sometimes special problems. The surface being rubbed may have sharp corners and moldings, as on table tops, legs, and sides of cabinets. It is difficult to rub from one end to the other, because obstructions prevent the completion of the rubbing stroke, and it is rather difficult to get into the corners or crevices. This difficulty may be overcome by rubbing the surface near the obstructions across the grain until that section is perfectly smooth. Next, remove the marks made by the cross-rubbing by rubbing in short strokes in the direction of the grain. Finally, finish off by rubbing the entire area with a few light strokes in the direction of the grain.

Advantages of rubbing compound

1. It is ideal for rubbing a lacquer finish. The surface is cut down rather quickly.
2. The compound may be obtained in an assortment of colors to match the finish being rubbed. This aids in getting a mellow appearance on the surface. Because the shade matches the surface, any of the compound remaining in the corners or crevices will not be conspicuous when the piece has been completely finished.

Disadvantages of rubbing compound

1. The grime from the surface is rather difficult to remove. It clogs the wiping cloth, and traces of it become imbedded in the finish.
2. The pad used also becomes clogged as you rub and must be cleaned often during the process to prevent scratches and friction.
3. Rubbing compound is comparatively expensive.

RUBBING WITH PUMICE STONE AND OIL

This type of rubbing is the professional finisher's way of obtaining a fine, smooth finish. You must have often heard it mentioned that this particular cabinet or that table has a hand-rubbed finish. This refers to pumice-stone rubbing done by hand. The process on shellacked, varnished, and lacquered surfaces is discussed in detail in Chapters 6, 7, and 8.

Pumice-stone rubbing, properly executed, will result in a finish which is beyond compare. It can produce the degree of luster or dullness desired. It can cut down so well that a perfectly true flat surface will be assured, provided proper filling of the wood has been done and an ample number of coats of material have been applied.

Pumice-stone rubbing requires the following materials:

1. Pumice stone (powdered)   —the abrasive
2. Rubbing pad   —to apply the abrasive
3. Oil or water   —the lubricant
4. Wiping cloth or sponge   —to remove the grime
5. Naphtha or gasoline   —to clean the surface

Let us discuss in detail the purpose and function of each of the materials just enumerated.

Pumice stone

Pumice stone is a white material obtained from the ashes of volcanic eruptions. The material is ground into powders of different degrees of coarseness; some of the powder is formed into solid bricks and the other is left in its powder form. The wood finisher uses the pumice stone in the powder form for most of his rubbing. The ranges of grit or coarseness are from very coarse, No. 2 or No. 1; fine, 2/0; to a very fine, FF. A medium-fine 2/0 pumice stone is recommended for the average rubbing job.

The wood finisher has selected pumice stone in preference to many other types of abrasives because of its very fine and fast-cutting qualities. It wears away the finish without leaving any unsightly scratches. It combines readily with either water or oil and, with these as a lubricant, cuts faster without itself wearing away.

The pumice-stone powder should be checked and sifted before it is used for rubbing. A small speck of foreign matter, or a grain of pumice stone larger than the others, will leave deep scratches on the surface.

The rubbing pad

Some medium for using the pumice stone should be available. It has been found that cloth, rags, and cotton waste, when used to apply the pumice stone, do not cut the surface fast enough, because the pumice stone imbeds itself in the fibers of the material and prevents a cutting action. A felt rubbing pad or a piece of burlap pad may be used for better rubbing action.

The felt pad is especially made for rubbing. It can be obtained in different thicknesses from 1/4" to 1" thick and in different degrees of coarseness. The

155

finer the weave, the smoother the net result. A medium-texture ¼" gray felt is recommended for most of rubbing. This can be obtained in any dimension from your local paint supply house. The rubbing felt is ideal for rubbing because it permits the fine pumice powder to move within the fibers of the felt, and this motion gives the pumice its good cutting action.

The rubbing felt has a flat surface and, when used, will help wear away the high ridges on the finish which have been made by dirt specks, orange-peel, and brush marks. This is a very important quality of the flat felt. Some finishers glue a piece of wood block to the upper side of the felt to give the felt more substance when rubbing a flat area.

When felt is not available, a piece of burlap bag folded several times to form a pad about ¼" thick and large enough to fit the palm of your hand may be used. The action with the pumice stone is about the same as with the felt. The felt, however, assures a more uniform, flat rubbing surface. The burlap should be clean and free of any imperfection which may injure the finish.

The lubricant (water or oil)

Rubbing a finish with dry pumice alone is not practical. Friction and heat will result which may injure the finish; also, no cutting action will take place because the pumice has a tendency to cake up. A lubricant is therefore essential with the dry pumice stone. This lubricant can be either water or oil.

Water may be used when you are rubbing a varnish or a lacquer finish. It should never be used when you are rubbing a shellac finish, because the water will affect the shellac film and turn it white. Remember shellac is not waterproof.

Water, when mixed with the pumice, helps in cutting the finish down very rapidly and should consequently be used with extreme care. Another reason for the use of water is that it does not leave an oily residue on the finish after the surface has been rubbed.

Any nonfatty oil can be used with pumice. Crude oil, a rather inexpensive mineral oil, is recommended. Any oil used should be thinned slightly with benzene to prevent unnecessary caking of the pumice while on the pad.

Shellac, varnish, and lacquer can be rubbed equally as well with oil. There is no danger to any of these finishes if oil is used as the lubricant. Oil does not cut as rapidly as water and, consequently, is safer to use, especially when the craftsman is not sufficiently skilled in the techniques of rubbing. As a matter of fact, oil is recommended for all types of rubbing situations to prevent any possible damage to the finish. The only drawback to the use of the oil is that it leaves an oily film on the finish which is rather difficult to eradicate. If not removed entirely, the finish will always appear oily and, after a while, turn dull.

Wiping materials (cloth, sponge, and chamois)

A soft, clean wiping cloth is recommended when wiping off the grime and residue after rubbing with oil. The cloth should be free of any stitching or creases, as these will leave impressions on the surface as the wiping is done. Those are the only requirements for the wiping cloth. You should go to no expense in obtaining it.

A sponge and chamois are essential for wiping the surface after it has been rubbed with pumice and water. In this type of rubbing, the water evaporates rapidly, leaving a chalky white pumice film on the surface. If a dry cloth were used to remove this film, you would be taking the risk of scratching the finish. The wet sponge softens the white film and cleans the surface, but it does not remove the excess water. A damp chamois is worked over the surface, following the direction of the grain, to remove all the excess water remaining on the finish.

Where neither of these materials is available, a wet cloth may be substituted for the sponge, and a clean, soft, dry cloth may be substituted for the chamois. The same precautions should be followed when using these.

Solvents (gasoline and naphtha)

Solvents are used primarily to remove traces of oil from the finish after it has been rubbed with pumice and oil. A soft cloth is dampened with the solvent and then rubbed on the already cleaned surface. This action will dissolve the oily film remaining. Waxes and other types of polishes may be used over surfaces so cleaned.

RUBBING WITH A BRUSH

There are areas and surfaces on furniture, like carvings, moldings, fretwork, and scrollwork, which are quite difficult to rub with any of the methods mentioned. There is always the fear that rubbing in the conventional manner will do more harm than good to these surfaces.

These areas may be rubbed with the aid of a stiff, short-haired brush. A brush or "scrubber" is available for this purpose in sizes from ¾" to 2" in diameter. A 1" scrubber is ideal for most brush rubbing. The bristle of the scrubber is very short, which tends to make it quite stiff. The stiff bristles aid in wearing away and dulling the finish when used for rubbing.

The brush is first soaked in oil or water and then the wet brush is pressed into the pumice-stone powder. The brush, saturated with the lubricant and the pumice stone, is held firmly in the hand and then scrubbed over the surface until the required effect is obtained. Occasionally, the brush should

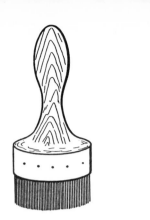

Left: The best way to rub carved and other irregular surfaces is with a scrubber. *Right:* A machine rubber can be improvised from a portable electric sander.

be refilled with the rubbing materials to continue the cutting action. Clean the surface with a clean cloth and then with a dry, soft brush to remove any excess pumice and lubricant that may have remained in these hard-to-get-at places. Dipping the clean brush in benzene will aid in obtaining a cleaner finish.

MACHINE RUBBING

The professional wood finisher has in recent years become accustomed to do most of his rubbing by mechanical means. Rubbing machines are operated by either air pressure or electricity. The machine has two oscillating pads covered with felt which move very rapidly. In some of the more simple types, the rubbing proceeds as follows. The pumice is sprinkled over the area to be rubbed so that a fine layer of pumice stone covers the surface. Water is sprinkled over the pumice. The oscillating pads are moistened and then placed over the area. The machine is then moved slowly from one end to the other and also laterally. This is continued until the entire area has been rubbed evenly. An occasional checking while the rubbing is proceeding is essential. Machine rubbing is faster than hand rubbing and, consequently, one must take the extra precautions. The surface is cleaned as indicated earlier in this chapter.

It is not suggested that you should involve yourself in any expense to secure a mechanical rubber. However, you may own an oscillating or vibrating power sander, and this may be used for rubbing if the appropriate attachments are part of the equipment or if they may be obtained at little cost. There is no doubt that, where this machine is available, much time and labor can be saved. A little experience and a little practice with it will prove very helpful.

PART THREE: SELECTING THE APPROPRIATE FINISH

CHAPTER 10

Bleached and Pickled Finishes

Within recent years new ideas in furniture design and finishing have appeared. Modern and contemporary designs of furniture have been introduced, and, although they did not attract public attention at first, they have become very popular. The newness of design and the trend away from the so-called drab traditional styles have appealed to all who have studied them. Thousands of homes today are decorated with furniture of the modern trend.

Among the most popular should be included the Scandinavian, French and Italian Provincial, and the Spanish and Mediterranean. In all these the trend has been toward a modification of the more traditional designs so as to simplify without losing the original flavor. Since most of these styles use such woods as pecan, walnut, teak, maple, and cherry, the finishing problem is a rather simple one. In most cases the pieces are finished in natural so as to bring out the beautiful characteristics of the grain. We find, for example, that Scandinavian furniture is "oil-finished" natural, Mediterranean is finished in natural but "distressed." Chapter 11 will describe these finishes more fully.

The craftsman also finds in these finishes a novelty which is quite intriguing. Here, through the process of bleaching and filling with contrasting fillers, he can produce a finish that is entirely different from the ones he has been accustomed to. The craftsman will find the market literally filled with projects made of wood in the modern design. He can avail himself of these without too much difficulty and then finish them in the natural or bleached finishes as the case may be. Various plywood manufacturers have developed new, simple ideas in furniture making and finishing to encourage the use of their products. Some of the ideas they have introduced are very helpful to the home craftsman. It is suggested that he refer to these manufacturers for ideas and suggestions in the use of their finishing materials.

Abiding by this new trend this chapter will be devoted to the procedures and methods used in producing the modern light finishes.

It should be emphasized at this point that all these finishes require more care in their execution than do the darker finishes. The wood surfaces to be finished in the natural or bleached finishes must be free of all imperfections. Blemishes, weather streaks, and contrasting shades of wood within the same piece of furniture must be avoided, for they become very conspicuous and annoying when the natural finishes are applied. Very little consideration must be given to these faults when finishing in the dark stains, because the dark stains hide many of them.

Thus, in selecting the woods for your job, make sure that you select only those that are free from all defects, have a uniform texture, and, if possible, have a uniform surface color.

These finishes can be divided into two groups: the blond finishes, and the pickled finishes. In the blond finishes, the wood is bleached and then finished in the natural state. The pickled finish requires the bleaching of the surface, the application of a light stain, and a contrasting colored pore filler.

BLOND FINISHES

As already indicated, these finishes require that the wood first be bleached and then finished in this natural shade. No stain, or very light stain, may be added to the surface before the finishing coats are applied. In this group may be included finishes like blond maple, blond mahogany, blond walnut, and natural pine. The process for finishing these is practically the same; therefore, the description of one may be applied to all the other woods mentioned.

Blond-finishing close-grain woods

1. The article to be finished should be carefully checked for defects, such as dents, bruises, scratches, and stains.

2. Sandpaper the surface carefully with No. 2/0 paper and remove all the imperfections observed.

3. Apply the preferred bleach carefully to the entire surface. Refer to Chapter 3 for details. Care must be exercised to make certain that the bleach is applied evenly on the surface. Flooding of one section and skimping on another will result in uneven shades when the wood dries.

4. Wash the surface with clear water to remove traces of chemicals.

5. After the surface has dried sufficiently, sandpaper with No. 3/0 garnet paper to remove the fuzz caused by the action of the water on the wood. Clean and dust thoroughly.

6. Apply a thin coat of water-white lacquer or a wash coat of white shellac to the entire surface. If possible, the water-white lacquer should be applied because it does not discolor the wood in any way, and it also helps to seal the surface in preparation for the next coat.

7. Apply a coat of clear gloss lacquer, if the water-white lacquer was used as the sealer. Refer to Chapter 8. If shellac was used as the sealer, another coat of white shellac may be applied or a coat of clear gloss varnish.

8. Apply a second and a third coat of the material used in step 7.

9. Rub the surface with No. 2/0 steel wool or with pumice stone and oil. If pumice stone and oil is used, make sure that all traces of oil and grime are completely removed. Any grime remaining will affect the light shade of the finish. See Chapter 9.

10. Clean the surface with a cloth dampened in benzene, and wipe thoroughly.

11. Apply wax and polish, as explained in Chapter 14.

Blond-finishing open-grain woods

If the wood of the job being finished blond is an open-grain wood, like mahogany, walnut, or oak, proceed with steps 1 to 6 above and then continue as follows:

7. Fill the surface pores with a natural filler paste. Allow this to set for about five minutes and then wipe off clean. The natural filler is recommended, because it has a neutral shade and it will not affect appreciably the shade of the bleached wood. Refer to Chapter 3.

8. Allow the surface to dry overnight and apply a wash coat of white shellac, as explained in Chapter 6.

9. At least two hours should elapse before the wash coat is sanded lightly and dusted.

10. Apply a finish top coat, shellac, varnish, or lacquer. Allow sufficient drying time, and sand the surface smooth.

11. Apply one or two more coats of finish coat the same as the coat applied in step 10.

12. Allow the final coat to dry at least twenty-four hours.

13. Rub the surface with No. 2/0 steel wool. Pumice stone and oil should not be used, because the grime has a tendency to imbed itself in the pores and spoil the effect of the light finish.

14. Clean and apply wax and polish.

When applying the top or finishing coats, remember to keep them to a minimum, because too many coats will allow a certain amount of yellowing of the surface and thus mar the appearance of this light finish.

PICKLED FINISHES

Pickled finishes are produced by the controlled wiping of colors on open-grain woods, like oak, mahogany, and walnut.

There is a very interesting story of how this pickling effect came into being. Some time ago a group purchased an old Colonial home, in which all of the woodwork was painted white. One of the purchasers decided to have this white paint removed from the surfaces and to have them refinished with another color. As the white paint was being removed, it was noted that a beautiful dark wood was being brought to light. Upon further examination, the wood was identified as mahogany. The workers were not successful in removing all of the paint from the mouldings and carvings, and the paint pigment was left in these places. The accidental effect of this contrast was so pleasing that it was admired by all who saw it. Before long this effect became one of the most popular of modern finishes.

The pickling effect, as has already been indicated, means that the pores of the open-grain wood, the corners, the crevices, are filled with a colored material that contrasts with the remainder of the surface.

Many different types of pickling effects are possible with the same kind of wood. Each is identified by the shade of the finish. For example, pickled finishes on oak include limed oak, gray limed oak, and wheat oak. Mahogany may be finished as pickled mahogany and rose pink. Pine may be finished as pickled pine and driftwood gray. The procedure involved in obtaining these special finishes is practically the same with all the woods. The differences are found in the shades of stain and the pickling color used.

Applying a pickled finish. First the surface is stained and sealed with shellac. Then the white material—paint or white lead—is spread on the surface. It is immediately wiped off with a cloth, so that traces remain in pores and crevices.

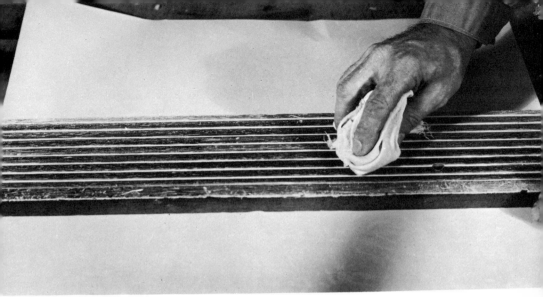

The following finishing schedules should serve as ready reference to obtain the desired pickled finish.

Tan Limed Oak (Wheat Oak)

For oak, chestnut, and ash.

1. Sandpaper. The surface should be carefully sanded with 2/0 garnet paper to remove all surface imperfections. Minor surface defects should be eliminated during this step.

2. Clean. The surface just sanded must be cleaned thoroughly. All dust on the surface and in the pores should be removed.

3. Bleach. If white oak is not used on the job, the wood surface should be bleached with an appropriate bleach. (Refer to Chapter 3.) The bleached surface should be washed with clean water to remove any trace of chemical remaining on the surface. If white oak is used for the job, bleaching of the wood is not necessary, but the surface should be sponged with clean water.

4. Sandpaper. The wood must be sandpapered with 3/0 paper to remove the fuzz on the surface.

5. Clean. The surface should be dusted free of all surface dust.

6. Stain. A light water stain is applied evenly on the surface. Dissolve a teaspoonful of walnut water-soluble crystals in ½ pint hot water. Use the same ratio when larger amounts are needed. Apply this light-tan stain to the surface evenly. Allow to dry.

7. Seal. Apply a wash coat (2-pound cut) of white shellac over the surface already stained. The nature of this coat is such that it helps in filling and sealing the surface without leaving a heavy deposit of the shellac on the surface.

8. Apply liming agent. This may be either a flat white paint, white undercoat, or a mixture of white lead dissolved in turpentine to the consistency of heavy cream. The white material preferred is brushed on to the surface and then is wiped off with a cloth or burlap. The wiping operation should be such that very little trace of the white paint remains on the top surface. A smeared look should be avoided on the surface, and it is for this reason that you must make certain that the surface, except for the pores, is wiped carefully.

9. Allow sufficient drying time. The white material applied requires from twelve to twenty-four hours to dry before any other material is applied. The oil base in the paint makes this imperative.

10. Seal. The surface is now coated with another wash coat of white shellac; or, if the job is to be finished in lacquer, a coat of water-white lacquer. This is allowed to dry two hours.

11. Sandpaper. The sealed surface is sanded carefully and lightly to remove any roughness remaining on the surface.

12. Apply a coat of clear shellac, varnish, or lacquer. Any one of these top clear glossy coats may be applied, provided the remaining coats are of the same material. The coat is applied evenly and carefully to the entire surface. Refer to the earlier sections in the book for the correct methods of application. Allow this coat to dry thoroughly.

13. Sandpaper. This top coat is sandpapered carefully to remove brush marks and other surface imperfections. It should be cleaned before the next coat is applied.

14. Apply second coat. This coat should be the same as the first coat of top finish. It is applied in the same manner as the first. Allow sufficient drying time.

15. Rub. No. 2/0 steel wool rubbing is preferred for this type of finish. The object of the rubbing is merely to remove any nibs and brush marks on the surface. No rubbing agent should be used, like pumice stone and oil, which tends to leave a residue in the pores to detract from the clean effect you want.

16. Wax. A light clear liquid wax is applied and the surface polished as explained in Chapter 14.

Gray Limed Oak

For oak, chestnut, and ash

1. Sandpaper. The surface should be carefully sanded with No. 2/0 garnet paper to remove all surface imperfections.

166

2. Clean. Dust the surface just sanded thoroughly.

3. Sponge. The entire area should be sponged with clean water. Allow several hours for drying.

4. Sandpaper. The sponged surface should be sanded with 3/0 garnet paper to remove the fuzz and roughness caused by the sponging.

5. Clean. The sanded surface should be cleaned of all dust.

6. Stain. A light water stain is applied evenly to the entire job. Dissolve ½ ounce of black water-soluble aniline in one quart of hot water, or dissolve ½ ounce of silver-gray water-soluble aniline in one quart of hot water. Either may be used for staining, but the silver-gray aniline will assure a better effect. It is well to try these stains on a piece of scrap wood, allow them to dry, and then apply the white color, before actually staining the job. The sample will give you a good indication of the results obtained with the stain. If you wish, you may alter the stain by adding more water or more aniline powder. A light stain is preferred.

7. Seal. The stained surface is now coated with a wash coat of shellac and allowed to dry at least two hours.

8. Sandpaper. The seal coat is sandpapered lightly to remove nibs.

9. Apply the liming agent. White flat paint, or white undercoat, or white lead thinned in turpentine to the consistency of heavy cream is brushed on to the surface evenly. Wipe off the excess color from the surface, using a piece of burlap or cloth. Make sure that the surface is absolutely clean and free of white paint. The white should appear in the pores only. Avoid a smeared surface effect by using care in wiping off the white paint.

10. Allow to dry. The surface limed white should be permitted to dry from twelve to twenty-four hours before the next application of material.

11. Seal. The colored surface should be sealed with a wash coat of white shellac. This seals the colored surface and provides a better surface for the next coats. Allow two hours' drying time.

12. Sandpaper. The sealed surface is slightly sanded to remove fuzz produced by the shellac.

13. Apply finish coat. A coat of white shellac, clear gloss varnish, or clear gloss lacquer is applied evenly on the entire surface. Refer to the earlier chapters for correct procedure. Allow this coat to dry.

14. Sandpaper. The finish coat should be sandpapered with No. 3/0 garnet paper evenly and smoothly.

15. Apply second coat. The second finish coat should be the same as the first coat. It is applied in the same manner as the first. Allow at least twenty-four hours of drying time.

16. Rub. The surface is rubbed with No. 2/0 steel wool. No rubbing agent should be used that will tend to leave a residue in the pores to detract from the clean effect you want.

17. Wax. A light clear liquid wax is applied and the surface polished, as explained in Chapter 14.

Pickled mahogany

For mahogany and Philippine mahogany

1. Sandpaper. The surface should be carefully sanded with No. 2/0 garnet paper to remove all surface imperfections.

2. Clean. Dust the surface just sanded thoroughly.

3. Bleach. The mahogany wood is bleached with an appropriate bleach to remove as much of the reddish color as possible. Refer to Chapter 3 for instructions in bleaching.

4. Wash. The bleached surface is washed with a cloth dampened in clean water to remove any trace of chemical remaining on the surface.

5. Sandpaper. After the surface has dried sufficiently, it should be sanded smooth with No. 3/0 garnet paper to remove the fuzz on the surface caused by the bleach and water.

6. Seal. The surface is now sealed with a wash coat of white shellac to prevent the next coat from penetrating too deeply. Sandpaper when dry.

7. Apply the liming agent. This can be white flat paint, white undercoat, or white lead thinned in turpentine to the consistency of heavy cream. A little chrome yellow medium may be added to the white for a better effect. Apply this paint on the surface evenly. With a piece of cloth or burlap, clean off the excess, but do not remove the color imbedded in the pores. Clean thoroughly in order not to leave a smeared effect on the surface.

8. Allow this pickled surface to dry overnight.

9. Seal. The pickled surface is sealed with a wash coat of white shellac. Allow to dry about two hours.

10. Sandpaper. The sealed surface is now sanded lightly to remove traces of fuzz.

11. Apply finish coat. White shellac, clear gloss varnish, or clear gloss lacquer may be applied. Refer to Chapters 6, 7, and 8 for instructions. Allow sufficient drying time.

12. Apply second coat. This coat should be the same as the first, and it is applied in the same way. Allow this final coat to dry at least twenty-four hours.

13. Rub. The surface is rubbed with No. 2/0 steel wool. No other rubbing agents should be used as they will leave a residue in the pores and thus spoil the pickling effect.

14. Wax. Wax with a clear liquid wax and then polish the surface.

Rose-Pink pickled effect

For mahogany, maple, poplar, pine, and gum

1. Sandpaper. The surface is carefully sanded with No. 2/0 garnet to remove all surface imperfections.

2. Clean. Remove all dust and dirt from the sanded surface.

3. Bleach. The wood is bleached with the appropriate bleach to remove as much color as possible. Refer to Chapter 3 for bleaching instructions.

4. Wash. The bleached surface is rinsed with a cloth soaked in clear water to remove all traces of chemicals remaining.

5. Sandpaper. After the surface has dried sufficiently sandpaper with No. 3/0 garnet paper to remove the fuzz caused by the water.

6. Stain. Apply a coat of light water stain evenly on the sanded surface. Dissolve about ¼ ounce of red mahogany water-soluble aniline in one quart of hot water. Apply this stain to the surface. It is a good idea to test the shade of stain on a piece of scrap wood of the type being finished, allow this to dry, and then coat with the white pickling agent. The shade of the stain may be controlled by adding more water or more aniline powder. Allow ample drying time after the stain is applied.

7. Seal. The stained surface is sealed with a wash coat of white shellac. Allow two hours of drying before applying the next coat.

8. Apply the pickling agent. Flat white paint, or white undercoat, or white lead dissolved in turpentine to the consistency of heavy cream may be applied. Apply uniformly on the surface and then wipe off the excess with a piece of cloth or burlap. Make sure that all traces of the paint are removed from the surface. A smeared muddy surface will result if this cleaning is not done carefully. Only the pores should show the effects of the pickling.

9. Seal. After the surface has dried at least twelve hours, it should be sealed with a wash coat of white shellac. Allow this to dry at least two hours.

10. Sandpaper. The sealed surface should now be sanded with 3/0 paper to remove all roughness. Clean and dust off the sanded surface.

11. Apply finish coat. White shellac, varnish, or clear gloss lacquer may be applied. Refer to Chapters 6, 7, and 8 for procedure in applying these finishing coats. Allow sufficient drying time.

12. Apply second finish coat. This should be the same as the first coat applied, and it should be applied in the same manner. Allow this final coat to dry at least twenty-four hours.

13. Rub. No. 2/0 steel wool should be used to rub the finish.

14. Wax. Apply a light clear liquid wax and polish, as explained in Chapter 14.

Silver-Gray pickled effect

For walnut, mahogany, pine, poplar, maple, and gum

1. Sandpaper. The surface is carefully sanded with No. 2/0 garnet paper to remove all surface imperfections.

2. Clean. Remove all dust and dirt from the sanded surface.

3. Bleach. Mahogany and walnut should be bleached with an appropriate bleach to remove all traces of color from the wood. Refer to Chapter 3 for details of the bleaching process.

4. Sponge. All woods, whether they have been bleached or not, should be sponged with clean water. Allow sufficient drying time after the sponging.

5. Sandpaper. The sponged surface should be sanded with 3/0 garnet paper to remove roughness caused by the water.

6. Stain. Apply a coat of light water stain. Dissolve ¼ ounce of silver-gray water-soluble aniline in one quart of hot water. Apply this stain evenly to the surface. It is a good idea to test the stain on a piece of scrap wood before applying it to the surface.

7. Seal. The stained surface is now sealed with a wash coat of white shellac. This is allowed to dry at least two hours.

8. Apply the pickling agent. White flat paint, white undercoat, or white lead thinned in turpentine to the consistency of heavy cream may be used for the pickling effect. Apply a coat evenly over the entire surface and then wipe off the excess with a cloth or a piece of burlap. Make sure that all traces of the paint are removed from the surface. A smeared and muddy surface will result if the cleaning is not done carefully. Only the pores should show the effect of the pickling.

9. Seal. The surface is sealed with a wash coat of shellac after the pickled surface has dried about twelve hours. Allow the shellac sealer at least two hours for drying.

10. Sandpaper. The sealed surface is sanded smooth with No. 3/0 garnet paper. Dust clean the sanded surface.

11. Apply finish coat. White shellac, clear gloss varnish, or lacquer may be applied as the finish coat. It should be applied evenly. Refer to the earlier chapters for detailed instructions. Allow sufficient drying time.

12. Sandpaper. This first coat of finish should be sanded carefully with No. 3/0 garnet paper before applying the next coat.

13. Apply second coat. The second coat of finish coat should be the same as the first, and it should be applied in the same manner. At least twenty-four hours should elapse before the next step.

14. Rub. Rub surface with No. 2/0 steel wool. Other rubbing agents should not be used, as they leave a residue in the pores and spoil the effect of the pickling.

15. Wax. Apply a light liquid wax and polish the surface, as explained in Chapter 14.

Pickled pine

1. Sandpaper. The wood surface should be carefully sanded with No. 2/0 garnet paper to remove all surface imperfections.

2. Clean. Remove all traces of dust and dirt from the sanded surface.

3. Bleach. Apply an appropriate bleach to obtain a uniform light color. Refer to Chapter 3 for detailed instruction in the use of bleaches.

4. Wash. The bleached surface is washed thoroughly with a cloth soaked in clean water. The surface is then allowed to dry.

5. Sandpaper. The surface is sanded with No. 3/0 garnet paper to a smooth finish. Dust and clean carefully.

6. Apply the pickling agent. White flat paint, white undercoat, or white lead thinned in turpentine may be used, but the one used should be tinted with a little Raw Umber and Drop Black before it is applied to the surface. Apply to the surface and then skillfully wipe off some of the agent so that a dust-like coating remains. Allow this surface to dry about twelve hours.

7. Seal. The surface should be sealed with a wash coat of white shellac. Care should be taken to make certain that the shellac covers every section of the surface. Allow this to dry about two hours.

8. Apply finish coat. A coat of white shellac is applied after the seal coat has been sanded carefully. This is allowed to dry for at least four hours.

9. Rub. The surface is rubbed lightly with No. 2/0 steel wool to get a relatively smooth surface.

10. Wax. The surface should be waxed and polished.

Note: This finish does not require too heavy a body; therefore, one coat of finish coat should be sufficient.

Driftwood-Gray pickled effect

For pine, maple, bass, poplar, and spruce

1. Sandpaper. The surface is sanded carefully with No. 2/0 garnet paper to remove all surface imperfections.

2. Clean. The surface just sanded is dusted and cleaned carefully.

3. Sponge. The cleaned surface is sponged with clean water to raise the grain in preparation for the water stain.

4. Sandpaper. The sponged surface is sanded smooth and free of all roughness.

5. Stain. Apply a light coat of water stain. Dissolve ¼ ounce of silver-gray or black water-soluble aniline in one quart of hot water. Apply this water stain evenly to the entire surface. Allow the surface to dry at least six hours.

6. Apply the pickling agent. The pickling agent is made as follows: melt ¼ pound of paraffin wax in a double boiler. While the wax is in liquid form, add enough zinc oxide (white) paste ground in japan to color the wax white. Add a little turpentine to the mixture to thin it to the consistency of heavy cream. Allow it to cool and then apply this mixture to the surface stained.

7. Rub. The surface is now wiped clean of excess wax and rubbed to a high gloss. No additional steps are necessary, as there is very little body to driftwood finish.

CHAPTER 11

Traditional, Mediterranean, and Scandinavian Finishes

It is the purpose of this chapter to present the basic schedules of the more common types of finishes in step-by-step fashion so that you may be able to follow them and obtain the desired results. Of course, merely following the steps in the procedures will not assure a professional job unless you make a determined effort to apply yourself to the best of your ability. At first your efforts may prove somewhat disappointing, but as you continue and progress, the results will show that your efforts have not been in vain.

NATURAL FINISHES

A natural finish usually refers to a surface which has been finished in the shade of the natural raw wood, with no stain or other coloring matter applied. The following steps may be followed.

Natural-finishing close-grain woods
For pine, maple, gum, birch, fir, and spruce
1. Prepare surface. Sand with No. 2/0 garnet paper to remove all surface imperfections. Make necessary minor repairs.
2. Clean. Dust the sanded surface free of dust, oil, and other dirt.
3. Apply a wash coat of white shellac. Allow two hours of drying time.
4. Sandpaper. Sand the sealed surface lightly with No. 5/0 garnet paper.
5. Apply finish coat. Shellac, lacquer, or clear varnish may be applied. Allow drying time depending on the material used.
6. Sandpaper. Sand the top coat with No. 5/0 garnet to remove brush marks and surface nibs. Clean thoroughly.
7. Apply finish coat. One or more coats of the same material used in step 5 are applied here. Allow sufficient drying time, depending on material used, between each coat. Permit final coat to dry overnight. Refer to Chapters 6, 7, and 8 for details.
8. Rub. Rub surface with No. 2/0 steel wool if a dull surface is desired. 2/0 pumice stone and oil rubbing may be resorted to if a satin-gloss and extremely smooth surface is desired. Wash surface with benzene to remove all traces of oil grime. Follow directions in Chapter 9.
9. Wax. A coat of light paste wax is applied. Allow this to set for a few minutes and then rub to the required polish.
10. Touch up. If necessary, touch up any rubbed-through spot or marks as indicated in Chapter 15.

Natural-finishing open-grain woods
For walnut, oak, mahogany, Philippine mahogany, ash, and chestnut
1. Prepare surface. Sandpaper surface thoroughly to remove all surface imperfections. Make necessary minor repairs as indicated in Chapter 2.
2. Clean. Dust the sanded surface free of dust, oil, or dirt.
3. Fill. Apply a natural paste filler, allow this to set, and then wipe off clean as described in Chapter 5. Allow twenty-four hours for drying of the filler.
4. Seal. Seal the surface with a wash coat of white shellac. Allow at least two hours for drying.

Hepplewhite commode: natural finish on open-grain wood. (Courtesy Smith & Watson)

5. Sandpaper. Sand the sealed surface lightly with No. 5/0 garnet paper to remove nibs and dust. Clean thoroughly.

6. Apply finish coat. Shellac, varnish, or lacquer may be applied as the finish coat. Refer to Chapters 6, 7, and 8 for details. Allow this coat to dry sufficiently.

7. Sandpaper. Sand the finish coat smooth with No. 5/0 garnet paper.

8. Apply finish coat. Apply one or more coats of the finish coat applied in step 6. If more than one coat is applied in this step, sandpaper with No. 5/0 garnet before the final coat is applied. Allow the final coat to dry at least twenty-four hours.

9. Rub. No. 2/0 steel wool may be used for rubbing the surface to a dull finish. Pumice stone and oil or water may be used if more than three coats of finish are applied. Rub as indicated in Chapter 9. Clean the surface of all traces of grime, and then wash with benzene to assure surface free from oil.

10. Wax. Apply a light paste wax, allow to set for a few minutes, and then rub to the desired luster.

11. Touch up. If necessary touch up any rubbed-through spot or mark as explained in Chapter 15.

Hepplewhite writing table, finished in Cordovan Mahogany. (Courtesy Smith & Watson)

WATER STAIN FINISHES

Cordovan mahogany

For African and Central American mahogany, gum, and birch

1. Prepare surface. Sandpaper surface with No. 2/0 garnet paper to remove all surface imperfections. Make necessary minor surface repairs.

2. Clean. Dust surface thoroughly.

3. Sponge. Sponge the surface with clear water to raise the grain in preparation of applying water stain. Allow two hours for drying.

4. Sandpaper. Sand rough surface with No. 3/0 garnet paper until the surface is absolutely smooth. Dust free of all traces of surface dust and dust in pores of wood.

5. Stain. Apply water stain evenly on the entire surface made according to the following formula:

½ oz. Brown Mahogany water-soluble aniline

½ oz. Red Mahogany water-soluble aniline

¼ oz. Nigrosene Black water-soluble aniline

Dissolve the above water-soluble anilines in one quart of hot water. More Nigrosene Black may be added if a darker shade of mahogany is desired. Refer to Chapter 4 for additional information.

6. Fill. After stained surface has dried overnight, apply a paste filler. The color of the filler should be slightly darker than the stained surface. Secure a dark Red Mahogany filler and darken to match the stained surface by adding Vandyke Brown oil color and a little lampblack. Clean off the filler as explained in Chapter 5. Allow at least twenty-four hours for drying.

7. Seal. Apply a wash coat of orange shellac. Allow two hours for drying.

8. Sandpaper. Sand the sealed surface lightly with No. 5/0 garnet paper, and dust clean.

9. Apply finish top coat. Apply coat of shellac, lacquer, or varnish evenly and carefully to the entire job. Allow appropriate drying time.

10. Sandpaper. Sand the first coat smooth with No. 5/0 garnet paper to remove brush marks and nibs on the surface. Use tack rag to clean surface if varnish is used. Clean surface thoroughly.

11. Apply finish coats. Apply at least two more coats of the same material applied in the first coat. Sandpaper between coats after sufficient drying time has elapsed. Allow the final coat at least twenty-four hours to dry before rubbing.

12. Rub. Rub with pumice stone and oil or water as indicated in Chapter 9. Clean the surface.

13. Wax or polish. Apply the appropriate polish if a high luster is desired. Refer to Chapter 14 for details.

14. Touch up. Touch up any minor surface defects made as a result of the finishing operations, as explained in Chapter 15.

Red mahogany

For mahogany, Philippine mahogany, poplar, maple, birch, and gum
Proceed with the step-by-step operations for Cordovan mahogany explained above with the following exceptions:

5. Stain with a Red Mahogany stain made by dissolving one ounce of Red Mahogany aniline powder soluble in water in one quart of hot water.

6. Fill with a Red Mahogany filler, ready-mixed. Color need not be added if the filler is a trifle darker than the stained surface.

Sheraton breakfront, finished in Brown Mahogany. (Courtesy Smith & Watson)

Brown mahogany

For mahogany, Philippine mahogany, poplar, maple, birch, and gum
Proceed with the step-by-step operations listed under Cordovan mahogany
finish with the following exceptions:

5. Stain with Brown Mahogany water stain made by dissolving one ounce
of Brown Mahogany aniline soluble in water in one quart of hot water.

6. Fill with Brown Mahogany paste filler ready-mixed. Color need not be
added if the shade of the brown filler is a trifle darker than the stained surface.

178

American walnut

For walnut, gum, birch, maple, and poplar

1. Prepare the surface by making necessary minor repairs and then sanding the surface smooth with No. 2/0 garnet paper.

2. Clean. Dust thoroughly.

3. Sponge. Wet surface evenly with sponge and clear water to raise the grain of the wood in preparation of application of water stain.

4. Sandpaper. Sand the sponged surface with No. 3/0 garnet paper. Dust off thoroughly. Remove dust from surface and pores.

5. Stain. Apply water stain evenly to the entire surface, made by dissolving one ounce of Walnut crystals soluble in water in one quart of hot water. *Note:* The shade of the stain may be controlled by the addition of more water to the solution. Chapter 4 gives a detailed discussion of water stains.

6. Fill. After the stained surface has dried, fill the surface with a walnut-colored filler ready prepared. Vandyke Brown may be added to the filler, if the shade of the prepared filler is lighter than the stained surface. Chapter 5 should be read for details of filling procedure.

7. Seal. Apply a wash coat of shellac mixed ½ orange and ½ white. Allow this to dry at least two hours.

8. Sandpaper. Sand the sealed surface with No. 5/0 garnet paper and clean thoroughly.

9. Apply finish coat. Shellac, lacquer, or varnish may be applied. Apply evenly over the entire surface as indicated in Chapters 6, 7, and 8.

10. Sandpaper. Sandpaper with No. 5/0 garnet paper after the first coat has dried sufficiently. Clean and dust.

11. Apply finish coat. At least two more coats of the same material as the first coat should be applied. Each coat should be sanded smooth before the application of the next coat. The last coat should be permitted to dry at least twenty-four hours before rubbing.

12. Rub. Rub the surface with pumice stone and water or oil. Clean thoroughly of all pumice grime. Wash with benzene, if necessary, as discussed in Chapter 9.

13. Wax. If a luster is desired, apply wax and then polish. Rottenstone and oil or water rubbing may be resorted to if a satin-smooth gloss is desired. Refer to Chapter 14 for additional details.

14. Touch up bare spots or any other imperfections.

Queen Anne chairs, finished in Antique American Walnut. (Courtesy Smith & Watson)

Antique American walnut
For walnut, maple, gum, birch, and poplar

1. Prepare the surface. Make necessary minor surface repairs, and then sandpaper with No. 3/0 garnet paper.
2. Clean. Dust the sanded surfaces thoroughly.
3. Sponge. Wet the surface by sponging with clean water to raise the grain in preparation of the application of water stain. Dry at least two hours.
4. Sandpaper. Sandpaper the sponged surface with No. 3/0 garnet paper until the roughness of the surface has been removed.
5. Stain. Apply a light Walnut water stain over the entire surface. Dissolve a little less than one ounce of Walnut crystal soluble in water in one quart of hot water. Apply to surface evenly. Dry at least six hours.

6. Fill. Apply light Walnut paste filler to the surface as indicated in Chapter 5. The filler should match the stained surface in color. It should be a lighter filler than used in the American Walnut finish.

7. Seal. After the filled surface has dried thoroughly, seal with a wash coat of white shellac. Allow this to dry at least two hours.

8. Sandpaper. Sandpaper lightly with No. 5/0 garnet paper.

9. Antique. Apply Walnut antique stain made and applied as follows:

> 1 oz. Vandyke Brown oil color
> 6 oz. turpentine
> 1 oz. boiled linseed oil
> 1 scoop drier

Mix these together to obtain the antique stain. Apply to the surface and then wipe off and brush to obtain the desired antique effect as illustrated in Chapter 13. Allow this antique to dry at least twenty-four hours.

10. Seal. Apply a wash coat of orange shellac to seal the surface and prevent washing off of the antique with the finish coats. Allow two hours for drying.

11. Steel wool. Steel wool the sealed surface lightly with No. 2/0 steel wool. Do not remove too much of the sealer coat, as you may affect the antique stain below.

12. Apply finish coat. Apply coat of shellac, varnish, or lacquer evenly to the entire surface. Allow sufficient drying time.

13. Sandpaper. Sand the first coat with No. 5/0 sandpaper to remove all brush marks and nibs on the surface.

14. Apply finish coats. Apply at least two coats of the same finish material used in the first coat. Each coat should be sanded before the next coat. The last coat should dry at least twenty-four hours before rubbing.

15. Rub. Rub the surface with pumice and water or oil to the desired texture. Clean the surface of all pumice-stone grime. Wash with benzene if necessary.

16. Polish. Rub with rottenstone and oil to obtain satin effect.

17. Wax. If desired apply wax and polish to high gloss.

Weathered oak

For oak and chestnut

1. Prepare the surface. Make necessary repairs and sandpaper the surface smooth with No. 2/0 garnet paper.

2. Clean. Dust the sanded area thoroughly.

3. Sponge. Wet the surface by sponging with clean water to raise the grain in preparation of the application of water stain. Allow to dry at least two hours.

4. Sandpaper. Sandpaper the sponged surface with No. 3/0 garnet paper until smooth.

5. Stain. Apply Weathered Oak water stain over the entire surface. Dissolve one ounce of Weathered Oak aniline soluble in water in one quart of water. Apply this to surface.

6. No filler is required, as this finish is open grained.

7. Seal. Apply a wash coat of orange shellac to the surface. Allow to dry at least six hours.

8. Sandpaper. Sandpaper the sealer lightly to remove fuzz.

9. Apply finish coat. Apply at least three coats of orange shellac. Sandpaper carefully in between each coat after sufficient drying time. *Note:* Two coats of glossy clear varnish may be applied, followed by a coat of flat varnish. No rubbing is then necessary.

10. Rub. Rub dull with pumice stone and oil.

Golden oak

For oak, chestnut, maple, poplar, and gum

1. Prepare the surface. Make necessary surface repairs and sandpaper the surface smooth with No. 2/0 garnet paper.

2. Clean. Dust the sanded area thoroughly.

3. Sponge. Wet the surface by sponging with clean water to raise the grain in preparation of the application of water stain. Allow at least two hours for drying.

4. Sandpaper. Sandpaper the sponged surface with No. 3/0 garnet paper until smooth.

5. Stain. Apply water stain over the entire surface. Dissolve about one ounce of Golden Oak water-soluble aniline in one quart of hot water. Apply this stain to the surface. Repeat the application if surface is stained too light. Allow overnight drying.

6. Fill. Apply paste filler, colored to match the stained surface, and clean the surface thoroughly as explained in Chapter 5. Dry at least twenty-four hours.

7. Seal. Apply a wash coat of shellac mixed one half white and one half orange. Allow two hours for drying.

8. Sandpaper. Sandpaper the sealed surface with No. 5/0 garnet paper. Clean and dust thoroughly.

9. Apply finish coat. Apply coat of clear gloss varnish or lacquer. Allow this to dry at least twenty-four hours if varnish, at least three hours if lacquer.

10. Sandpaper. Sandpaper with No. 5/0 garnet paper to remove brush marks and nibs on surface.

11. Apply finish coats. Apply at least two coats of the material applied in the first coat. Sandpaper between coats. Allow overnight drying before rubbing.

182

12. Rub. Rub with pumice stone and water or oil for a satin-smooth finish. Clean surface by washing with benzene if oil was used as the lubricant. Refer to Chapter 9 for details.

13. Rub with rottenstone and water or oil to obtain gloss surface. Clean surface free of all grime.

14. Wax. Apply paste wax; allow it to set for a few minutes, and rub to a high luster.

Colonial maple
For maple, birch, poplar, gum, and beech

1. Prepare the surface. Make necessary minor repairs and then sandpaper surface with No. 2/0 garnet paper to smooth finish.

2. Clean. Dust the sanded surface thoroughly.

3. Sponge. Wet the surface by sponging with clean water to raise the grain in preparation of application of water stain. Allow several hours for drying.

4. Sandpaper. Sandpaper the sponged surface with No. 3/0 paper to remove roughness caused by sponging. Clean and dust smooth.

5. Stain. Make water stain by dissolving one ounce Reddish Maple water-soluble aniline in one quart of hot water, and apply to entire surface. *Note:* If stain is too red, add yellow aniline. Brown aniline may also be added if an orange-brown stain is desired. A little experimenting will help in getting the desired shade of stain.

6. Seal. Apply a wash coat of orange shellac to the stained surface after it has dried sufficiently. Allow this to dry about two hours.

7. Sandpaper. Sand the sealed surface lightly with 5/0 garnet paper. Clean thoroughly.

8. Apply antique. Antique stain is made as follows:

> 1 oz. Burnt Sienna in oil
> ½ oz. Burnt Umber in oil
> 6 oz. turpentine
> 1 oz. boiled linseed oil
> 1 scoop drier

Mix these together to obtain the antiquing stain. Apply to the surface, then wipe off and brush with dry brush to obtain the desired antique effect. Refer to Chapter 13 for detailed description of antiquing. Allow this antique to dry at least twenty-four hours.

9. Seal. Apply a wash coat of orange shellac. Allow this to dry two hours.

10. Apply finish coat. Apply shellac, lacquer, or varnish. Allow to dry sufficiently.

11. Apply finish coat. Apply at least two more coats of material used in first coat. Sandpaper with No. 5/0 garnet paper between coats. Allow at least twenty-four hours' drying time before rubbing.

12. Rub. Rub with 2/0 steel wool to a smooth semi-gloss finish.

13. Wax. Wax surface with colored wax to match the finish. Polish to obtain desired luster.

Golden maple

For maple, gum, poplar, and birch

Proceed as in Colonial Maple finish with the following exceptions:

5. Stain. Apply water stain to the entire surface. Dissolve one ounce of Yellow Maple water-soluble aniline powder in one quart of hot water. Apply this stain to surface.

6. Seal. The surface is sealed with a wash coat of white shellac. Allow at least two hours for drying.

7. Sandpaper. Sand the sealed surface with No. 5/0 garnet paper.

8. Apply finish coat. Apply finish coat of white shellac, lacquer, or varnish. Allow sufficient drying time.

9. Apply finish coats. Apply at least two more coats of the same material used in first coat. Sandpaper between coats with No. 5/0 sandpaper. Allow at least twenty-four hours before rubbing.

10. Rub. Rub with pumice stone and water or oil to desired smoothness and luster. Clean surface of all pumice grime.

11. Wax. Apply light-colored paste wax. Allow to set and then rub to the desired luster.

PENETRATING OIL STAINS

All the water-stain finishes listed above may be achieved by using penetrating oil stains as explained in Chapter 4. These stains may be secured already mixed from your local paint dealer. The basic finishing procedure for these stains is given, and all that is required is to substitute oil stain for the water stain.

1. Prepare the surface. Make the necessary minor surface repairs and sandpaper with No. 2/0 garnet paper.

2. Clean. Dust and clean the surface thoroughly.

3. Stain. Apply the desired penetrating oil stain.

4. Seal. Apply a wash coat of shellac, the color depending upon the shade of the stained surface. Refer to Chapter 6.

5. Sandpaper. Sand the sealed surface carefully with No. 5/0 garnet paper. Dust clean.

6. Fill. If surface finished is open-grain wood, apply a paste filler, the color of which is to be slightly darker than the shade of the stained surface, as explained in Chapter 5. Filling may be eliminated when a close-grain wood is being finished, and liquid filler may be used in place of the paste filler. Refer to Chapter 5 for detailed discussion.

7. Seal. Apply a wash coat of shellac. Sandpaper after the surface has dried at least two hours. Dust clean.

8. Apply finish coat. Shellac, lacquer, or varnish may be applied as the first coat. Allow sufficient drying time.

9. Sandpaper. Sandpaper with No. 5/0 garnet paper to remove brush marks and surface nibs. Clean thoroughly.

10. Apply finish coat. Apply at least two more coats of the material used in the first coat. Allow sufficient drying time and sandpaper between coats. Allow at least twenty-four hours of drying before rubbing.

11. Rub. Rub with No. 2/0 steel wool, or with pumice stone and oil or water. Clean surface of all pumice grime.

12. Rub. Rub with rottenstone if desired to produce a higher gloss.

13. Wax. Wax surface and polish to desired luster.

PIGMENT OIL STAINS

In Chapter 4 much space was given to the making of pigment oil stains. It would do well for you to refer to that section. These stains may be used effectively in staining a surface. The formulas given there are practical for all types of woods and may be used in place of any of the other stains which have already been discussed.

The basic finishing procedure is similar to the procedure described for finishing with penetrating oil stains, with one exception: the pigment oil stains should be wiped clean after they are applied. Merely substitute the pigment oil stains of the desired shade for the penetrating oil stains in step 3. All the other steps are the same.

LINSEED OIL FINISH

Boiled linseed oil has been used for centuries as a finishing material. The early American colonists used it effectively in finishing all their homemade furniture. Many coats of heated linseed oil were used to produce a beautiful golden natural finish. The finish was not only durable, but it was also waterproof and heatproof. It lasted for many many years and new life was added to it by rubbing more oil into the surface from time to time. This finish may be duplicated today. Proceed as follows:

1. Check all surfaces and make necessary repairs.
2. Sandpaper with 3/0 garnet paper and dust off thoroughly.
3. Prepare oil mixture as follows: to one pint of linseed oil add one ounce of Burnt Sienna oil color and two tablespoons of japan drier. Heat the mixture in a double cooker. *Do not heat mixture over an open flame.*
4. Apply the heated mixture to the surface and permit it to soak into the wood for a few hours. Then wipe off the excess.
5. Allow overnight drying.
6. Repeat coating the surface with a second coat, and allow overnight drying.
7. Repeat if additional body is desired, and allow overnight drying.
8. Apply paste-wax polish and buff to smooth satin gloss.

SOME CLASSIC OIL FINISHES

Distressed French Provincial, Italian Provincial, Spanish, and Mediterranean

For pecan, maple, beech, and cherry

1. Sandpaper. The surface is sanded carefully with 3/0 garnet paper to remove all imperfections and smooth the surface.
2. Clean and dust all surfaces.
3. Apply a wash coat of white shellac.
4. Sandpaper with 5/0 garnet and dust.
5. Prepare a pigment oil stain using Van Dyke Brown as the base. See Chapter 4.
6. Apply pigment oil stain to sections of the job and wipe off excess with clean rag. Some of the stain should be left in crevices and moldings.
7. Use a wide clean brush to feather remaining stain on surface. See the discussion of antiquing in Chapter 13.
8. Allow overnight drying.
9. Apply distressed finish, as described in Chapter 13.
10. Spray on two coats of clear gloss lacquer. Sand with 3/0 garnet between coats.
11. Rub with 2/0 steel wool and wax.

186

Scandinavian oil finish using lacquer

For teak and walnut

1. Check all surfaces and make necessary repairs.
2. Sand with 3/0 garnet paper and dust thoroughly.
3. Spray on a coat of clear wood lacquer sealer.
4. Allow to dry and sand with 5/0 garnet paper. Dust carefully.
5. Apply coat of clear flat wood lacquer.
6. Allow to dry and sand with 5/0 garnet paper.
7. Apply second coat of clear flat wood lacquer.
8. Rubbing is not necessary if sprayed surface is smooth. If it is not, rub with steel wool and paraffin oil. Clean thoroughly.
9. Apply dull polish cream wax and buff.

Scandinavian oil finish

For teak, walnut, and rosewood

1. Check all surfaces and make necessary repairs.
2. Sand with 3/0 garnet paper and dust thoroughly.
3. Prepare oil-base finishing material as follows: Mix equal parts of boiled linseed oil and four-hour-drying synthetic varnish. Place in double cooker and heat.
4. Apply heated mixture to surface with a wide flat brush.
5. Allow solution to be absorbed by surface and then wipe off the excess. Rub in the direction of the grain. Change cloth as frequently as required.
6. Allow overnight drying.
7. Apply a second coat in the manner described above and allow overnight drying.
8. Apply cream liquid wax and buff slightly for additional protection. This step assures a smooth mar-proof surface.

Italian Provincial—Mediterranean finish

1. Sandpaper the surface carefully with 3/0 garnet paper.
2. Clean and dust surface. Check for bruises, blemishes, etc.
3. Prepare a pigment oil stain as follows: Mix 8 ounces white lead, 1 pint of turpentine, 6 ounces linseed oil (boiled), 1 ounce japan drier.
4. Apply this stain to a section at a time and carefully wipe off excess with rag.
5. Proceed with this operation until entire job has been stained.
6. Allow overnight drying.
7. Apply a wash coat of white shellac and sand lightly with 5/0 garnet after four hours.

8. Apply Vandyke Brown antiquing stain. See Chapter 3. Stain should be applied to a small section at a time. Wipe off excess and feather with dry brush.
9. Allow overnight drying and apply wash coat of white shellac.
10. Apply distressed finish. Refer to Chapter 13.
11. Apply wash coat of white shellac. Sand lightly when dry. If wood lacquer is used, this step may be eliminated, and instead spray one coat of clear wood lacquer sealer and finish off by spraying one or two coats of clear gloss lacquer.
12. Apply two coats of four-hour-drying varnish. Sand between coats with 5/0 garnet. *Note:* Step 11 may be substituted for the varnish.
13. Allow overnight drying and rub to suit with steel wool, then pumice and oil.

French Provincial finish
For maple, beech, and pecan
1. Check all surfaces and make necessary repairs.
2. Sand with 3/0 garnet paper and dust thoroughly.
3. Prepare base stain as follows: Dissolve 6 ounces of white lead and 1 ounce of Chrome Yellow medium oil colors in 1 pint of turpentine. Add 4 ounces of linseed oil and 1 ounce of japan drier to mixture.
4. Brush this base stain on surface and wipe off excess. Use dry brush in corners.
5. Allow overnight drying.
6. Spray or brush on a coat of thinned white shellac.
7. Sandpaper lightly with 5/0 garnet and dust.
8. Prepare pigment oil stain as follows: Dissolve 4 ounces of Raw Sienna and 2 ounces of Burnt Umber oil color in 1 pint of turpentine. Add 4 ounces of boiled linseed oil and 1 ounce of japan drier to mixture.
9. Apply this stain to a small section at a time with a brush.
10. Wipe off excess with a dry cloth and feather remaining surface stain with a flat dry brush.
11. Continue until entire job has been stained.
12. Allow overnight drying and apply a wash coat of white shellac.
13. Spray or brush on two coats of four-hour-drying synthetic varnish. Two coats of lacquer may be sprayed on instead of the varnish.
14. Sand between coats. Rub the final coat with steel wool and paraffin oil.
15. Clean and apply a cream wax polish.

PART FOUR: PAINTING, DECORATING, AND ANTIQUING

CHAPTER 12

Painting Finished and Unfinished Surfaces

Paints and enamels are used today for many effects. The homes we live in, the kitchen equipment, and some of the furniture are covered with paint in one form or another.

The term "painting" means that an opaque liquid material is applied to the surface. This opaque material, unlike transparent materials, hides the grain and the other characteristics of the wood, leaving a uniform colored surface.

It goes without saying that painting is a very useful process in the finishing of wood and other products. The reasons should be obvious to all. Paint hides inferior wood. Paint comes in any color, and many wood products can be made much more attractive and appealing with paint than with other finishes—and this includes certain antique pieces, such as early French styles. Painting also facilitates cleaning of the article painted. Any painted surface may be washed clean with soap and water without in any way harming the painted film. It is for this reason that many articles of furniture are painted, especially those used in the kitchen and children's rooms.

TYPES OF PAINT AND ENAMEL

At this point, a distinction should be made between paint and enamel. Although they are both used for the same purpose, the composition of paint is slightly different from that of enamel. These differences are pointed out to enable you to choose the more appropriate material for your job.

Paint is composed of the following ingredients: pigment oil color, oil, drier, and thinner. The pigment, usually ground in linseed oil, gives the paint its color and body. The oil, usually linseed oil or oil varnish, gives the paint the vehicle in which the color is dispersed. The drier is added to hasten the oxidation of the paint and hence shorten the drying time. Finally, the thinner, usually turpentine, is added to reduce the paint so that it can be brushed easily on the surface.

The variety of colors in which paint is available is too great to mention here. Any paint store will supply you with color cards of paints held in stock. Where the desired shade is not available in the ready-mixed paints, instructions from your dealer will help you in blending colors to obtain the shade that you request.

Paints may be obtained that will dry with a flat finish. These are called flat paints. They may also be obtained to dry with a decided gloss finish. These are designated as glossy paints. Wherever possible, the gloss paints should be used in preference to the flat paints. The glossy paints may be rubbed down with steel wool if a flat finish is desired.

Enamels

Enamels are actually colored varnishes. In some the color pigment is ground in varnish rather than oil. Drier is added and finally a thinner. These will make brushing easier and drying faster. In the more modern types such pigment solids as titanium calcium or titanium oxide are added to alkyd resins, linseed oil, and drier. These enamels require special tinting colors for tinting and special solvents as thinners. Oil-ground colors or turpentine may not be used. Both types of enamels produce a smooth, glossy, hard, durable surface devoid of brush marks. They can also be rubbed like any clear-gloss varnish to produce a beautiful satin-smooth surface. They are available in a large variety of colors. Your local paint dealer will show you hundreds of different colors from which to choose. However, when the desired shade cannot be obtained, colors ground in japan may be added to the enamel to produce the shade required. Enamels may also be obtained to dry flat. The flat enamels, like flat varnishes, will dry with a dull appearance. The gloss enamels dry to a very high gloss, and rubbing is needed to tone down the luster.

If you will refer to Chapter 7, you will note that varnishes are divided into slow-drying oil varnishes and fast-drying synthetic-resin varnishes. Enamels are also divided into these two groups. Like the oil varnishes, the oil enamels take a long time to dry. At least twenty-four hours should elapse before another coat is applied. The precautions given for oil enamels apply as well to oil varnishes. Both have good covering and lasting qualities.

The synthetic four-hour-drying enamels have proved to be more popular with the wood finisher and the amateur finisher, because, as with the synthetic varnishes, application is easier and the drying much faster. These enamels dry dustproof in a matter of hours. Another coat may be applied within twelve hours. Your paint dealer stocks these enamels in preference to the others, because they are more in demand and also because they give excellent results whether they are used by the amateur or the wood finisher. A large assortment of colors is available, but, where the color desired is not obtainable, japan or alkyd colors may be added to the enamel to obtain the exact shade.

Lacquer enamels

Lacquer enamels, their characteristics and method of application, are discussed in Chapter 8, and if you will refer to it you will note that these enamels are equivalent in quality and results obtained to the oil and synthetic varnishes. Their lasting and covering qualities compare well with those of the enamels discussed in the foregoing paragraph. Of course, there is no comparison when drying qualities are concerned. Lacquer enamel will dry dustproof in a matter of minutes, and when subjected to forced-heat drying will dry hard enough for another coat in about fifteen minutes. There is only one drawback in the use of these, as far as the craftsman is concerned: they cannot be applied without a spraying system. Brushing lacquer enamels are available, but the results do not compare with the spraying lacquers.

Undercoats

As the name implies, these materials are used for the coat under the paint or enamel. They differ somewhat, both in composition and application, from the paints and enamels already discussed. They are compounded so that when they are applied to the raw wood, they will seal the surface and form a hard film for the succeeding coats. They will also sand easily when they have dried hard, and this smooth surface provides an excellent bond for the coats of paint or enamel to be applied later.

Some finishers like to use flat paint instead of these prepared undercoats. Others prefer to use pure white lead thinned with turpentine as the undercoat. Still others prefer to use shellac. In any event, although these materials have some merit as undercoats, it is better to apply the prepared undercoats before the enamels or paints are applied. The manufacturers of paints recommend that prepared undercoats be used for their paints or enamels.

Lacquer undercoats should be used when lacquer enamels are used as the finishing materials. These undercoats are made of the same ingredients as the lacquers, so that the succeeding coats of colored lacquers will adhere properly. Oil-paint undercoats should be used when oil paints are to be used as the finishing coats—never with lacquers.

Water-soluble latex paints can also be used for undercoats. As is well known, these water paints have excellent covering qualities in addition to being opaque and fast-drying. They adhere well to finished and unfinished woods. They are applied over a raw wood surface in the same manner as the conventional undercoats. After they have dried sufficiently, they are sanded smooth. Enamels may be applied directly over this coat. A discussion of latex paints will be found later in this chapter.

APPLYING AN ENAMEL FINISH

1. Prepare the bare wood surface by sanding it thoroughly with fine finishing sandpaper to remove all surface scratches, small dents, and other minor faults.

2. If the wood contains knots or sap streaks, apply a wash coat of shellac over them to prevent later discoloration of the surface. Either white or orange shellac may be used for this purpose.

3. Allow the shellac to dry and then sand lightly to remove the wood fuzz.

4. Apply a coat of undercoat that has been tinted to match the final color of the painted surface. The undercoat should be applied with a wide, clean, bristle, flat brush, evenly, to the entire surface. Cross-brushing may be done to build up the body of the undercoat, but the final result should be a smooth and even coat. Allow this to dry at least twelve hours before the surface is prepared for the next operation.

5. If necessary cover with putty any nail hole, dent, or other imperfection not covered with the first operation. Allow this putty to dry hard before sanding the entire surface smooth with 3/0 garnet paper. Make sure that the under-coated surface is thoroughly sanded and cleaned before continuing with the next step.

6. A second coat of undercoat may be applied now. This coat should be prepared by mixing one half the undercoat and one half the enamel to be used in the final coat. It is applied as was the undercoat in step 4. Allow this surface to dry thoroughly and sandpaper with No. 2/0 garnet paper. Dust and clean carefully.

7. The coat of white or colored enamel is now applied. Here the same precautions should be followed as in applying clear varnish. The brush should be clean and so should the surface. Apply the enamel as you did the clear varnish. Brush it on freely and evenly to the entire surface. Work the enamel across grain to pick up all excess material on the surface. Dry your brush and go over the freshly enameled surface with it in straight, even, light strokes. Pick up any runs or sags which may have appeared on the surface by working over them with a dry brush.

8. At least twelve hours should be allowed for drying before the next step is attempted.

9. The surface should now be sandpapered with "wet or dry" finishing paper or with garnet paper soaked in benzene. This will assure a fine, smooth surface, free from any brush marks and dust specks. Careful sanding is very important at this stage. The surface should be cleaned thoroughly with a tack rag or with a rag moistened in benzene, after it has been sanded.

10. A second coat of enamel is now applied as was explained in step 7. This coat should dry for at least twenty-four hours before the rubbing procedure is begun.

11. The surface is now rubbed with pumice stone and water. Follow the instructions for rubbing in Chapter 9. One additional point should be made clear in rubbing an enameled surface. Inasmuch as no grain is visible on the colored surface, there is no grain to indicate the direction of the rubbing action. In this case, the rubbing should also be done in one direction. Rub in the direction of the longer edge. To illustrate, if you are rubbing the top of a colored bookcase, the direction of the rubbing should follow the length of the bookcase and not its width. This direction should be followed on the other sections of the article being rubbed. Changing the direction will produce conspicuous marks.

Note: The steps enumerated above will assure an excellent enameled surface, full of body, with no open-grain showing. These steps may be shortened somewhat if a quicker job is required. To illustrate, step 10 and step 11 can be eliminated. If a better surface is desired, step 10 may be repeated so that another coat of enamel is applied to the surface. Step 11 is then followed.

The same procedure is followed when lacquer enamels are applied. The lacquer undercoats and enamels are substituted for the oil enamels.

Enameling open-grain wood

At times you may be confronted with the problem of whether to use open-grain wood, like oak or chestnut, for a particular piece to be finished in colored enamel. The large, open pores of these woods do not provide a good surface for the finish desired. The uniform mirrorlike finish essential to an enameled surface is not easily obtained. Therefore, wherever possible, open-grain woods should not be used. Too much work is involved in preparing the surface and filling the pores before the enamel is applied.

Where open-grain wood has been used and it is to be painted or enameled, the surface should be prepared in the following manner. After the surface has been sanded smooth and dusted clean, a natural paste filler is applied to the entire surface. The filler is permitted to set for a few minutes and then the excess is cleaned off with excelsior or a coarse wiping rag. All traces of filler still remaining on the surface are cleaned off with a soft wiping rag. Refer to Chapter 5 if additional information is required regarding the filling operation.

The filler fills the many fine open pores in the wood and helps to produce a flat, smooth surface. If the open grain were permitted to remain, the paint would enter into the open pores and the finished surface would show the design of the open grain, even though the surface was uniform in color.

PAINTING OR ENAMELING A FINISHED SURFACE

It is quite simple to paint or enamel over a surface which has already been painted or has been finished in a natural finish. The important point is to know the kind of surface which is to be repainted. If the surface has been painted in oil paint or finished in shellac or varnish, there is no problem. Select the appropriate shade of paint or enamel for the job and then proceed as follows:

1. Sandpaper the surface with No. 2/0 garnet finish paper in order to remove scratches, dirt, stains. Dust off the surface.
2. Wash the surface with a cloth dampened in benzene to remove all traces of grease, wax, and oil. This is very important, for uneven drying will result if the surface is not perfectly free of these materials.
3. Apply a coat of white undercoat so that every section of the piece has been adequately covered with it.
4. Allow sufficient drying time and then sandpaper with 3/0 garnet paper.
5. Apply a coat of the colored paint or enamel desired. See step 7 under "Applying an enamel finish."
6. Repeat step 5 if desired, but sandpaper the surface before applying this second coat.
7. Rub with pumice and water if desired.

Note: Where the surface to be repainted has been previously finished in lacquer or lacquer enamel, the same procedure is followed, but lacquer enamels and undercoats should be used instead of the oil or synthetic paints or enamels.

PAINTING OR ENAMELING A REFINISHED SURFACE

This type of surface presents a situation slightly different from the one mentioned above. Here the surface to be repainted is so badly marred and damaged that the old finish must be removed in order to obtain a smooth enameled surface. Thus the surface must be cleaned of all of the old finish. You may proceed as follows:

1. Remove the old, damaged finish with paint and varnish remover. You will find detailed instructions for this operation in Chapter 3.
2. After the finish has been removed to the bare wood, make all necessary repairs, like filling in dents, removing scratches and other faults Sandpaper the surface with No. 2/0 garnet paper.
3. Now proceed with steps 2 to 12 detailed in the section on "Applying an enamel finish." *Note:* All the detailed precautions listed in Chapter 3 should be considered when removing the old finish and preparing it for the paint or enamel.

WATER LATEX PAINTS

Recent developments in paint manufacturing have resulted in the introduction of a new class of paints which are water-soluble. These are called latex paints. Their composition includes titanium dioxide, silicates, soya alkyd resins, emulsions, and water. They are now produced in flat, semi-gloss, and gloss finishes, both for interior and exterior work.

Although they have been used extensively for interior wall painting, they may be used for painting unfinished furniture. They can be obtained in a myriad of colors, and if a particular color is not available, special blending with tinting colors is possible. These paints may be applied with a roller or a nylon brush.

Advantages of latex paints
1. They have excellent covering qualities. Usually one coat will suffice.
2. They dry touch-proof in half an hour.

3. A second coat may be applied after overnight drying. Sanding between coats is recommended.

4. Brushes and rollers can be cleaned by washing in water.

Disadvantages of latex paints

1. Gloss paints are not available in all colors.

2. Antique stains may be applied over these paints only after the surface has been given a wash coat of clear white shellac.

Applying latex paints

1. Surface should be cleaned of all dirt and grease. Glossy surfaces should be sanded dull before paint is applied.

2. Brush on coat by flowing the paint directly to the raw wood surface. No undercoat is necessary.

3. Allow overnight drying; sand with 5/0 finishing paper.

4. Apply second coat of latex as before.

5. If glazing or antiquing is required, apply a wash coat of white shellac.

6. Apply antique finish as explained later in the next chapter.

CHAPTER 13

Antiquing and Other Special Decorative Effects

In addition to using colored paints and enamels for obtaining decorative effects on your furniture, you may obtain still other interesting effects on these painted surfaces by supplementing them with any one or more of the methods discussed in this chapter.

Antiquing, or glazing, makes a newly painted object appear old and mellow. It emphasizes carvings, moldings, and other irregular surfaces by bringing out the elevated portion of the object and darkening the crevices and corners. It helps to soften and tone down highly decorated surfaces and make them more subdued and mellow. And finally, antiquing helps to hide some of the imperfections which may be present on the painted surfaces.

This form of decoration is especially effective on surfaces which have been painted in the light shades. White, buff, green, and red surfaces antique exceptionally well because the stains used in antiquing bring out a contrast which adds to the richness of the surface. Exceptionally appropriate, too, is the antiquing of objects painted with various shades of gold bronze and silver. Picture frames, for example, finished in gold and then antiqued with Raw Umber stain gain an appearance of age and mellowness.

Antiquing is a handy device when you want a surface to show the appearance of age and wear and to have high lights. This process is used in many of the modern finishes found today. Such furniture styles as French and Italian Provincial, Mediterranean, and Spanish use this type of finish quite extensively.

Antiquing has become so popular that many manufacturers are producing antique kits for the buying public. You may try them. The results, although not professional, may prove satisfactory. The professional finisher prefers to make his own antique and glazing mixtures. These are more effective and less expensive than those prepared by the manufacturers.

ANTIQUING

The materials required for antiquing are an antiquing stain, a brush, another dry brush for cleaning the surface, and a wiping cloth. The stain is not unlike the pigment oil stain described in Chapter 4. It may be made by mixing the appropriate oil color with a little linseed oil, then thinning slightly with turpentine, and adding a few drops of drier. The texture of this mixture should be not too watery but more like the consistency of light cream. The deepness or lightness of the shade may be controlled by the addition or elimination of oil color while the mixture is being made. Just enough of the stain should be made for the job on hand. At times, this may be not more than an ounce.

The shade of oil color to use is very important, for the effectiveness of the antiquing depends upon the proper contrasting stain. When mixing these antique stains, note the following:
1. Use Raw Umber oil color in making the stain where the surface to be antiqued is painted or enameled in white, buff, or other light shade.
2. If desired, Raw Sienna (a yellow-brown) may be used in place of the Raw Umber.
3. Lampblack oil color should be used in making antiquing stain where the surface to be antiqued is painted or enameled in red, green, or blue. The Raw Umber stain, if used, would tend to discolor this background. The black antique or glaze merely tones down these colors.
4. Burnt Umber or Raw Umber oil color is used in making the stain if the surface to be antiqued is painted in gold.
5. Lampblack oil color is used in making the antique if the surface to be antiqued is finished in aluminum or silver.

The brush used in applying the glaze should be large enough for the surface being antiqued. Naturally, the larger the surface, the larger the brush to use. A round 1½" bristle brush is suggested for most antiquing jobs.

The dry brush is not to be confused with the brush used for applying the stain. This brush has a specific duty in the antiquing process—the removal of excess glaze in the depressions of the job. A 2" or 3" flat, double-chisel brush is suggested because of its picking and holding properties. The brush should be absolutely clean and free of all traces of old paint, oil, or stain. An unclean brush will damage the glazed surface.

For a wiping cloth, a piece of cheesecloth, clean and free from oil and grease, is suggested. It is to be used for wiping off the excess glaze and for high-lighting.

Antiquing a flat enameled surface

Before this operation can be performed, you must make certain that the surface enameled is absolutely dry. At least twenty-four hours should elapse from the time the last coat was applied to the antiquing operation. If the surface is not dry enough, the antiquing stain will soften the surface and damage the enamel beyond repair.

The object to be antiqued should be placed in such a position that it can be worked on from all sides. If you are working on a large object, select one section of it at a time for antiquing. Do not attempt to antique the entire job all at once. For example, if you are antiquing a small table, you should stain each leg separately, and finally the top. When these preparations have been made, begin antiquing as indicated below.

1. Apply the glaze already prepared to a section of the surface as indicated. The glaze should be applied evenly, but not excessively, with a brush. Work the stain into corners and moldings.

2. With a clean, soft rag, wipe off as much of the glaze as desired immediately after it has been applied with the brush. Wipe the glaze off evenly and uniformly. Usually the more wiped off, the better and cleaner the surface. Too much antique gives the surface a muddy appearance.

3. Remove more of the glaze from the center of the section than from the edges. It is better to wipe the center clean of all stain and leave just a light film around the edges.

4. Now use your clean brush to spread the antique at the outer edges in order to remove the jagged edges of stain left by the wiping cloth. This brushing is done very lightly and should be from the clean center toward the darker edges. If this method does not give a feathered effect (the gradual change from light to dark), clean your brush by wiping it over a piece of clean cloth and stipple the dark edges near the center. This stippling (dabbing the brush

Antiquing glaze is brushed onto an enameled surface. Immediately most of it is wiped off, leaving more at the edges of sections than in the middle. Then a clean brush is used to remove streaks left by the wiping cloth and to make the transitions from light to dark as gradual as possible.

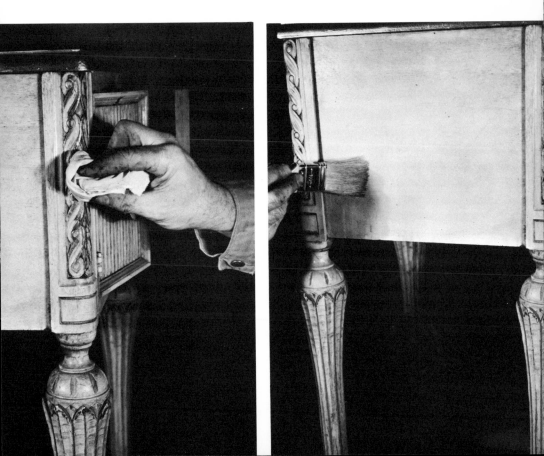

on the surface) picks up traces of the stain and leaves a lighter area than could be obtained by spreading the stain with the brush.

5. Continue doing this, cleaning the brush and stippling, until the center blends gradually with the outer edges. There should be no abrupt change from a light center to dark corners.

6. If your first attempt does not give the results anticipated, wipe off the remaining antique with a clean rag and restain as step 1. Proceed as before, but this time try to avoid the mistakes made in the first attempt.

7. After the job has been antiqued to the desired effect, it should be allowed to dry overnight.

8. A coat of white shellac is next applied and permitted to dry.

9. The surface may now be rubbed with No. 2/0 steel wool, then cleaned and wax-polished.

Antiquing a transparent finish

This operation is performed on all types of transparent finishes where mellowness, age, and high-lighting are required. The furniture to be glazed is first given a light stain and then sealed with a wash coat of shellac. The antique glaze is applied over this preparation.

1. Prepare the glaze (antiquing stain) appropriate to the finish desired.

2. Sand the sealed surface very lightly.

3. Apply the glaze, a section at a time—legs, sides, drawer fronts, and so on.

4. With a clean rag, wipe off as much of the glaze as desired.

5. Remove more of the glaze on parts which normally have greater wear, such as centers, panels and tops, knees of legs, and outer curves of turnings.

6. Use a clean dry brush to spread the glaze in order to remove the conspicuous edges produced by the cloth.

7. Work the dry brush from the light center to the darker edges. This should give a feathered effect—a gradual change from light to dark.

8. Dry the brush from time to time by rubbing it on a dry cloth, and continue to feather.

9. Continue this operation on the other parts of the job. The top should be the last surface to antique.

10. Allow surfaces to dry overnight.

11. Apply a coat of shellac or a sealer.

12. Proceed to apply transparent finishes as directed.

202

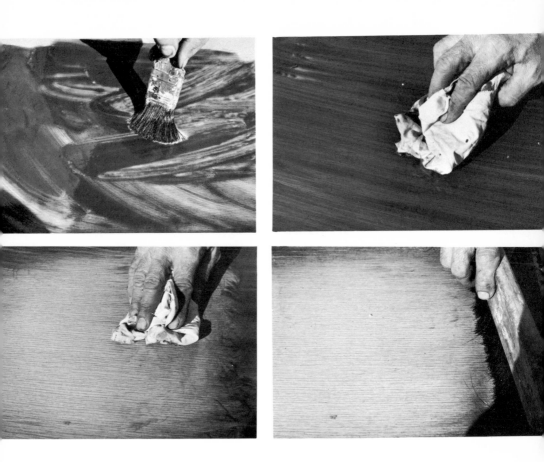

When antiquing over a transparent finish, the surface is first sealed with shellac. Then the glaze is applied with a brush, spread evenly with a rag, and wiped off with a clean rag. More glaze is left at the edges and in the crevices, which normally would be protected from wear, than on the centers of flat areas and on protrusions, which normally would show considerable wear. A wide feathering brush removes streaks and sharp transitions.

203

Antiquing a carved surface

The surface must be absolutely dry before the antique is applied.

1. The stain is applied as above.

2. With a clean, soft rag, wipe off the excess stain wherever possible.

3. With a clean brush, pick up the excess stain remaining in the depressions and crevices of the carvings. The brush should be kept clean by wiping it on a clean cloth as more stain is removed from these corners.

4. The remaining stain is now spread evenly on the surface with the dry brush.

5. Shape a piece of wiping cloth into a wad or ball and wipe off the antique from the elevated areas. The wiping cloth may be dampened in turpentine from time to time to facilitate the removal of the stain from the high spots. The depressed areas should not be cleaned of the glaze. The result of following these steps should be a contrast in colors—dark corners, crevices, and depressions of the carving, and light elevated sections and high spots.

6. If an additional mellow effect is desired, powdered rottenstone may be dusted into the carvings while the antique is still damp. Wipe off the excess powder.

Hints for better antiquing

1. It is wise to antique a small piece of scrap to get the feel before attempting a large job.

2. When a large area is to be antiqued at one time, adding a little more linseed oil to the mixture will slow the drying time and make the glazing easier.

3. Too much oil, however, slows the drying to such an extent that the surface will remain moist for a long time, thus delaying the application of the protective coat.

4. When the glazed surface has dried thoroughly, a coat of clear varnish may be applied. This varnish will serve as a protective coat over the glaze. The varnish film may be rubbed with steel wool when it has dried hard.

5. A cloth dampened in turpentine will help in removing the excess glaze from the surface. Use a clean, dry cloth when the first wiping is done.

6. Apply the glaze thin. Too heavy a glaze will provide too sharp a contrast between light and dark.

7. Always feather the glaze from the light clean center to the darker edges. The change from the light center to the dark corners should not be abrupt, but gradual.

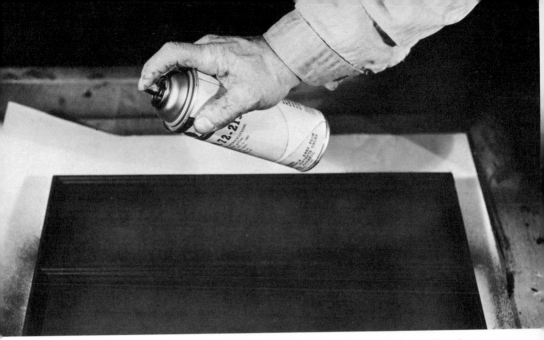

Lacquer shading stains are available in aerosol cans, but they cannot be worked or feathered after they are applied, so they are not suitable for carved surfaces.

Antiquing with lacquer shading stains

Lacquer shading stains may be substituted for the antiquing materials already discussed. These shading stains are lacquer-base transparent or opaque stains in aerosol spray cans. They are available in a large variety of shading colors similar to the glaze colors used in antiquing. Since they are very fast-drying they cannot be worked or feathered after they are applied. Consequently they can be used on flat surfaces only. They cannot be used on carved pieces, moldings, or other surfaces with indentations and designs.

1. The surface to be shaded should be prepared as in the above instructions for "Antiquing a transparent finish."
2. Select the appropriate shade of stain.
3. Before using the spray can on the job, make a few practice tries on a piece of scrap wood.
4. Hold nozzle about 8 inches from outer surface around the perimeter.
5. Hold spray nozzle about 10 inches from surface and spray toward the center from the perimeter. This movement will give you the feathered appearance obtained in the hand glazing.
6. Protective coats may be applied directly over this stain. No waiting time is required, since these stains are very fast-drying.

Antique gold and silver

This type of finish is ideal for picture frames and carved pieces. It accentuates the carving designs and gives the surface a general appearance of richness and beauty. If the frame or other article is in the raw wood, it should be prepared as follows:

1. Sandpaper with No. 2/0 garnet paper and clean thoroughly.
2. Brush a wash coat of shellac on the entire surface. Allow it to dry, then sand and clean.
3. Apply undercoat to the entire surface, evenly and carefully. Allow it to dry, then sand smooth and clean.
4. Apply another coat of undercoat, but this should be tinted slightly red before it is applied. Allow this to dry sufficiently and then sandpaper and clean.
5. Apply gold bronze to the entire surface. *Note:* Gold bronze may be purchased ready-mixed or it may be prepared by you as follows. Purchase an ounce of gold bronze powder from your local paint dealer. The finer the powder the better the surface will be covered. Also obtain from your local dealer about half a pint of bronzing liquid. Now mix part of the gold powder with the bronzing liquid to form a gold paint. This resultant paint should be heavy enough to cover the area in one application. You can judge the covering qualities of your mixture by testing it on a piece of scrap. If the surface covered seems watery, add more bronze powder. Stir the mixture from time to time to prevent the heavy metal from settling. This mixture is applied evenly on the surface with a small, soft brush. If necessary, you may go over the area several times to obtain a uniform coat.
6. Allow this gold bronze mixture to dry on the surface overnight.
7. Brush on a wash coat of orange shellac and allow it to dry about two hours.
8. Apply Burnt Umber glaze as explained earlier in this chapter under the heading "Antiquing a carved surface."
9. Dust rottenstone powder on the freshly antiqued frame if a more mellow effect is desired. Wipe off the excess powder.

When antiquing a carved surface, two of the steps are reversed. Excess stain is picked up with a dry brush and the remainder is spread evenly on the surface. Then a rag is used to remove the stain from the high spots.

Gold bronze is available in aerosol cans. Several light coats will give better results than one heavy one.

Aerosol bronzes

There are many shades of bronzes available in aerosol cans for bronzing picture frames and other articles. They range in color from pale gold to reddish copper. For most bronzing jobs a pale yellow-gold is recommended.

After the usual preparatory steps, the aerosol can may be used for applying the bronze, but observe the following:

1. Before using an aerosol spray can make certain that there is ample ventilation and ample room to move about.

2. Shake the can well before using.

3. Experiment by directing spray on a piece of paper at various distances from 10 to 18 inches. Note how the distance from the paper affects the amount of liquid sprayed. Select a distance which will spray enough bronze without running or sagging.

4. Lay picture frame horizontally on a table covered with paper and away from other objects.

5. Begin spraying, using the distance from the can to frame already decided upon, in a slow even stroke from left to right. Spray the entire frame. It is better to spray a number of light coats than to spray one heavy coat. Parts of the frame may be sprayed if desired. Use masking tape to cover those parts which need no bronzing and then spray the entire frame. Remove masking tape and antique as discussed earlier.

6. Repeat the operation several times until an even coat has been applied.

7. Allow half an hour drying time. Remove masking tape.

8. Follow the steps discussed in antiquing a gold frame.

Applying gold leaf

This method of gilding is used by professional finishers to obtain an Old World gilt finish. It is used particularly on picture frames. There are two methods which can be used to produce this type of finish. One requires considerable preparation and experience. The other method is simpler, and is recommended.

To gild a frame the following supplies are needed: Several booklets of gold leaf or imitation-gold leaf (a book of gold leaf contains 20 sheets of finely hammered gold, 1/10,000 of an inch thick), a razor blade or gilder's knife, and a gilder's tip—a thin flat brush with very thin layers of hair 2¼″ long (to pick up the leaf and place it on the work), and a quick-drying japan gold size (the adhesive to hold the leaf in place).

The first step in applying gold leaf: an even coat of japan gold size is brushed on and allowed to dry to the tacky stage.

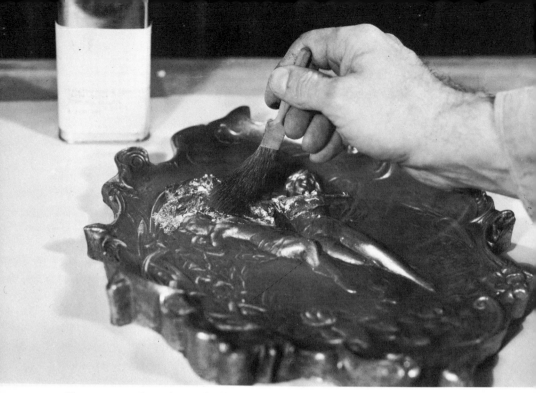

Then, one at a time, pieces of gold leaf are picked up with the gilder's tip and put in place.

The surface can then be antiqued like any carved surface.

1. Check the frame for bruises, dents, etc., make necessary repairs.
2. Sand thoroughly with 3/0 garnet paper, clean, and dust.
3. Apply several coats of 3-pound cut white shellac. Sand with 5/0 garnet paper before applying a second coat. Dust and clean.
4. Apply an even coat of japan gold size to the entire frame. Check to make certain that all spots have been covered.
5. Allow at least two hours' drying time. The frame should feel tacky to touch before the next step is taken.
6. Cut the gold leaf, one piece at a time, to fit the space to be covered.
7. Use the gilder's tip to pick up the leaf and put it in place. Press the leaf down with the tip of the brush.
8. In the same manner lay the other leaves alongside each other, until the entire piece has been covered.
9. Check piece for skips. Pick up small sheets of leaf and press them into the places skipped, using the gilder's brush to force the leaf into position.
10. Place a little gold bronze powder on a sheet of paper, and with a small wad of cotton pick up the powder and work it over the gilded frame.
11. Allow overnight drying. Apply a wash coat of orange shellac.
12. Antique to suit, as described earlier in this chapter.

OTHER EFFECTS

Mottled two-tone effect on painted surfaces

This is an interesting device for decorating painted or enameled novelties, toys, knickknack shelves, and picture frames. This type of finish requires the application of two different shades of color. One is for the background effect, and the other, which is applied over this, is for contrast. This effect is obtained in the following manner:
1. The object is prepared in the usual manner.
2. Apply the colored enamel. The color of this coat should be light enough to afford a dark contrasting color. Buff or tan are very appropriate shades for this ground coat.
3. Allow the surface to dry overnight.
4. Now apply a coat of contrasting colored enamel (preferably brown) over the surface.

Using crumpled newspaper to obtain a mottled effect with enamel.

5. While the surface is still wet, go over it with a piece of crumbled newspaper as follows: Obtain a sheet of newspaper and crumble it into a ball. Now roll this ball over the surface. The sharp edges of the paper will pick the fresh paint at random, leaving the mottled effect. The newspaper should be changed from time to time as it becomes saturated with the fresh paint.
6. Allow this mottled surface to dry overnight.
7. Apply a coat of clear varnish over the surface to protect the design.
8. Rub with No. 2/0 steel wool, if desired, after the varnish has dried.

Textured effect on painted surfaces

This decorative device has found many uses in the finishing of articles of furniture of the modern period of design. The material is applied to the surface rather heavily, thus giving the appearance of roughness and depth. In some designs, the brush marks are purposely made deep and heavy to accentuate them. Several methods can be used to attain these effects with equally good results. One is the thick-paint method:

1. Seal the surface by applying a wash coat of shellac or a coat of paint undercoat. Allow this to dry sufficiently.
2. Into the next coat of undercoat, mix enough plaster of Paris to make a heavy liquid. The plaster of Paris is sifted slowly into the undercoat, and the mixture is stirred while the plaster is being poured.
3. Stir the mixture thoroughly and apply a heavy coat to the surface with a stiff-haired brush. While the surface is still wet, use a whisk broom or some other stiff-haired brush to make the desired designs. These designs depend on the individual. Some prefer straight parallel lines, and others prefer an irregular or wavy design.
4. Allow the surface to dry overnight. Sandpaper lightly with No. 2/0 paper.
5. Apply a coat of enamel or paint of the desired shade.
6. After sufficient time has been allowed for drying, apply a Raw Umber antique stain as explained earlier in this chapter.
7. Apply a coat of flat varnish if desired.

A prepared plaster-base powder known as Graftex may be used in place of the thick paint. This powder consists of fine plaster and a slow-drying adhesive. When mixed with water a paste is formed. The thickness depends on the amount of water used. A good paste mixture should leave a coat at least 1/16 inch thick when it is brushed or spread on with a putty knife. It dries slowly enough to permit making any textured design. The steps are as follows:

1. Apply a wash coat of shellac as in step 1 above.
2. Secure about one pound of Graftex from your local paint dealer and mix enough in water to produce a heavy paste.
3. Brush this heavy paste on the surface with a stiff brush, or apply it with a putty knife.
4. While the surface is still wet, run over it with a fine comb, sponge, or stiff brush, to obtain the desired textured design.
5. Allow this to dry overnight and then sandpaper lightly with No. 0 paper to remove the sharp edges on the surface.
6. Seal this textured surface with a wash coat of shellac, and allow it to dry.

A textured effect is achieved by spreading a mixture of paint and plaster of paris and making patterns in it with a comb or stiff brush. When the surface is thoroughly dry it is sanded lightly. Then after the piece has been enameled the desired color, it can be antiqued; the tiny grooves will hold more glaze than the ridges, accentuating the texture.

7. Brush on two coats of the desired shade of enamel.

8. Apply the antique stain and wipe off the excess as described earlier in this chapter.

9. Brush on a coat of flat clear varnish to protect the antique.

10. Wax if desired

Decalcomanias

One of the simplest and yet most effective ways of decorating an article of furniture is with decals. They are available in all types of designs from floral pieces to scrolls, pictures, figures, and lettering. They are available for all periods of furniture styles from the traditional eighteenth century to the modern and contemporary. Thus, their use is not limited to any one design or style.

A decalcomania (decal) is a thin film of oil paint and lacquer. It is so constructed that it can be applied to practically any object, be it painted with oil paint or lacquer. Once it is applied it retains its brilliancy of color and accuracy in design, and it becomes a permanent part of the surface.

There are many types of decals on the market today. You should concern yourself only with those which meet the requirements of your decorative problem. Applying this decal to any surface is quite simple, as you will note from the steps listed here. The only precaution to take is to make sure that the surface to which they are to be applied is perfectly clean, free from grease, oil, and wax.

1. Make sure that the surface has already received the appropriate finish.

2. Locate the spot where the decal is to be placed. Make a light mark on the surface which is to serve as the boundary outline of the decal.

3. Dip the decal into water for about fifteen seconds. Make sure that the entire decal is well soaked with water.

4. Test the color film on the soaked decal. If it moves on the paper with the slightest pressure it is ready to be transferred.

5. Slide off the film design face up into the position which has already been marked on the surface.

6. Press the design down with a roller or soft cloth. You should now make sure that all air bubbles between the surface and the design have been removed. Press further if all air has not been eliminated.

7. Allow this design to dry thoroughly.

8. Apply a thin coat of clear varnish or lacquer to protect the decal. *Note:* The decal may be applied to a natural finish before the final coat of clear lacquer, varnish, or shellac has been applied. The final coat will cover the decal and the surface simultaneously.

A decal should be moistened for a few seconds, then slid gently off its paper backing onto the finished surface. After it has dried in place it can be protected with a thin coat of clear varnish or lacquer.

PLASTIC-COATED PAPERS

A close examination of tables, boxes, radio, TV, and hi-fi cabinets will often show that what appears to be a fine wood surface is nothing more than photoprinted representations of the actual woods. So refined has the process become that it is almost impossible to tell whether the wood surface being viewed is actual wood. The grain and color characteristics in these papers appear almost real. Of course, the open pores, softness of texture, and feel of warm wood are missing.

In commercial furniture the overlays are bonded to plywood, hardboard, and chipboard at the factory before the cabinets or tables are constructed. However, it is possible to obtain these overlay papers in sheet form from hardware stores, department stores, and finishing-supply houses. They can be applied to the surface of an already finished piece of furniture without too much difficulty. It is possible to obtain these overlay papers with the characteristics of practically any cabinet wood, including walnut, teak, oak, cherry, mahogany, and maple, and finished in a variety of shades from natural to antique. Prints of other materials, such as marble, leather, and cloth, are also available.

These overlays are precoated with an adhesive similar to the one found on scotch tape. The adhesive side is covered with a heavy easily removed paper for the protection of the adhesive. The papers can be applied on any type of surface, finished or unfinished. They are applied as follows:

1. Check surface and make such repairs as filling dents, bruises, and deep scratches. Level smooth.
2. Sandpaper with 3/0 finishing paper and clean thoroughly.
3. If a finished surface is being covered, wash with alcohol or benzene to remove traces of wax, oil, and grease.
4. Note direction of grain on overlay. It is important that grain be consistent on object being covered. Grain should always follow the length of the object.
5. Lay out parts on reverse side of overlay and cut the pieces, allowing ¼" for trimming.
6. Remove protective backing and place overlay on section intended. Use roller to remove air pockets and wrinkles. Work from center toward edges.
7. Trim overhanging edges carefully with sharp razor.
8. Follow steps 6 and 7 for remaining parts of job.
9. There is no need for a protective coating once the paper has been applied; these papers are treated with a plastic coating. However, a coat of spray wax may be applied for additional luster and protection.

English desk with a distressed finish. (Courtesy Smith & Watson)

Distressed finishes

The term "distressed" refers to a method of imitating an appearance of age and wear on the finish of the furniture of the Provincial and Mediterranean styles. The finished surface may show fine dark lines, splattered spots, dark dents, and hammer marks. Several methods may be used to accomplish these effects. Some of these are discussed below.

Splattering

1. Prepare the splatter stain: dissolve japan Vandyke Brown in turpentine to make a thin but dark stain. Japan color is used instead of oil color in order to prevent the stain from spreading once it is splattered on the surface.
2. Select a long-haired bristle brush.
3. Dip the brush in the prepared stain and remove the excess by rubbing the brush on the side of the can.
4. Take a short stick or rod and hold on to one end and rest the other end on the surface to be splattered.
5. Hit the ferrule of the brush on the stick, splattering the stain on the surface. The size and frequency of the splatter spots may be adjusted by increasing or reducing the amount of stain in the brush and the pressure used when hitting the brush on the stick.
6. Continue to refill the brush and splatter until the entire area is covered.
7. After the surface has dried protect with one or two coats of clear lacquer.

There are several methods of distressing a finish. Splattering makes small blots all over the surface.

Pounding the surface with chain or coral rock produces small dark indentations—smooth dents with chain, sharper impressions with coral rock.

Chain Marking

This method marks and dents the surface in one step.

1. Prepare the stain as discussed under "Splattering."

2. Obtain a piece of iron chain with links about 1" long. Make a ball of the chain, about 5" in diameter.

3. Cover the chain with the Vandyke Brown stain by brushing stain on all parts.

4. Hold ball of chain in hand and begin pounding surface. As the pounding proceeds you will note that small irregular stained impressions are being made on the surface. The depth and size of the impressions depend upon the amount of force used in pounding. The darkness of the spots depends upon the amount of stain brushed on to the chain. Avoid making all impressions the same size and shade.

5. Rotate the chain as you move about the surface.

6. Continue to refill the ball of chain as the need arises. Pound until the entire surface has been marked.

7. One or two coats of clear gloss lacquer may be applied after the spots have dried.

220

Coral-rock distressing
Coral rock is like a hard sponge with large open pockets. Where deeper and sharper impressions are desired, coral rock should be used. It may be obtained from the wood-finishing supplier. It is used just like the chain above.

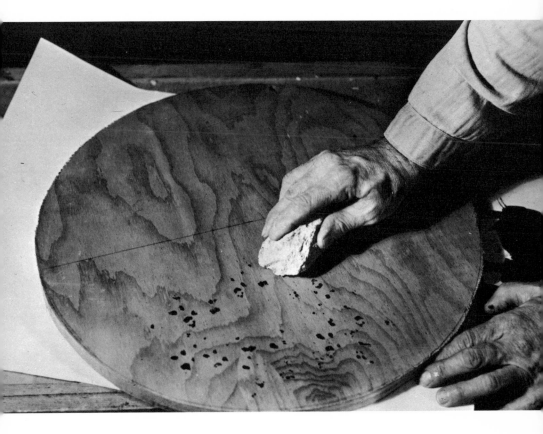

Brush distressing produces irregular fine lines such as might be caused by decades of use.

Brush distressing
1. Obtain several fine long camel's-hair brushes with diameters ranging from 1/16" to 3/16"
2. Prepare the Vandyke stain as in "Splattering," above.
3. Carefully fill a brush and clean off excess.
4. With the brush make irregular fine line markings on the surface at random.
5. Continue this with various brushes until the surface has been covered. These lines may be made after the surface has been distressed with one of the methods discussed. It is best not to make the markings uniform in size and shape. The more irregular the more natural they will look.

222

PART FIVE: PRESERVING THE FINISHED SURFACE

CHAPTER 14

Cleaning and Polishing

From time to time, it becomes necessary to produce a gloss on a surface which has already been rubbed. On other occasions, you will note that a piece of furniture in your home appears cloudy, without life and newness. You can restore the original appearances of these articles by polishing the finished surfaces. Polishing usually means that the surface is first cleaned and then rubbed to a luster. In some instances, polishing may mean the wearing away of a very fine film of the finish with a fine abrasive. In other instances, it may mean the application of a light oil or a wax to the finished surface. Finally, it may mean the application of a thin coat of shellac on the finish.

At the outset of this discussion, it should be emphasized that it is not possible to obtain a polish on the surface unless the surface finish has ample body. A thin layer of finish or a finish that has lost its body through age will not polish well regardless of the amount of effort. Where such a situation exists, additional coats of finishing materials must be applied to build up this poor finish.

Polishes may be classified into the following groups:

Oil polishes

Oil mixture polishes

Wax polishes

Rottenstone polishes

Spiriting

French polishing

Qualasole polishing

Let us describe each of these polishes in some detail.

OIL POLISHES

These are among the most inexpensive polishes used by the wood finisher and the home craftsman. They are easily available and very simple to apply. Among the most common are: crude oil, a dark brown mineral oil; paraffin oil, a water-white mineral oil; lemon oil, a yellowish oil; and a combination of paraffin and boiled linseed oil. They are applied as follows:

1. Dampen piece of cheesecloth in neutral soapy water.

2. Rub briskly on surface to be polished. Note dirt and grime collected on cheesecloth.

3. Replenish cheesecloth and clean entire job.

4. Dampen fresh cheesecloth in clear water and go over surface already cleaned to remove traces of soap remaining on surface.

5. Soak another cloth in the oil selected and wring out excess oil.

6. Rub oil cloth on surface just cleaned. Cover the entire area, replenishing the cloth from time to time.

7. Take another piece of dry, clean cheesecloth and rub briskly on oiled surface to remove all traces of free oil remaining.

At best, these oil polishes are short-lived. They will not last long regardless of the amount of effort used in applying them. If the oil film is not wiped off completely, it will sweat and attract dust and dirt to the finish. The oil has a tendency to soak through the finish, especially if the finish is quite old and dried out, and it will eventually destroy any luster left on the surface.

OIL MIXTURE POLISHES

In order to overcome some of the faults of the oil polishes just mentioned, some finishers have devised polishes which clean and polish and still do not leave an oily film on the surface. These polishes are mixtures of more than one oil, blended with wax or vinegar. Most of these are quite simple to make, and whenever possible you should mix and use them instead of the oil polishes. Several of the more simple formulas are given here in order that you may be able to discover the ease in making them.

Polish No. 1

1 pint raw linseed oil

1 pint turpentine

1 oz. beeswax

Dissolve the beeswax in linseed oil by heating the oil slightly in a double cooker; that is, the oil is placed in one small can and this is then placed in a second can containing hot water. When the wax has dissolved in the oil, remove from the source of heat and add the turpentine. When the solution has cooled, apply it to the surface by pouring some on a soft rag and then rubbing it briskly. Wipe off the excess with a clean cloth, and then polish the surface to the desired luster.

Polish No. 2

1 pint linseed oil (raw)

3 pints clean water

1 pint denatured alcohol

Add the oil to the water and stir briskly. Then add the alcohol to the solution. You will note that this mixture is not a perfect solution, but an emulsion. The component parts will separate when the mixture is allowed to settle. It should be stirred well before it is used as a polish. Alcohol not mixed in the solution may damage the finish. Now proceed as follows:

1. Prepare the surface to be polished by washing with a cloth dampened in soapy water. Clean surface with clean water and wipe dry.

2. Soak a piece of cheesecloth with the polish and rub briskly on the surface.

3. Wipe off the excess polish by wiping the surface with a clean cloth.

4. Continue to rub briskly until the desired luster is obtained.

Polish No. 3

½ pint acetic acid (vinegar)

½ pint denatured alcohol

½ pint paraffin oil

226

Mix these together in order and in the quantities given. Shake well to assure a good mixture.

Prepare the surface by cleaning with a cloth dampened in soapy water. Rinse the surface with a cloth dampened in clear water. Dry the surface thoroughly.

Soak a piece of cheesecloth in the polish and then rub the cloth on the surface to be polished. Allow the polish to remain on the surface for a few minutes. Rub off the remaining polish from the surface briskly with a clean piece of cheesecloth. Continue the polishing until the desired luster is obtained.

Polish No. 4

    4 parts linseed oil
    1 part denatured alcohol
    1 part turpentine
    1 part acetic acid (vinegar)
    ¼ part butter of antimony

You will note that most of the ingredients in the formula given above are quite common and easily available. Only the butter of antimony is unusual, but this may be obtained without too much difficulty from the better wood-finishing supply houses. It increases the effectiveness of the polish.

Mix all the ingredients in the order given above. Stir the solution as the various ingredients are being combined together. Finally add the butter of antimony and mix this well in the solution. Store the mixture in a glass container.

Clean the surface thoroughly, and then soak a piece of cheesecloth in the solution and rub it briskly over the entire surface. Allow the solution to remain on the finish for several minutes. Next, wipe the surface briskly with a piece of clean cloth. Make sure that none of the polish remains on the surface. Continue rubbing until the surface has acquired a high gloss. This polish should give excellent results if it is applied carefully and the instructions followed.

Polish No. 5

    1 pint paraffin oil
    1 pint denatured alcohol
    1 pint acetic acid (vinegar)
    3 oz. sifted rottenstone powder

Mix the above ingredients in the order given. Stir the solution as the ingredients are being added. Add the sifted rottenstone powder after the other ingredients have been mixed together. Stir until the rottenstone powder has become dispersed throughout the solution. Proceed polishing as follows:

1. Dust off and clean the surface thoroughly.
2. Shake the solution well and apply some to a piece of cheesecloth.
3. Rub the surface with the saturated cloth in a circular and straight motion.
4. Briskly wipe off the excess polish remaining on the surface with a clean soft cloth. Follow the direction of the grain. Continue until the desired luster has been obtained.
5. The rottenstone increases the abrasive action. Therefore, make certain that the final polishing action is in the direction of the grain.

PASTE WAX POLISHES

Wax polishes are longer-lasting than oil polishes, for the obvious reason that the wax leaves a very thin film on the surface. Wax enhances the natural beauty of the wood. It provides protection, since it absorbs the wear and abrasion which otherwise must be borne by the finish. Wax reduces maintenance and leaves a dry clean film to which dust and grime cannot cling.

Polishing waxes are available in paste and liquid form. Practically all paste waxes contain a proportion of carnauba wax. The more carnauba wax in the mixture, the harder the resulting film and the higher the luster. Paste waxes are applied with a cloth and must be buffed or rubbed to obtain the desired luster. It is suggested by some manufacturers that paste wax be used for antique and worn furniture. You can prepare your own polishing wax by using any of the formulas given below.

Wax Polish No. 1 Beeswax
  1 lb. beeswax
  ½ pint turpentine

Beeswax is the product of the honey bee. There are two types available—the white beeswax and the brown beeswax. Either may be used for general waxing purposes.

Cut the beeswax into thin shavings with a knife, then dissolve it in the turpentine. In order to allow it to dissolve much faster, place flaked beeswax in a container and then place this container in another container holding water. Place this double cooker over a flame or any other source of heat until the wax has dissolved completely. Now remove the liquid wax from the source of heat and add the turpentine. Stir the solution slowly as the turpentine is added. Allow this to cool. Incidentally, never place the wax can directly over the source of heat as the wax may overflow and start a fire.

Secure a piece of cheesecloth and fill with the wax just made. Apply the cloth to the surface evenly and preferably in a circular motion. Do not apply the wax to the entire job. A small area at a time will make the polishing easier. Now allow the wax to set for several minutes and then polish with a clean, soft cloth. Continue polishing until all streaks from the surface have been removed and a high gloss has been obtained.

Wax Polish No. 2

- 1 lb. carnauba wax
- 1 lb. paraffin wax
- 1 pint turpentine

The carnauba wax included in the above formula is one of the hardest waxes known. It is the product of a palm tree which grows in Brazil. Because of its hardness it cannot be used alone as a wax polish. However, when it is combined with other waxes, like the paraffin wax included in the formula, the resulting combination will give excellent results. It will leave a hard surface on the finish and will polish to a very high gloss. To make this wax, follow the instructions below.

Break the carnauba wax into small pieces. With a knife, cut the paraffin wax into thin shavings. Place both waxes in a container, and then put this container into another container filled with water. Place this double container over a source of heat. Allow the heated water to melt the wax. Be extremely careful of fire. The wax should never be placed directly over an open flame. When the wax has melted completely, remove the source of heat and slowly add the turpentine. Stir the mixture as you are doing this. Allow it to cool into a paste. If the wax mixture dries too hard and not into a soft paste, the solution may be heated as before and a little more turpentine added while the wax is in the liquid form.

This wax is applied like any other wax. Secure a soft cloth and pick up some of the wax with it. Work the wax into the cloth and then rub it evenly on the surface being polished. Allow the wax to set for a few minutes and then begin rubbing the area briskly with a piece of clean cloth. Continue to do this until the desired luster has been obtained.

Colored waxes

All light-colored waxes, whether they are purchased already prepared or are made by you, will dry light in carvings, crevices, and moldings. A great deal of effort is required to remove these traces of wax. In order to prevent this and also to help hide any light surface scratch, color is added to the wax.

Oil color of the appropriate shade is mixed with the wax while it is in the liquid or paste form. The color used is the same as that used in the making of pigment oil stain. Dissolve enough of the oil color in the wax to give color to the wax. Too much color, however, will affect the polishing qualities of the wax. Some of the more popular colored waxes are discussed here with their matching surface finish.

When waxing a walnut finish, add Raw Umber or Burnt Umber oil paste to the wax. When waxing a mahogany finish, add Vandyke Brown oil color paste to the wax. When waxing a pickled finish, add white lead to the wax. When waxing light oak, add Chrome Yellow to the wax. You may add, in a similar manner, any other oil color to the wax to give you the shade to match the color of the surface being waxed.

Hints when polishing with wax
1. The surface to be waxed should be free of oil, dirt, and grease.
2. Apply the wax to a limited area at a time. Allow that to set and then polish. Avoid waxing a large area at one time as the wax sets too hard to be polished adequately.
3. Use a ball made of cheesecloth when polishing wax. A cloth containing wrinkles, creases, and stitching will leave deep streaks on the waxed surface which are difficult to remove.
4. The rubbing may be done in any direction on the surface as long as no streaks remain after the polishing has been done. If the streaks cannot be removed by polishing with the grain, remove the wax film with a little turpentine and then rewax the surface.
5. Use a colored wax whenever possible.
6. Another coat of wax may be applied after the first, if the desired amount of luster has not been obtained. The second coat is polished in the same manner as the first.

LIQUID WAX POLISHES

Many wax manufacturers have moved away from the paste waxes and have developed a series of liquid waxes which clean and polish at the same time. At first the paste waxes were diluted with solvents and such cleaning agents as water and naphtha to form a solution. Although this form of liquid wax cleaned and polished, it did not last as long as the paste wax polishes once on the surface.

The problem of increasing hardness and durability was solved with the development of silicones. These are obtained from silicon compounds such as flint and silex. Combining these silicones with other materials produces a harder compound. Thus when silicone is combined with wax a polish is produced which is easy to apply and wipe off, giving a lasting coat and a high gloss.

Silicones were incorporated into the spray wax polishes for furniture. These new spray polishes make possible instant waxing with a minimum of effort, and they provide a protective coating like that of paste wax. The manufacturer's instructions should be followed when using these polishes. The following are also important:

1. Shake the spray can before using.
2. Make sure that the spray tip faces the object to be polished.
3. Spray lightly about 6 inches from the surface. Use the spray sparingly.
4. Wipe the mist off immediately with a soft lint-free cloth.
5. When polishing a small area, spray the wax on the polishing cloth and then rub the cloth on the surface.
6. Use care in spraying. Do not spray toward the face. Do not spray near a hot radiator or an open flame.

ROTTENSTONE

The professional wood finisher obtains a high gloss on his finishes by rubbing the surface with rottenstone and water or oil. Although the process is very slow, requiring much effort and time, the results obtained are indeed worth the added effort.

In Chapter 9, the statement is made that the finer the scratch produced by an abrasive on the finish the higher the gloss obtained. In other words, the size of the scratch determines the amount of gloss on the finish. Pumice-stone rubbing, at best, produces a medium scratch and gives the surface a satiny, semi-gloss appearance. Extremely high-polished surfaces are not possible with pumice stone, because the pumice stone is not fine enough to give a fine scratch.

Rottenstone is a very fine abrasive powder which can be used for this purpose. This gray powder is derived from slate. If you rub some of it between your fingers, you will note that it feels like talcum powder. Yet, despite this smoothness of feel, it has remarkable abrasive qualities; and, when used as a polishing agent on a finish, a beautiful high luster will be obtained. The steps are as follows:

1. Place some powdered rottenstone in a shallow saucer.
2. Have a container of crude oil if the polishing is to be done with oil, or water if the polishing is to be done with water.

3. Get a piece of soft felt about 4″ x 4″. Part of an old felt hat is ideal for this purpose.
4. Soak the felt in the oil and place the saturated felt on the rottenstone.
5. Work the rottenstone into the saturated felt with your hands.
6. Sprinkle a little oil or water and rottenstone on the surface.
7. Place pad on the surface and begin rubbing with a moderate pressure in the direction of the grain.
8. As you continue rubbing refill the felt with oil and rottenstone. Rub the surface evenly from one edge to the next.
9. Check the surface periodically by wiping the grime from a section of the surface to note the degree of luster. The more rubbing the higher the gloss.
10. When the desired degree of luster has been obtained, carefully wipe off the grime with a soft clean cloth in the direction of the grain.
11. Finish by wiping the surface with the palm of your hand.
12. A wax or oil polish may be used to acquire a higher gloss. This step may not be required if the desired polish has been obtained.

You will notice that oil is suggested as the lubricant. Water can be used in place of the oil, but greater care must be exercised and the surface being rubbed must be finished in either lacquer or varnish. Water should never be used when a shellac surface is being polished with rottenstone. However, either may be used on the other two finishes with equally good results.

Rottenstone polishing may be performed immediately after the surface has been rubbed with pumice stone. Better results will be obtained then than if the method is used on an old finish. The new finish is rubbed with pumice stone as directed in the earlier chapters until the surface has acquired a smooth texture. The surface is then cleaned of the residue and the rotten-stone rubbing follows. The result will be an exceptionally smooth and polished surface.

ALCOHOL POLISH (SPIRITING)

Another method of producing a polish on a finished surface, especially a varnished surface, is spiriting. A piece of lint-free washed linen is shaped into a ball and then dipped into alcohol. The pad, wrung free of all liquid alcohol, is held between your thumb and fingers.

Rub the pad briskly on the finished surface in a circular motion and in the direction of the grain. As you are rubbing you will notice that a luster is beginning to appear on the surface. Continue rubbing and, from time to time, refill the pad with alcohol as before. No further polishing is required after the finish has attained the desired luster.

232

Great care should be exercised with this method of rubbing. Too much alcohol on the rubbing pad may damage the finish seriously. Therefore, make certain that the pad is free of all liquid alcohol before applying it to the surface. Test the pad by pressing it against your hand. If the pad feels wet, wring out the excess alcohol. The pad must be constantly in motion while it is on the surface. Do not rest the alcohol pad on the surface for any reason, for if the pad comes to a rest on the surface, the alcohol vapor will soften the finish, causing serious damage to the film.

Some finishers use this method of polishing after the surface has been polished with oil. The "spiriting off" will remove all traces of oil from the finish and leave a clean polished surface.

FRENCH POLISHING

Making the rubbing pad

Secure a piece of washed linen about 6 inches square. Lay it flat on your table and place a piece of cotton waste or cheesecloth in the center of it. Enough cotton waste should be placed in the cloth to make a ball about 2 inches in diameter. Now pick up the four ends of the linen square and twist them together. The pad is held with your fingers and then the hand is closed into a fist. The pad is thus supported by the palm of your hand and pressure is applied in this fashion.

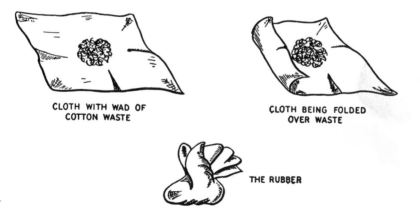

CLOTH WITH WAD OF COTTON WASTE

CLOTH BEING FOLDED OVER WASTE

THE RUBBER

This method of polishing is one of the oldest. It was first used by the French during the seventeenth and eighteenth centuries. They used it primarily to apply coats of shellac to their beautiful furniture. The shellac was built up slowly with a pad, layer upon layer, until the desired body was reached. In

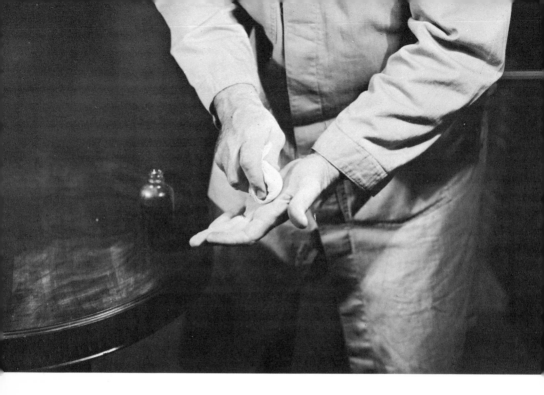

Alcohol, shellac, and oil are worked into the French-polishing pad until it is moist. Then the surface is padded in either a circular or a figure-eight pattern, adding more shellac from time to time and more oil if the pad begins to stick.

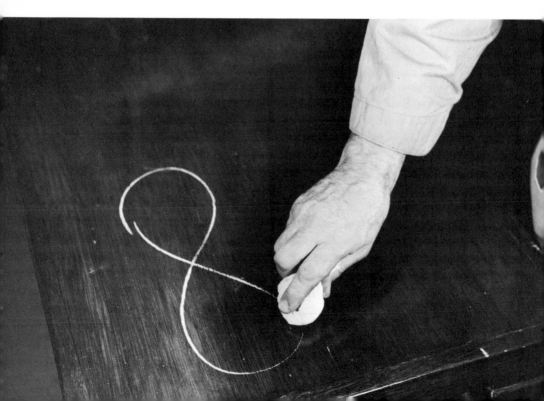

When a sufficient coat of shellac has built up, the pad is moistened with a few drops of alcohol and the surface is padded in the direction of the grain to remove the circular marks.

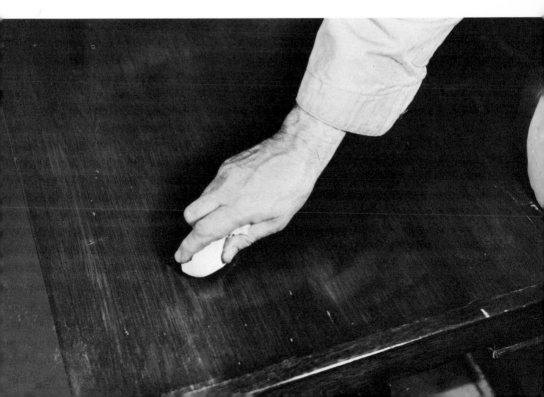

recent years, however, the method has been used mostly for obtaining a high gloss on a finish and also for patching up a damaged area.

By French polishing is meant the application of thin layers of shellac or French varnish to a finished surface with a cloth pad, until a nigh, smooth gloss is obtained. This form of polishing is complete in itself. No other form of polish is required after it.

Materials required for French polishing

1. French varnish or shellac—to provide the body of the polish.
2. Linseed oil—to act as the lubricant.
3. A rubbing pad—a piece of washed linen in the shape of an egg to apply the shellac.
4. Denatured alcohol—to act as the solvent and thin the shellac.

Provide yourself with three small bottles and label them "alcohol," "shellac," and "oil." Pour the materials in each bottle as designated and then cover each with a stopper. Make several holes in each stopper in order to permit the sprinkling of the liquid.

The surface to be polished should first be cleaned of dirt, grease, and wax. Light sanding of the surface with No. 5/0 garnet paper will aid in cleaning and removing some of the scratches. Dust the surface clean.

Applying the French polish

1. Hold pad in hand and shake a few drops of alcohol into it.
2. Work alcohol into pad by rubbing with hand.
3. Shake a few drops of shellac into the pad and work shellac into pad with hand.
4. Sprinkle a few drops of oil into pad.
5. Check pad. It should feel moist to touch.
6. Add additional ingredients if necessary.
7. Hold pad in hand as indicated and begin rubbing on the surface with a moderate pressure and in a circular or "figure 8" motion. *Note:* the diameter of circle should be not less than 8 inches.
8. Continue polishing in this manner and move in all directions on the surface.
9. Refill the pad and move in all directions on the surface.
10. Note how the body is beginning to build up as you rub.
11. Continue refilling and rubbing to obtain the desired body.
12. If rubbing becomes difficult, add a few drops of oil to pad. This will reduce friction while finish is building up.

13. When the desired luster has been obtained, shake a few drops of alcohol on the pad and rub the entire surface in the direction of the grain. This will remove the circular marks made while polishing.

14. Continue this step until all circular traces have been removed.

Hints to assure good French polishing

1. Use a 5-pound cut shellac or French varnish.

2. Always make sure that the oil on the surface is enough to prevent friction and sticking of the pad. Do not use too much oil, however.

3. The rubbing motion should consist of circle not less than 8 inches in diameter. A smaller circle will keep the pad on a small area and this prevents the building up of the shellac. If the circle is too small the pad will soften whatever shellac has been applied and remove it.

4. Use only a lint-free cloth in making your pad. The pad should be in the shape of an egg, at least 2 inches in diameter.

5. Do not soak the pad with the ingredients listed, as this will merely flood them on the surface and leave a smeared and muddy effect.

6. The pad should always be in motion while it is being used. Avoid resting the pad on the surface for any length of time. If not moved constantly, the pad will stick to the surface and pick up the material just applied.

7. The final polishing should always be done in the direction of the grain, to remove all the traces of the circular streaks. A little alcohol added to the pad will make this easier.

QUALASOLE POLISHING

Within recent years improvements in French-polishing techniques have been made through the introduction of new materials. Qualasole is one of these. The ingredients in this material are a trade secret. The results obtained when it is applied to the surface compare well with conventional French polishing.

Qualasole is basically a one-liquid polish. However, a solvent may be used if during the polishing circular streaks appear on the surface. A few drops on the pad will remove these streaks when the pad is moved in the direction of the grain.

Qualasole is applied to the surface with a pad and worked as the French polish. The surface produced by this method of polishing has a high, long-lasting luster which seems to improve with age. It can be used on all types of finished surfaces with no ill effects. The results produced have met with the approval of the trade, and it is for this reason that Qualasole is used in

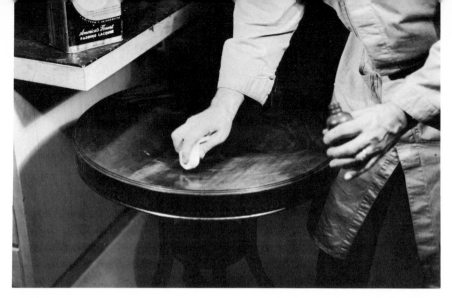

Qualasole is a good substitute for conventional French polishing and is somewhat easier to apply.

place of French polish in many wood-finishing shops. The craftsman would do well to familiarize himself with this material.

Applying Qualasole

The surface to be polished should be thoroughly cleaned of all wax, grease, and oil. Light sanding with No. 5/0 garnet paper after the cleaning will aid in removing light surface scratches and other imperfections. Proceed with the padding as follows:

1. Prepare a rubbing pad made of lint-free linen and packed with cotton waste. Refer to the procedure for making a French-polishing pad.
2. Apply a small quantity of Qualasole to the pad.
3. Flatten pad against the palm of your hand to ensure equal dispersion of the liquid into the pad.
4. Press the pad to the surface and begin rubbing in a figure-8 motion with a medium pressure.
5. Continue replenishing the pad and rubbing until the desired luster has been obtained.
6. Replenish the pad with a few drops of Qualasole solvent and rub in the direction of the grain to remove the circular marks made by the initial rubbing.
7. If a higher gloss is desired, rub the surface with the pad using Qualasole solvent only.

Hints to assure good Qualasole polishing

1. Do not soak the pad with Qualasole, because the excess material will smear the surface and leave a muddy appearance. The pad should be just dampened with the material and then rubbed on to the surface.

2. The scrubbing should be done in a circular motion with the circle not less than 8 inches in diameter. A smaller circle will not produce the desired results.

3. Never allow the pad to rest on the surface while rubbing. The pad will stick to the wet surface and remove the thin layer.

4. Do not add any oil to the pad while the polishing is progressing. Oil on the surface will prevent the drying of the material. Remember, Qualasole is a one-liquid padding and polishing material.

PIGMENT OIL STAIN POLISH

Pigment oil stain may be used as a furniture polish with excellent results. If you will refer to Chapter 4 you will note the various formulas for mixing the different shades of pigment oil stains. The only difference between the pigment oil stains used for staining wood and the pigment oil stain used for polishing is that more japan drier is added to the polishing mixture.

The shade of the stain you select for the polish should be as close to the shade of the finished surface as possible. Thus, if you intend to use the stain for polishing mahogany, use a Mahogany stain. If walnut is to be polished, use a Walnut stain. Do not use a stain for polishing that is much lighter or darker than the shade of the surface being polished.

The main advantage of this colored stain used as a polish is that it will color any surface scratches, thus making them inconspicuous. The polish also colors the corners of moldings and crevices and gives them a mellow appearance. It leaves a uniform satin gloss on the surface which may be enhanced from time to time with further rubbing. It is quite simple to make and very easy to use.

The surface should be cleaned thoroughly before the polishing is attempted. Secure a piece of soft cloth and wet it with the stain polish you have selected. Rub this dampened cloth over the finish to be polished. Make sure that the entire area is adequately covered with the stain. Use a stiff brush to get into the corners of moldings or carvings. After a section has been covered in this manner, obtain a clean piece of soft cloth and wipe off the excess. Use another clean piece of cloth to dry the surface free of all remaining stain. Naturally, the more you rub at this time the higher the luster obtained on the surface.

CHAPTER 15

Making Minor Repairs

No matter how careful you may be with your finishing work or the completed job, occasions always arise where some slight damage appears on the surface. The table or chest may have been pushed along the floor and accidentally hit another object, resulting in a scratch or dent. During the rubbing operation you may have rubbed the sharp corners of the finished piece to the bare wood. You may have dropped a blunt article on another piece of furniture, causing surface bruises. Then, again, you may be called upon to polish your furniture and in the process you discover that the polish does not remove the scratches and other marks on the surface.

These and other problems always confront the home finisher. Consequently, it is advisable to familiarize yourself with the techniques of making minor repairs. There is no doubt that you will be improving the quality of your work if you make these simple corrections.

"Touching up" means the painting of small surface damages, like scratches, bare spots, and spots which have been rubbed through, with colored shellac, a fast-drying finishing material. The process of touching up also includes patching a defective area so that it resembles the surrounding surface so well that it cannot be recognized by the inexperienced eye.

In order to perform these operations, the craftsman should assemble a repair kit containing the essential materials required. The cost of the materials in this kit is very small.

Minimum materials for touching-up kit

1. Assorted sizes of round camel's-hair pencil brushes, ⅛", 3/16", and ¼" being most essential.
2. Two flat camel's-hair brushes, ½" and 1"
3. Assorted shades of dry powder colors, about an ounce of each, stored in covered, small, wide-mouth bottles. Shades should include: Burnt Umber, Raw Umber, Zinc White, Black, Chrome Yellow, French Ochre, and Vermilion Red.
4. Assorted shades of aniline powder colors soluble in alcohol; about one ounce of each, stored in small, wide-mouth bottles. Assortment should include: Red Mahogany, Brown Mahogany, Black, Chrome Yellow, Walnut, Fumed Oak, Light Oak.
5. ½ pint of white shellac, stored in small can.
6. ½ pint of orange shellac, stored in small can.
7. ½ pint of denatured alcohol, stored in small can.
8. One package of cheesecloth.
9. One alcohol lamp.
10. One burning-in knife.
11. Assorted colors of burning-in stick shellac, including Red Mahogany, Brown Mahogany, Light Natural, Dark Natural Oak, Maple, White.
12. Assorted grits of finishing sandpaper.
13. Rubbing materials—see Chapter 9.
14. Quick touch-up patching sticks in a variety of colors.

PROCEDURE IN TOUCHING UP

Let us suppose that you have just completed rubbing a mahogany table and you find that some of the edges have been rubbed through to the bare wood. They look ugly and mar the general appearance of the table. Your problem,

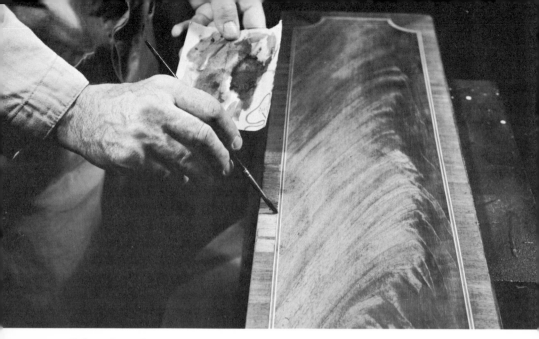

If the edges of a piece have accidentally been rubbed through to the bare wood here and there, shellac colored to match the finish will make the flaws almost invisible.

therefore, is to touch up these edges so that they will match the remainder of the surface. This may be done by the following procedure:

Rubbed-through edges
1. Pour a small amount of white shellac in a small paper cup.
2. Have available the dry colors listed above.
3. Dip pencil brush in the shellac and with the tip pick up a bit of the dry color which matches the surface.
4. Work the saturated brush on a clean piece of white paper in order to mix the color and shellac thoroughly.
5. Match this color with the color of the surface. Add other shades if necessary.
6. Pick up some of the colored shellac with the pencil brush and carefully brush on the bare spot, using the side of the brush. Several applications may be necessary at times.
7. If color does not match, remove by rubbing lightly with a little steel wool. Prepare a new mixture and try again.
8. Rub the touched-up area carefully with a little steel wool and oil.

242

Surface scratches

1. Select a very small pencil brush and dip into white shellac.
2. Use saturated pencil brush to pick up dry powdered colors.
3. Mix colors and shellac on brush on sheet of white paper. Add other dry colors if necessary to match the surface around the scratch.
4. Very carefully, and using only the tip of the brush, cover the scratch with the prepared mixture.
5. Wipe off with finger any color which may have spread to surrounding surface.
6. Clean brush by washing in alcohol.
7. Pick up some clear white shellac with brush and cover the scratch just touched up. Allow to dry.
8. Continue doing this until the depth of the scratch has built up flush to surface.
9. Allow sufficient drying time.
10. Rub with pumice and oil.

Scratches in a finished surface can be filled with colored shellac, using a delicate pointed brush.

Some hints for touching up

1. The shade blended with the dry colors should match the damaged area as closely as possible.

2. When using the brush to apply the colored shellac, do not cover more of the area than the spot affected. Do not spread the damaged area more than necessary.

3. If the color applied to the affected area is not correct, remove by washing it off with a small pad soaked in alcohol, but be careful not to damage any other area with the alcohol pad.

4. Do not use any other material than white shellac for making the colored touching-up liquid. Varnish does not dry for at least twelve hours and, consequently, is not practical for touching up. Lacquer, if used for this purpose, would dry too rapidly to be applied well.

5. Thin the shellac with denatured alcohol if it begins to set (harden) while you are blending the powders to get the desired color.

6. Allow sufficient time for the patched area to dry before attempting to rub it down smooth.

Patching a lacquered surface with lacquer

When a surface has been finished in lacquer, scratches and small deep defects may be repaired by using lacquer as the repair medium.

1. When color has been removed from base of scratch, make a little alcohol stain to match the base color, and with a fine pencil brush stain the base of the scratch.

2. Pour some clear glossy lacquer in a small paper cup. Do not use a waxed cup.

3. Pick up the lacquer with a fine pencil brush and very carefully begin to build up the scratch.

4. Since lacquer dries very rapidly, several coats may be applied at short intervals.

5. Continue building up in this manner until the scratch has been filled.

6. After drying rub with pumice and oil.

Removing fine scratches

Fine scratches on a finished surface are quite common and, at times, very annoying. A finely rubbed finish is so delicate that the slightest movement of an object placed over it leaves a mark or a scratch. They are indeed difficult to avoid. However, removing them is not too difficult.

1. Obtain a small piece of soft felt and soak it in crude oil.

2. Sprinkle some fine rottenstone over the affected area.

3. Place the saturated felt over the rottenstone and begin carefully to rub the affected area in the direction of the grain.

4. Make the rubbing strokes a little longer than the scratches.

5. Repeat the rubbing operation with additional oil and rottenstone until the scratches have been removed.

6. Clean off the grime. You will note that the affected area now has a cleaner appearance than the remainder of the surface.

7. Repeat the rubbing operation to cover the entire area. This will give a uniform sheen to the surface.

Several precautions should be taken when removing fine scratches. Avoid considerable rubbing if the scratch does not seem to disappear. This may indicate that the scratch is deeper than the finished surface. Refer to the steps illustrated earlier in the chapter to remove deep scratches. Regardless of the direction of the scratch, the rubbing should always be done in the direction of the grain. Rubbing against the grain will make any scratch more conspicuous.

Padding to patch a surface

Padding a damaged area with colored shellac is another method which may be used for making minor repairs on a finished surface. This procedure is not unlike the French polishing discussed in Chapter 14.

In a situation where an area larger than a scratch requires patching, using the touch-up brush to apply the correct color to the area would not work out too well, because the brush would leave an opaque paint on the surface, thus hiding the grain of the wood. In padding with a colored shellac, the damaged area is covered without hiding the grain beneath it. Let us assume that, after rubbing the side of a desk, you notice that you have accidentally rubbed through the finish at one point. In order to repair this area, proceed as follows:

1. Shape a piece of lint-free linen into a ball about 2 inches in diameter.

2. Sprinkle a small amount of alcohol-soluble aniline color to match the finished surface on a piece of white paper.

3. Moisten the rubbing ball with 2-pound cut shellac by working the shellac with the palm of the hand.

4. Press the dampened pad on the color sprinkled on the paper and work the color into the pad by rubbing it on the paper. This action causes the color to dissolve in the saturated ball.

5. Begin rubbing the colored ball on the damaged section of the finish with a light pressure and raising the pad before and after each stroke.

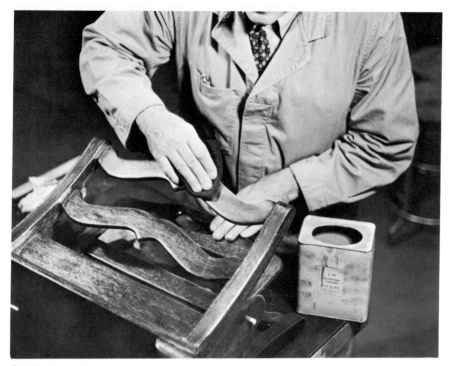

Padding is used to touch up larger areas that have been rubbed bare. If properly applied, the colored shellac repairs the area without concealing the grain.

6. Continue this action until the surface acquires the shade of the colored ball.

7. If not enough color is adhering to the surface add more aniline to the ball saturated with shellac and again work the color in by rubbing on the paper. Pad the ball on the surface.

8. Attempt to blend the color with the surrounding unaffected area. Avoid a sharp demarcation.

9. If the ball feels dry and is sticking to the surface, add a few drops of linseed oil to the affected area.

10. After the desired shade has been padded on the surface, allow the surface two hours of drying time before it is carefully rubbed with pumice stone and oil.

11. Rub the entire surface with rottenstone and oil to assure an even texture.

246

Qualasole padding

The manufacturers of Qualasole have made available about fifteen different shades of colored anilines which can be used to match a surface when the padding is done with the Qualasole. The variety of shades meets most of the requirements of the finisher, because among them are included the shades of the most popular wood finishes. Here is a partial list of the anilines available:

Champagne	Red Brown Mahogany	Light Walnut
Red Maple	White	Dark Walnut
Orange Red Maple	Blond Glaze	Medium Walnut
Medium Red Mahogany	Limed Oak	Black

You can see from this list that practically any color of finish may be padded up merely by using the most appropriate shade. The directions for using these aniline stains are very simple and easy to follow. You first apply Qualasole to the damaged area with a small pad, in order to provide a base for the color. Then dip the pad moistened in the Qualasole into the correct shade of aniline. With the pad filled in this way, continue to pad over the affected surface until it has acquired the shade desired. Repeat this operation until the affected area has been filled level with the surrounding surface. As a final step, go over the entire surface with clear Qualasole to refresh the finish and make the patched area less conspicuous.

Qualasole and aniline colors can also be used for touch-up padding.

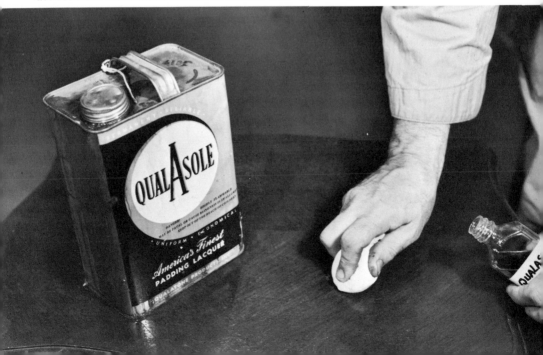

BURNING-IN A DAMAGED AREA

This is perhaps one of the most important operations in the repairing of minor surface defects. Burning-in is filling in a dent, deep scratch, or a chipped surface with melted stick shellac or lacquer. The liquid shellac hardens within a few seconds, adheres to the affected area, and fills it.

Materials required for burning-in
1. Assorted colors of stick shellac and stick lacquer
2. Alcohol lamp
3. Spatula or burning-in knife
4. 5/0 garnet paper and a small block
5. Rubbing materials—pumice, etc.

A knowledge of the use of each of these items in the operation is very important. The following description should aid in understanding the importance of each.

Stick shellac and stick lacquer. These are made by melting shellac or lacquer and pouring it into a mold. The sticks are then available in about thirty different shades—the shades matching most of the popular shades of finished surfaces. An indication of the variety of shades available are listed here.

Red Mahogany	Walnut
Brown Mahogany	Maple
Natural Light—transparent	Oak
Natural Dark—transparent	Red
Black	White

You should provide yourself with an assortment of colors both in shellac stick and in lacquer stick for your repair kit, so that you are always prepared to make a burning-in repair, regardless of the shade of finish. The shellac sticks should be used for filling dents on shellac or varnished surfaces, and the lacquer sticks for filling dents on lacquered surfaces.

Alcohol lamp. A source of heat is required to heat the spatula or burning-in knife, which, in turn, is to melt the stick shellac or lacquer. A small alcohol lamp would be the most appropriate. A good-quality alcohol lamp is quite expensive; but, if you desire to save this expense, one can be made very easily. Purchase a small oil can and cut the spout to 1″ above the cap. Be careful not to close the sides of the spout when cutting it. Now make a wick with a piece of cotton rope or cloth to fit into the spout opening. Insert the wick into the spout. The can is now filled with denatured alcohol and the cap fastened to it. Do not fill the can with benzene or turpentine, as both of these

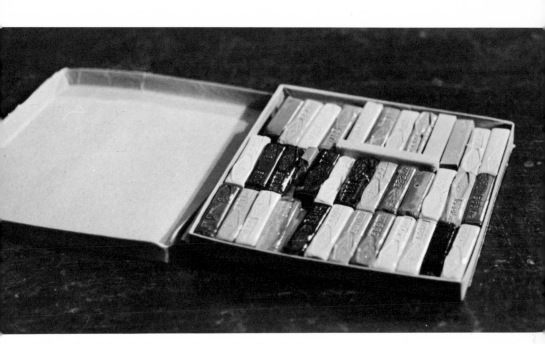

Stick shellac for burning-in comes in a great variety of colors.

burn with a yellow flame and give off a black smoke which will discolor the stick shellac. You will notice a clean blue flame from the alcohol after the lamp is ignited. This will not affect the stick shellac.

The spatula or burning-in knife. A flexible steel blade or spatula is essential for the melting of the stick shellac. A heavy blade is not suitable for this purpose, because it is not flexible enough to smooth the melted stick shellac when it is forced into the depression. The blade must be thick enough to carry the heat for a while and work in the shellac. A piece of bandsaw blade, ¼" wide with the teeth removed and the end filed round, would be very appropriate as a burning-in knife.

Sandpaper and small block. As you will note later in the description, the stick shellac which has melted into the dent does not leave a smooth surface. It must be sanded smooth and flush with the surrounding finish. Consequently, No. 5/0 garnet paper, soaked in crude oil and then backed by a small block of wood, is used to sandpaper the uneven hard shellac.

Rubbing materials. If you will refer to Chapter 9, the materials required for this operation are discussed. These are used to give the filled-in surface a gloss and smooth finish.

The burning-in operation

Assuming that you have a deep dent on the finished surface that requires filling-in with stick shellac, select the stick shellac whose color best matches the shade of the defective area.

1. Light the alcohol lamp. Make sure it is away from flammable materials.
2. Place the burning-in knife over the flame and heat sufficiently to melt the stick shellac. Do not overheat the knife; if it is too hot it will burn the stick shellac and turn it black.
3. Carry the liquefied shellac on the knife to the spot to be filled and work it into the dented area with the point of the knife. Make sure, however, that you do not touch the surrounding finish with the heated knife, because it may scorch the finish.
4. If the first attempt has not succeeded in filling the area, reheat the knife and melt additional shellac. Repeat step 3, then moisten your finger tip and carefully press the melted shellac into the dent. *Note:* Make sure the finger tip is wet when pressing down the melted shellac. A serious burn may result otherwise.
5. After the spot has been completely filled, heat the tip of the knife and press it over the spot. This will flatten the excess shellac on the surface.
6. Scuff the surface with a small piece of 5/0 garnet paper to remove the sharp crystals.
7. Soak the paper in crude oil, wrap it around a small flat block of wood, and carefully sandpaper the affected area flush to the surrounding surface. Do not sandpaper more than necessary or you may damage the surrounding area.
8. Rub the entire area with rottenstone and oil to produce a uniform unblemished sheen. If the burning-in has been done properly, no trace of the damaged spot should appear on the surface,

Precautions when burning-in

1. Do not overheat the burning-in knife. A knife heated red-hot will burn the stick shellac and scorch the surface finish. A properly heated knife should melt the. shellac slowly. If the shellac smokes or bubbles while it is being melted, you may assume that the knife is too hot. Allow it to cool slightly before attempting to melt the shellac again.
2. Do not overfill the dent with shellac, for the more shellac that hardens over the dent the more labor is involved in removing it.
3. Do not allow the melted shellac to overflow the dent. The heated shellac touching the finish may scorch and damage it.

Burning-in is a delicate operation. First the knife is heated just enough to melt the shellac. Then the shellac is forced into the dent; be careful not to touch the surrounding area. When the dent is filled, it is sanded very gently, and then the entire area is rubbed with rottenstone and oil so that the patch will blend in.

4. Do not touch the surface with the heated knife. It may soften or burn the finish. Work the knife over the dent as much as possible.

5. Avoid sandpapering the hardened shellac more than necessary. You should remember that the surface film surrounding the damaged area is quite thin, and undue sanding may wear away this thin film, thus causing more serious damage to the surface.

6. Avoid rubbing too much with the pumice, for the same reasons.

7. Select the color of stick shellac which matches the finished surface best. You must remember that no matter how good the results of the burning-in, the spot will be conspicuous unless the shellac used matches well.

HOT-AND-COLD TREATMENT FOR REMOVING DENTS

This method, although not as sure as the burning method of filling in dents, should be attempted, and if it works out well the dented area will rise to the surface and there will be no need for burning-in. The steps involved are quite simple. Very little equipment is necessary to perform the operation. It is worth trying before any other method is given consideration. The principle involved is the sudden change of temperature on the finished surface from high to low. This change affects the surface and causes the wood fibers underneath the finish to rise. Study the procedure and then make the attempt.

1. Heat a piece of wool cloth over a radiator or by pressing it with a hot iron. An electric heating pad may be used.

2. Pack a few pieces of cracked ice in a cellophane bag.

3. Press the heated cloth or pad over the damaged area firmly for a few minutes.

4. Remove the heated cloth or pad and replace immediately with the cracked ice.

5. Allow the ice to remain on the surface for a few minutes.

6. Repeat these hot and cold applications until the dented area shows signs of change. Continue until the dented surface is flush with the rest of the area.

7. Clean off all traces of water and rub slightly with rottenstone and oil to freshen up the entire surface.

Advantages of the hot-and-cold method

1. If successful, the dent may be removed without undue damage to the finish and without the necessity of burning-in.

2. The surface is free from the blemishes and discoloration which may be caused by the stick shellac. The grain is not hidden at the dented area.

252

The hot-and-cold method of removing dents: first the iron, then the icebag. Here the iron is applied directly to the cloth on the wood, but it is safer to use an electric heating pad or to warm the cloth away from the wood and then press it to the damaged area.

3. It is a rather simple operation to perform and no special tools or equipment are necessary.

4. The only precaution to bear in mind is that no heated material should be applied which will in any way damage the delicate finish.

TOUCH-UP PATCHING STICKS

These sticks are made from a waxlike material and resemble a crayon pencil. They may be obtained in any color to match the finish or painted surface to be repaired. They are used where a quick fill-up job is required. Proceed as follows:

1. Select the correct shade for the surface to be repaired.

2. Work the stick into the marred area until a sufficient amount has been forced into the area.

3. Remove the excess material by rubbing the area with a cloth.

4. Carefully pad the area and the surrounding surface with Qualasole or shellac.

Patching sticks cannot replace the use of stick shellac and the burning process. The area will never dry hard enough to permit rubbing and polishing as with the other filling materials.

Making your own patch wax

1. Carefully melt a small amount of beeswax in a double cooker.

2. Add oil color to match the shade of surface to be repaired. Only a small amount of oil color is required.

3. Allow the mixture to cool.

4. Scoop out enough of the colored beeswax to fill the damaged area.

5. Rub off the excess with a soft cloth.

REPAIRING BLISTERED VENEER ON FINISHED SURFACES

Blistered veneer on a finished piece may be caused by the accumulation of an amount of water on the veneered top, or the continuous presence of an excessive amount of heat. Actually the glue holding the veneer in place has dissolved. In order to remove the blister, the thin layer of veneer should be reglued. Chapter 3 discusses the procedure of repairing a blister in detail. However, additional precautions should be taken when this operation is done on a finished surface. They are as follows:

1. After the glue has set the damaged area should be sanded lightly with 5/0

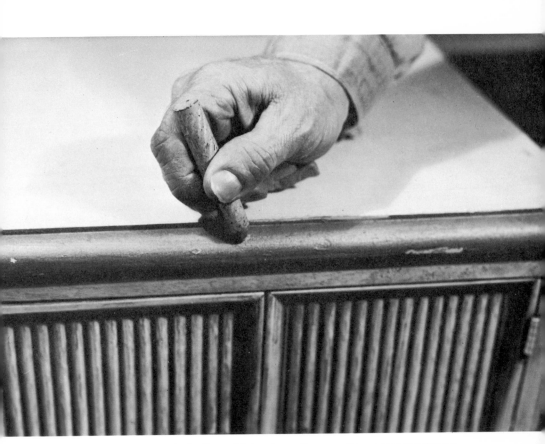

The patching stick—an easy and effective quick touch-up. However, the waxy material never dries hard.

garnet paper saturated in oil. The sanding should be done carefully and in the direction of the grain. Care should be taken not to damage the finish while sanding.

2. If some of the finish is removed, the surface should be touched up to match the remainder of the top and then padded with shellac or Qualasole.

3. The entire surface should be rubbed with pumice or rottenstone to avoid a contrast between the damaged area and the rest of the surface.

APPENDIX: SETTING UP A WOOD-FINISHING SHOP

To a large extent, good finishing results will depend upon the quality of material you use, the equipment that you have, and the working area you have set aside for that purpose. The importance of these has been stressed from time to time in this book. There is very little justification for spending money and hours of your time in finishing an article of furniture, unless the finish produced shows signs of quality and workmanship. Surprising as it may seem, these results are easily obtainable, without involving yourself in too much expense and without the need of too large a working area. Simple basic fundamentals in planning a work area and providing ample space for storage of materials will assure you the fine results that your labor deserves.

Work area

You should select a section of your shop for your wood-finishing operations. The area need not be too large, and it need not take the best part of your shop. All that is required is that the section should be away from your wood-working machines and your woodworking bench. A wood-finishing area near these will invariably be clouded with dust and shavings, and any attempt to keep the area clean is doomed.

Locate the finishing section in a corner of your room away from all dust-creating devices. If possible, select the corner which has a window so that natural light may be available during the day hours, and also so that the window can be a source of ventilation and an outlet for fumes of paint or spray. A good type of artificial illumination should also be provided directly over the work station. A fluorescent fixture with two 40-watt tubes would suffice.

Provide yourself with a finishing table on which to put your work during the finishing process. The table should be about 28 inches high, 30 inches wide, and 48 inches long. Of course, there is no need of going to the expense of making one of these, but if something is available it should be as near to these dimensions as possible. A larger table will be difficult to move. A smaller table may not be large enough to hold the articles you are finishing. If possible, place this table as near to the window as practical. Good finishing results are obtained when the light source is directly in front of you.

A pair of wooden horses about 28 inches high will also prove helpful. A table of any dimension may be easily made by placing a wide board over these horses. It can be moved from place to place as the situation arises. If desired, large articles of furniture, such as a sofa or a dining-room table, may be placed directly on the horses.

Storage area

Proper storage facilities are very important. You will find that with time you will have accumulated many types of materials. These require proper storage and handling. Oil colors, for example, dry unless stored properly. Aniline and dry powders become dusty and caked. Paint, shellac, varnish, and lacquer require proper storage facilities, because they too dry with time.

You should, therefore, have a metal storage closet with ample space to store those materials which are used occasionally, and those materials which are used more frequently. All oil-color-paste containers should be stored in one location with their labels in easy sight. Dry colors and anilines should be stored in covered metal or paper containers so that dust and moisture will not affect them. Fillers should be stored separately. Shellac, varnish, and lacquer should be properly labeled and stored away from possible danger of fire, and the containers covered tightly to prevent evaporation and oxidation. Your rubbing materials should be stored by themselves. The pumice stone, rottenstone, rubbing felt, and wiping materials should be stored so that they are easily accessible.

A fireproof waste receptacle should also be available. A five-gallon type with spring snap cover should be selected. Here all your waste materials, such as wiping rags, paper, and dirt, are stored until they are removed from the premises. Remember to destroy all wiping rags immediately after use, to prevent the possibility of fire.

Bleaching materials should also be stored separately. It is important that these be labeled properly and not within reach of children. Place your rubber gloves alongside of these bleaches so that they are handy whenever any bleaching operation is to be performed.

Finally, every precaution should be taken to prevent fire. You no doubt know that many of the materials used in wood finishing are highly flammable. Proper storage of these materials will aid in the prevention of fire, but the proper handling is also necessary. Finishing materials should never be used near an open flame or in places where there is danger of fire. Do not smoke while using such flammables as lacquer, benzene, gasoline, turpentine, and lacquer thinner.

ESSENTIAL FINISHING MATERIALS

The list of materials given below is not presented with the idea that you should immediately set out to purchase every item on the list. It is given to indicate the materials a well-equipped home-finishing shop should have. These can be obtained as the need for each arises. They should be purchased in quantities large enough to permit their use on other occasions. Of course, you should not go to the extreme and purchase quantities which not even large finishing shops would consider. Certain items like shellac, varnish, and lacquer should be purchased in small quantities unless they are to be used often. A quart of each should be sufficient for the ordinary finishing situations. Purchasing more than is needed is a waste as most of the materials deteriorate with time.

Top-coat finishing materials—about a quart of each
   White shellac, 5-pound cut
   Orange shellac, 5-pound cut
   Varnish, four-hour drying, clear glossy
   Varnish, flat
   Lacquer, clear glossy
   Lacquer, flat
   Lacquer, sealer
Solvents—about a quart of each
   Benzene—for paste filler and oil stains
   Turpentine
   Alcohol, denatured
   Lacquer thinner
Oils—about one pint of each
   Boiled linseed oil
   Crude oil
   Paraffin oil
Oil-color paste—in ½ pint containers
   Burnt Umber
   Raw Umber
   Vandyke Brown
   Lamp Black
   Chrome Yellow, medium
   Chrome Green, medium
   White Lead

Dry powder colors, for touching-up—¼ pound of each
- Raw Umber
- Burnt Umber
- Red Vermilion
- Vandyke Brown
- Zinc White
- Black
- French Ochre

Aniline (water-soluble) powders for water stain—¼ pound of each
- Walnut
- Red Mahogany
- Brown Mahogany
- Golden Maple
- Red Maple
- Dark Oak
- Light Oak
- Silver Gray
- Black, Nigrosene

Aniline (alcohol-soluble) powders for touching-up—1 ounce of each
- Brown
- Red Mahogany
- Lemon Yellow
- Black

Touch-up patching sticks
- Walnut
- Red and Brown Mahogany
- Maple
- Mediterranean colors
- Oak
- Teak
- Natural

Burning-in, 1 of each
- Alcohol lamp
- Burning-in knife
- Stick shellac:
  - transparent light
  - transparent dark
  - Walnut
  - Red Mahogany

Brown
Light Maple
White
Light Oak

Rubbing materials

No. 2/0 steel wool—1 pound package
No. 2/0 pumice stone—1 pound
Rottenstone—1 pound
Rubbing felt ¼″—¼ pound
Rubbing compound—1 pint container
Cheesecloth—¼ pound package
Polishing wax paste—1 pound
Paint removers—1 quart
Putty knife—1¼″ wide
Wire brush
Japan drier, for oil stain—1 pint

Sandpapers

No. 1 Garnet paper—6 sheets
No. 0 Garnet paper—6 sheets
No. 3/0 Garnet paper—24 sheets
No. 5/0 Garnet paper—24 sheets

Wet-or-dry papers

No. 320—12 sheets
No. 220—12 sheets

Brushes

2″ double-chisel, fitch, chisel edge
2½″ double-chisel, fitch, chisel edge
1½″ flat, single fitch
1″ flat, single fitch
½″ flat, single camel's-hair
¼″ round bristle
⅛″ pencil brush, camel's-hair—at least six
2″ scrubber-fitch
4″ round duster

Optional equipment

Complete spraying outfit capable of obtaining 45- to 60-pound pressure
Portable oscillating sander and rubbing combination

BRUSHES AND THEIR CARE

Brushes are a very important part of the finishing operation. They are used in almost every step of the finishing process. It is, therefore, very important that you select the appropriate brush for the various operations, and that care be exercised in keeping the brushes clean and in good condition.

Inexpensive brushes made of cheap and inferior hair products should be avoided, because they do not spread the material well, and they do not stand up well under constant use.

The best general-purpose brush is made of bristle and is called a fitch brush. These brushes, imported from China, are made from selected hair of the Chinese boar. The bristles are selected, shaped, and fastened together with vulcanized rubber. The brush has excellent holding and spreading qualities. Shellac, varnish, and lacquer may be applied without the bristle spreading or softening.

The fitch XXX chisel brush is used most by the wood finisher, because its thickness and shape permit the spreading of much material rapidly and evenly. XXX means simply that the brush consists of three rows of hair instead of one. "Chisel" refers to the shape of the bristle formation at the tip of the brush.

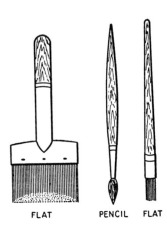

FLAT   PENCIL   FLAT

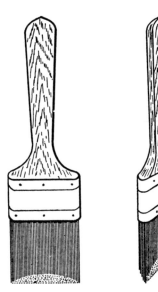

Left: Common types of camel's-hair brushes.

Right: A fitch chisel brush. Like other types of brushes, these are available in nylon as well as bristle, but one must remember that nylon will dissolve in alcohol or lacquer thinner.

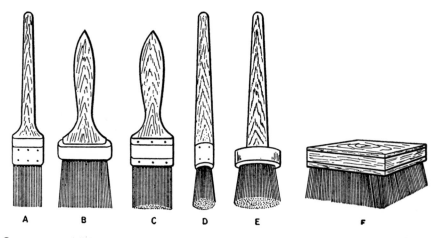

Common wood-finishing brushes. A: trim brush, 1″-2″, for fine brushing. B: camel's-hair brush, 1″-4″, for shellac. C: fitch XXX oxhair brush, 1″-4″, for shellac, varnish, and stain. D: Round oxhair brush, 1″-2″, for stain. E: round horsehair brush, 3″, for dusting. F: rectangular brush, 2″ x 4″, for stippling.

The edges of the brush are shaped like a double beveled-edge chisel. The bristles used in making the chisel-type brush are selected according to length and then arranged in a beveled edge before they are vulcanized in rubber. Brushes whose edge is cut to a bevel are not as good as those whose edges have been arranged purposely in this manner.

Perhaps the first good habit the wood finisher should develop is proper care of brushes. A clean dry brush that has been wrapped as shown will last indefinitely.

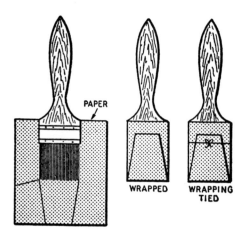

Camel's-hair brushes are also recommended. These brushes, made from the tail hair of the Siberian squirrel, are very soft and flexible. Available in many sizes, they are used for lacquering and touching-up purposes.

Nylon-filament brushes have the same characteristics as bristle brushes and are obtained in the same widths and lengths as the other brushes. Care should be taken when using them; although they may be used in applying practically all finishing materials, they should not be used when shellac or lacquer is to be brushed on a surface. The nylon filaments will disintegrate when they come in contact with alcohol and lacquer thinners.

Brushes should be cleaned immediately after they have been used. This, more than any other single step, assures the brush a long life. More brushes are made worthless because of neglect than because of use.

The brush should be cleaned immediately in the solvent of the material which was applied by the brush. For example:

1. A water-stain brush should be washed with hot water and allowed to dry.
2. A brush used for alcohol staining should be washed in alcohol.
3. A brush used in applying filler should be washed in benzene.
4. A shellac brush should be cleaned in alcohol and then allowed to dry.
5. A varnish brush should be cleaned with turpentine and then stored in a container filled partly with brush-keeper varnish.
6. A lacquer brush should be thoroughly cleaned in lacquer thinner and then dried.
7. Paint brushes should be cleaned with benzene and then stored in a container half-filled with raw linseed oil.

Cleaners

Any brush which has hardened because of neglect can be restored to use by washing in a brush cleaner. There are many types of prepared commercial brush cleaners on the market which give excellent results. They may be used in preference to the ones listed below.

Trisodium phosphate dissolved in hot water is a good cleaner. The brush is allowed to soak in the solution for twenty-four hours and then washed with yellow soap and water and allowed to dry.

A chemical brush cleaner may be made by using the following solvents:

1 pint benzol
½ pint alcohol
½ pint acetone

The brush is allowed to remain in the solution for twenty-four hours or until the bristles are free of paint. An occasional turn of the brush while in the solution will hasten the cleaning action. The brush should be cleaned with a wire comb after it has been removed from the solution. Wash with soap and water to assure absolute cleanness.

The paint and varnish removers discussed earlier in this book can also be used to good advantage when cleaning a brush. Use the same procedure as was described in the previous paragraphs.

A few words of caution. When immersing a brush in these liquids, allow the liquid to cover only the bristles. Placing the entire brush in the liquid may affect the rubber or ferrule holding the bristles together and thus cause the brush to come apart. It is not a good practice to keep paint brushes in water for an extended time. The water will make the bristles soft and flabby and is likely to swell and crack the wood handle. Brushes should be hung up by the handle to dry. A brush which is not to be used for an indefinite period should be cleaned carefully as indicated earlier and then dried thoroughly. It should be wrapped with newspaper before being stored away.

Index

268

684
G   Gibbia, S.W.

Wood Finishing & Refinishing

Date Due   761243

APR 1 8			